MW00611457

New York's Poop Scoop Law

Dogs, the Dirt, and Due Process

By Michael Brandow

Purdue University Press
West Lafayette, Indiana

Library of Congress Cataloging-in-Publication Data

Brandow, Michael, 1959–
    New York's poop scoop law : dogs, the dirt, and due process / by Michael Brandow.
        p.   cm.
    Includes bibliographical references.
    ISBN 978-1-55753-492-7
    1. Dogs—Cleaning—New York (State)—New York. 2. Dogs—Manure—
Handling—New York (State)—New York. 3. Pet cleanup—New York (State)—
New York.   I. Title.
SF427.48.B73 2008

636.7'0887097471—dc22   2008013915

For my sweet Samantha,
who goes more than any other dog I know.

TABLE OF CONTENTS

ACKNOWLEDGMENTS

Many thanks to:

- Catherine Laur-White for her insight, knowledge of the English language, and devotion.
- Joseph Caldwell for his eternal optimism.
- Mary Connelly and Stacy Alldredge for their love and help in finding work to support my writing.
- All my friends and family for their encouragement.
- The La Guardia and Wagner Archives for lending me access to buried treasure.
- All my sources for their enthusiasm for this unsavory topic and their willingness to dig up the past.
- Alan Beck and Purdue University for giving me a break when so many New Yorkers were saying that no one would want to read a book about New York.
- All the dogs in this town, every shape, size, color, and creed. Thanks for being here.

PERMISSIONS

INTRODUCTION

"Science and superstition were agreed as to the horror."
—Victor Hugo, *Les Misérables*, on the sewers of Paris[1]

I began writing this book after adopting a dog in New York City and spending more time than ever before on the sidewalks in my Greenwich Village neighborhood. Suddenly and to my dismay, I became aware of the kind of hysteria that's generated by the few stray turds left uncollected on public walkways. You'd think it was the end of the world. People growl as they pass the smelly clumps positioned across the pavement like landmines, muttering things that ought not be repeated here, sometimes even going after me and my dog when we aren't the guilty parties. Traditionally, it's said to be good luck to step into dog doo, though I doubt that anyone has ever believed this. Who could have coined that phrase?* Anyone unlucky enough to put a foot into a mess is likely to launch into an uncontrollable fit of rage right there on the curb, a sort of temper tantrum for adults. The culprit is long gone and there's nothing that any sane and rational person can do but reach into a trash can and grab a piece of newspaper to wipe it off. But some of these unfortunate pedestrians lose all composure and decide, instead, to lash out

---

*The association of feces with good fortune is deeply rooted due to the undeniable fact that the dirty business makes things grow. "Where there's muck, there's luck," went an old English adage.

"Howard, I think the dog wants to go out."

at the next person carrying a leash. I've been traveling these sidewalks for 25 years and know of no other aspect of urban life that manages to summon this sort of response. Not the sight of a little old lady being mugged, a child being molested, or a dog being beaten—nothing seems to hold the key to making New Yorkers stop whatever they're doing and "get involved" like this does. I don't like stepping into an unexpected surprise any more than the next guy. And I've always picked up after my own. But anything as emotionally charged as this single concern, I've long suspected, just has to be about something more than the obvious— or is a little crap really all that people are so upset over?

In all fairness, I'd also have to ask: What's the big deal about picking up after a dog? Proud, poop-scooping pet owners of the present day have grown so accustomed to performing this task that hardly anyone thinks about it anymore. Sure, a few stragglers still leave the mess on the pavement, making the rest of us look bad. But they're the exceptions, not the rule. Most modern and enlightened dog owners have no problem doing their civic duty. On the contrary, they're almost eager to stoop to the ground, plastic bag in hand, and remove the offending matter. Over the years, this dirty deed—unpleasant, unsavory, and sometimes a bit embarrassing—has become a normal part of daily life in many places, a decent and respectable act that's often encouraged with wild enthusiasm. Scooping has become a central part of dog ownership and is performed an average of about 6,000 to 11,000 times over the life of a dog. However hard they try, people can't seem to remember a time when they might have held back if no one was watching. But there was a time, not long ago, when they might have. In fact, it took years before New Yorkers could face the responsibility without flinching, and cities throughout the world would dare to take this bold example and expect their own citizens to start acting like New Yorkers. Setting this trend wasn't easy. Scooping begins to sound like a big deal again when you talk to Manhattanites old enough to have endured those wretched, pre-scoop days. They're so proud of their law, and the standard it helped to establish for the rest of the world, that they've actually started believing the whole thing was their idea.

Sorry. As eager as New Yorkers are to take credit for having invented everything under the sun, we were not the first people in the world to pick up after our dogs. Contrary to popular opinion, and as much as it hurts to admit, the idea was, like Bruce Springsteen and so much else that cowers in our shadow, from nearby New Jersey.

It all began one morning in 1971 when a man was out walking his Great Dane in a small town called Nutley. Neighbors had been putting up with finding dog doo on their lawns for as long as they could remember. But this was the last straw. A meeting was called. News spread to other neighborhoods. A law was passed, and after a few years of unpleasant encounters, most local dog owners were complying. "We got calls from people all over the world," recalls one city official, proudly. "They told us this was the greatest thing since the Emancipation Proclamation."[2]

New York casts a long shadow. Before this revolutionary step forward, however brilliant and impressive, could take hold, it would need the official seal of approval. The problem was that life in New York has always been a bit more complicated than it is in Nutley. Like everything else in this crazy place, a simple solution to an obvious problem became hellishly complex. Before it was solved, our own poop problem became *political*. We'd need a lot more than a few complaints from disgruntled citizens with dirt on their shoes to pass a new dog law. For years the stuff just sat there on the pavement while people argued about whose responsibility it was. Unlike Californians, who have forged light-years ahead of us by converting canine waste into energy, New Yorkers used the matter to fuel bad feelings, to further careers, and to advance secret agendas. We may not have been the first ones in the world to do something about our pet problem, but this story of how our poop scoop law was slowly and agonizingly put into practice is proof that no one can deny: This only could have happened here.

It's hard to imagine: 8 million people stepping into dog crap—and no one could agree on what to do. But poop became the focus of daily life back in the 1970s when New York's dog problem reached a critical point, though dog owners had no reason to assume that picking up would become a basic duty. At first, they thought the idea was absurd and they had many supporters. Animal rights activists were unanimously opposed to scooping. The ASPCA condemned the law on the grounds that it would impose undue hardship! Everyone seems to have forgotten that New York's City Council passed over the proposal on several occasions before shelving the idea. And that Ed Koch eventually had to go to the state level to back a law that local leaders thought was too dangerous to support publicly. Passing this risky piece of legislation was tough enough—what about enforcement? After five or six years of struggling to get dog owners in line with the program, the law was finally working. Big-city mayors from around the world looked on with amazement and asked: What was New York's secret? How had a poop scoop law been enforced when similar laws had failed so miserably most everywhere else? And how did those pushy, arrogant New Yorkers, who don't like being told what to do, manage to convince each other that picking up after a dog was a good thing to do?

New York was, indeed, the first major city to have a truly successful poop scoop law. We proved that it could be done, which was enough to inspire other municipal governments to renew their own campaigns and embrace a cause they'd pretty much given up on. Little did they know that we paid a high price for finding the answer to our fecal dilemma. The question of what to do with a dog's droppings managed to occupy the center stage of daily life, and of New York politics, for nearly 20 years. Poop made the cover of the *New York Times* before dog owners finally agreed, begrudgingly, to start picking up. Politicians risked their careers by addressing this hot potato. Over the years, many shoes were soiled and feelings hurt. Despite the emphasis on sanitation and public health, clearing the sidewalks and parks was almost a secondary concern. The poop scoop law was viewed as a last hope to resolve what was being called a "civil war" over dogs.

How quickly we've forgotten the long and ugly fight that took place on our pavements, as easily as we've forgotten that the struggle to accommodate unprecedented numbers of pets came during a phase of urban decay and alarming civil unrest. New York was on the brink of bankruptcy by the 1970s. We had the highest violent crime rate of any city in the world (after Detroit). During these traumatic times, a combination of pressures, most having nothing whatsoever to do with pets, tended to inflate certain trivial matters like their feces beyond the limits of common sense. Dogs, and the problems they were said to be causing, were actually blamed for the city's downfall. Despite the long list of pressing issues facing us during the nationwide urban crisis—crime, unemployment, the flight of taxpayers and corporations, drastic cutbacks in basic services from trash collection to police protection—dogs emerged as a leading cause for complaint. And the number one complaint was number two.

The endless fighting on pavements and in parks would color the entire experience of owning a dog in New York for decades to come. Sure, our poop scoop law eventually became a success. In time, most dog owners were trained to remove those pungent piles before anyone could step into them. But resentment on both sides of the issue would remain, lingering and festering, shaping our policies and practices concerning pets. How, after all this talk of civic duty, did the people so proud of their poop scoop law create one of the most horrific animal disposal plants in the world? Is it random coincidence that one recent mayor placed a specialist in Solid Waste Management in charge of animal welfare? Considering how superficially pleasant our city has become in recent years, it's easy to ignore our tradition of favoring sanitation and health issues over more humane concerns.

A closer look at a seemingly trivial subject brings us into a grey area where science meets politics, facts can be distorted by fear, and altruism and self-interest are sometimes difficult to distinguish from one another. There can be no doubt: New York really did need a poop scoop law. But beyond the obvious reasons—that feces smell bad, they mar the landscape, and they contain some organisms that are potentially harmful to human health—subtler and more potent forces have always been at work. That old and rusty institutional concept of "mental hygiene"— still a subdivision of many health departments—keeps coming back to haunt us. By broadening our scope, and examining a loaded topic in his- torical, political, economic, esthetic, cultural, and psychological terms, it's possible to arrive at more interesting conclusions than the one that says: "Dog owners have to pick up because that's the only decent thing to do." How did we arrive at this assumption in the first place?

Any student of human nature with a taste for the absurd, a deep and abiding love for other animals, and a stomach for tragedy will con- nect with this tale of New York's struggle to come to terms with canine waste and—let's not forget—the dogs themselves. New Yorkers were among the first people in the world to bend over and bag the unspeak- able. But the years leading up to this dubious honor should remind us that even the most straightforward issues contain more than meets the eye or nose. Yes, the situation in New York was unique, as it so often is. The crusade to keep an ungovernable city feces-free shows the extremes to which New Yorkers are willing to go in order to get what they want. This need to be heard, and the willingness to take that first bold step forward (hopefully, without stepping into anything), have earned us a lasting place on the cutting edge (and plenty of walking space on the rightful side of the curb).

But still—an entire book about dog crap? Some readers will no doubt find the topic trivial, perhaps even distasteful. They need to rise above their gut reactions, keeping sight of the true order of human concerns. Trying to bury recent history is pointless, however upsetting or embarrassing it may be. If only people could shed their schoolgirl shyness over shit, this tale of New York's scatological fixation and the struggle to come to terms with a very real urban problem might reveal the inner workings of those forces that shape our thoughts and lives.

This is the social history of an act, and a comedy of manners about the long and difficult process of bringing this strange custom into the fold of daily life.

Michael Brandow
New York City
2008

Chapter 1

Invasion of the Dog People

"This is no joke."

—Office of the Mayor, 1978[1]

Someone new was in City Hall and he was tired of fooling around. Just days before a controversial law was scheduled to go into effect, dog owners couldn't believe that Koch was actually serious. This was an outrage. As far as anyone knew, no society on the face of the earth had been reduced to performing such a bizarre and loathsome task, an act so foul, so despicable, so humiliating as handling dog doo. It simply wasn't done. Cities like Chicago and Denver had been trying for years to force people to pick up, and these attempts had failed miserably. So why wouldn't New York take the helpful hints and give up on what seemed, at best, a well-intentioned but impractical idea?

Koch made it painfully clear that he meant business. New Yorkers would be forced to set a daring new example for cities around the world. They would have a new rule *and* learn to follow it. "Cleaning up after your pet is no longer a courtesy," he reminded hundreds of thousands of rebellious dog owners. "It's the law."[2] Saying so was easy enough. The real battle remained to be fought. After a decade-long struggle to push through this arguable piece of legislation, tension filled the air like the smell of feces that radiated from the pavement. Koch had no illusions. He prepared for a rough ride, instructing the departments of Police, Sanitation, Parks, and Traffic to give Health Law 1310—affectionately known as "the poop scoop law" in years to come—the utmost priority. A standing army of civil servants awaited that historic day, armed with the right to issue warnings and summonses, even to arrest any resisters who might laugh in their faces or perhaps react violently. But most people were more stunned than anything else, unable to believe this was even happening. "It shall be the duty of each dog owner," read the strange new decree, "to remove any feces left by his dog on any sidewalk, gutter, street, or other public area." This had to be a joke! Dog poop was something you bought in novelty shops in Times Square, a gag gift on the shelf next to the whoopee cushions! Were human beings actually going to be ordered to bend over and grab some nasty business, then bring it home in a handbag or a back pocket for disposal? Under no circumstances, they were told by their mayor, was anyone to use public waste receptacles. Clearly, the logistics of the operation had yet to be worked out—they wouldn't have to handle the stuff with their bare hands, would they?

All that perplexed pet owners knew for certain was that, very soon, they'd be coerced into doing the unthinkable. On the eve of the new law, they lined up panic-stricken by the thousands in front of Gimbels department store and supermarkets like Red Apple, Sloan's, and Gristede's to purchase one of several different patented "pooper-scooper" devices. These gizmos ranged in price from 15 cents to $10.98, and included a variety of models from a simple cardboard box to an elaborate plastic contraption with a flashlight attachment. Stores ran out of all items within a few hours, and people still lined up on the sidewalk went home terrified at the thought that, come the next morning, they'd be left holding the bag.

"Like the Jews of Nazi Germany," said the head of New York's Dog Owners Guild, "we citizens, including the old and infirm, are being humiliated by being forced to pick up excrement from the gutter."[3] In time, some dog owners would appeal to the courts to declare the poop scoop law unconstitutional. But however unfairly they believed they were being treated, no one could deny that the problem had gotten out of hand. People were sick and tired of dodging the landmines that spread across the sidewalks and public greens. "The serendipitous pleasure in strolling streets and parks," wrote the *New York Times* in an endless cycle of laments on crap, "is considerably diminished by the need to keep eyes down and steps high."[4] The stuff was everywhere you tried to go. And the stench! . . . Despite the best efforts to navigate through this mess, every New Yorker had a personal collection of war stories about sliding into a pungent pile and then tracking the matter into a restaurant, shop, subway, bus, cab, or high-rise apartment building. Angry voters sent letters to City Council and to local papers demanding that a law be passed without delay. One woman wrote that she was tired of doing "the New Yorker walk," always looking down, eyes glued to the pavement for fear of slipping and falling.

The problem wasn't new. Technically, it was said, dogs were forbidden by an ancient City ordinance from relieving themselves in public places at all. Section 755 (2) 7.0 of the City's Administrative Code, and Section 153.09 of the Health Code, had long outlawed the depositing of any "offensive animal matter" on public property. But practical considerations had led to a special interpretation of that law, which wasn't originally intended to mean canine waste but slaughterhouse carrion left at roadsides.[*] By the newly expanded definition, dogs were

---

[*]New Yorkers might have been even angrier had they considered recent history and another animal-related horror. During the 19th century, a dramatic increase in horse-driven traffic had bogged down city streets with dung and urine. The latter was left to evaporate and the former was often sold as fertilizer. The Second Avenue Street Railway is said to have earned an extra $4.80 per horse from manure sales in 1866. But many of these public deposits were not recycled and simply sat stinking up the streets. So much feces was dumped that pedestrians had difficulty crossing, or rather wading, though the mess. Rain and melting snow created seas of liquid manure. In dry weather, dung dust filled the air. Fly, rat, and pigeon populations, which fed on excrement or on the portion of indigested grain, flourished. As late as the early 20th century, New York still had approximately 200,000 horses and was struggling to clear not only untold millions of tons of dung each year, but about 15,000 carcasses because horses were being worked to death.

As horses were gradually replaced by automobiles, other pollutants, far more toxic than animal waste products, began to threaten cities. By the time that New

Stray dog populations and canine waste are double-trouble for many cities.
Source: Alan M. Beck

allowed to do their business in public places but only after their owners guided them off the edge of the sidewalk where they could evacuate directly into a gutter.[†] The fine for not "curbing" a dog was $25 but was rarely imposed. New York had long been proud of its very original idea, quite revolutionary when first put into effect in 1937 as a kind of social experiment. One Sanitation worker was so excited that he actually built a float and decorated it with signs reading "Curb Your Dog." He drove his creation around the city while the rest of the nation looked on with amazement at this bold step for mankind. Chicago, impressed as always, praised New York, "truly a doggity city," for its progressive move, and for having the courage "to compel the indifferent dog owner to consider public welfare."[5] But hardly any New York dog owners actually took this law seriously, and by the 1970s it was an official failure.

York's canine waste problem became critical, urban residents had already been forced to face the possibility that automobiles were a questionable advance. But at least the pavements were more or less walkable. Then a new wave of dogs arrived and added insult to injury. Now New Yorkers had to contend not only with air pollution, but with animal feces all over again.

[†]The still popular expression "It's raining cats and dogs" suggests that pets have long been associated with urban gutters. The precise origin of the phrase, however, has been debated. Some say it comes from a famous storm in 18th-century England that drowned both animals and swept them along the streets in a raging torrent. It's also possible the image comes from Germanic mythology, which saw cats as foretellers of storms and associated dogs with rain.

Even if they could be made to "curb" their animals—to willingly drag them off the sidewalk and into oncoming traffic—it would have cost the City more money than it had to flush the gutters daily.

The poop scoop law, however self-evident it might seem today, came only as a last resort. Over the years, other ideas had been tried but failed. In 1958, an experimental "dog toilet" was installed at 92nd Street and York Avenue in the hope that pooches might be trained to relieve themselves more hygienically. This strange invention was really no more than a hole in the ground and resembled a Turkish toilet. The dogs, however, were not interested and the hole was plugged a year later. And it wasn't just the sidewalks that stayed dirty. Despite a leash law enacted in 1969, dog owners continued letting their beasts run il-legally every morning in Central Park, where they left a trail of turds like jelly beans in an Easter egg hunt.

The problem worsened before it was solved. As New York's dog population continued to grow exponentially, littering parks and pavements, the question of what to do with canine waste was caus-ing some of the fiercest disputes to be heard in public places. To most dog owners, the answer was simple: Why, they asked, weren't street cleaners handling this unwholesome mess? After all, they argued, civil servants had once collected the droppings of horses, and now that these animals had been replaced by automobiles, workers might as well use the extra time to pick up after dogs. The drivers of carriages and wagons had never been expected to stop and clean up after their own horses. So why should dog owners be forced to pick up when street cleaners could easily do the job? The Department of Sanitation begged to differ. "First of all, we're being paid to clean the streets, not the sidewalks,"[6] Com-missioner Herbert Elish declared in no uncertain terms.

Secondly, Elish might have added, the gutters were technically part of the streets. But flushing them daily would have cost the De-partment of Sanitation an annual $18.5 million (in 1972 dollars). If New York had been in better shape financially, simply enforcing the "curbing" interpretation of the original waste law might have been enough to take care of the problem, assuming most dog owners could be made to comply. A poop scoop law wouldn't have been necessary. But New York was in the midst of a fiscal crisis, street cleaning had been scaled back along with other City services, and it wasn't likely that municipal government would bear any more than the load it was already carrying.

If Sanitation wasn't going to do the job, then who exactly would lift the brown shroud that seemed to cover the earth's surface, like that landscape in the *New Yorker* cartoon, for as far as the eye could see—or the nose could smell? Most everyone agreed that something had to be done about the mess. But what? "For a city as financially strapped as New York," wrote the editors of the *Times*, "it is fatuous to suggest additional services that might be undertaken. However, there are certain self-services that residents can perform which will improve the city's livability without burdening the treasury."[7] The press was suggesting that dog owners themselves might be convinced to volunteer to help keep the sidewalks clean—the implication being, of course, that whether they scooped or simply "curbed" their dogs, once New York got back on its feet again, the responsibility for keeping the pavements clean would eventually revert to government.

"Curbing" dogs against oncoming traffic was one thing—now the owners were being asked to crawl into the gutter themselves and retrieve the poop? They were shocked and appalled by the suggestion.

New York was discussing dog laws in the 1970s because it had never seen so many of these animals before. In fact, dog ownership on a mass scale, and the problems surrounding this urban phenomenon, were quite recent developments. Across the nation, the dramatic increase in canine populations came in the post-war years as a result of a new prosperity. People had money enough to buy family pets, among many other new luxuries. They could also afford to take care of them. As the nation's disposable income rose, so did the number of dogs. This wasn't so much of a problem in the suburbs. But cities like New York were unprepared to accommodate the vast numbers of canines finding urban homes, not to mention the tens of thousands abandoned on the streets each year by people who'd changed their minds about impulse purchases.

This overabundance of dogs, some loved, some discarded, would have many repercussions. As New York and other American cities fell upon hard times, canine populations continued to grow, though for precisely the opposite reason than post-war prosperity. Dogs were now being brought in to protect people when crime rates soared and budget cuts scaled back the level of police protection. New York's dog population doubled during the 1960s to reach upwards of 1 million by the 1970s. Though estimates varied widely, the rule of thumb was one dog for every six humans—in a city of 8 million, that was a lot of dogs.

To make matters more complicated, as American cities fell into a downward spiral, a new trend in politics tended to give priority to suburban concerns, often leaving big cities to fend more or less for themselves. Crime, unemployment, pollution, racial tensions, and a host of other problems contributed to "the urban crisis" that was forcing people to flee cities and begin new lives in the suburbs. American families were choosing the more wholesome environments supposedly offered in these new settings. They bought sprawling, ranch-style houses and said good-bye to cramped, stuffy apartments. They parked big, gas-guzzling cars in the garage, which meant no more waiting for subways and buses or fighting for cabs at rush hour. They had finely manicured front lawns in place of pavement, and peace and quiet instead of the constant roar of passing traffic. In their own private backyards sprawled big, drooly dogs, not rats in the hall or pigeons on the fire escape. Rover or Spot was often tied to a tree and all but ignored by the family. But that didn't seem to matter. The domestic dog, like all the other civilized amenities, became an indispensable part of the American dream. "Lassie" became a household name. While her distant cousins sat alone, tied up "out back" and left to entertain themselves, her adventures across the wide open country unfolded weekly on television, that new and powerful medium installed as a permanent fixture at the center of American households.

The loveable collie played no small role in shaping attitudes toward dogs of all kinds. Lassie's efforts to save little Timmy made her the stuff of legends, and made pet ownership all the more popular. She was faithful, brave, noble—in short, Lassie was a kind of four-legged war hero.

The only problem was that Lassie lived in the country. Before World War II, large dogs were typically kept in rural areas where they often roamed freely and where doing their business seldom bothered anyone. In the newly created suburbs, dogs could eliminate on their own property. If Beaver Cleaver didn't pick up, then he had only himself to blame for stepping in a mound and then dragging it into the house.

But there was no "out back" in city apartments. Moreover, the highest concentration of the nation's dogs was not in the suburbs or in the country, but in the city. As millions of Americans took flight from the great metropolises for the promise of suburban bliss, others clung to the ideal of the modern city and the very different kinds of pleasures that it offered. As long as they had dogs to take some of the edge off daily life by protecting them and providing companionship in a harsh urban environment, these die-hard pueblo dwellers stayed immune to the allure of greener pastures. But New Yorkers hadn't escaped the national trend of dog ownership. On the contrary, they had more dogs than anyone else.

Humorist Russell Baker observed the strange new culture of dog people that had reached a critical mass by 1975. "New Yorkers are partial to dogs," he wrote perplexedly, "which they harbor in all sizes and shapes, keeping them imprisoned most of the day in tiny apartments and bringing them out morning and evening to evacuate on sidewalks and streets. The dogs vary from mammoth beasts capable of consuming a policeman in three bites to creatures no larger than mice, and come in a startling variety of forms. There is one breed that resembles a woman's wig. The first time I saw one at the curb on Second Avenue, I undertook to retrieve it for its owner, mistaking it for an escaped wig, before I discovered that it had four legs and was being walked."[8] New York's dog population had grown dramatically, not only in number but also in size. No longer were New Yorkers content with the fluffy little Malteses so popular on the Upper West Side, or the fragile Yorkies of the Upper East. At a time when suburbanites seemed to need big metal tanks to make themselves feel secure, New York pedestrians wanted larger dogs. Collies, Labrador retrievers, German shepherds, St. Bernards, Great Danes, and "the ubiquitous golden retrievers,"[9] as Anna Quindlen called the latest name-brand breed to be churned out like sausage links—animals created specifically for herding sheep, hunting in marshlands, or guarding country estates—were now to be seen promenading on New York pavements or running loose in public parks. These beasts were bringing endless joy to the lives of their human guardians for whom they provided love, companionship, and protection against other humans. But New York was physically unprepared to handle all these animals.

"The dog has been made a sacred cow,"[10] said Alan Beck, head of the City's Bureau of Animal Affairs, in 1974 when it became necessary for government to create this office. Lassie was apparently leaving some 500,000 pounds of feces on city surfaces each and every day of the year, and the problem wasn't being addressed. "The responsibilities, expenses, and public health implications have been minimized and ownership has been given status and an aura of freedom and patriotism."[11] It was wonderful that so many New Yorkers loved dogs. But owning them didn't necessarily make them good people. Lassie was much-admired but she was causing tremendous problems. The streets, sidewalks, and parks had become so disgusting that one Greenwich Village woman told a paper that she had stopped taking her dog out for its own safety—the ground, she said, was too filthy. Other New Yorkers, however, weren't so fond of dogs or concerned about their welfare. Instead, they worried about the safety of their children and health concerns in general. "It may be that the hordes of New York dogs," wrote Claire Berman in the *Times*, "pose a greater threat to city dwellers, young and old, than do the double-parkers or the muggers. If we can send men to litter the moon, we should be able to keep our city from being inundated by dog excrement."[12]

Canine feces soon emerged as a major cultural theme in New York and other cities across the nation. "Got to scrape the shit right off your shoes"[13] went the lyrics to a Rolling Stones song in 1972, when poop was very much on people's minds. While it may have been considered fertilizer in more natural settings, it was viewed as "pollution" in the city, and nobody was fond of stepping in the stuff. Whether you loved the four-legged beasts, hated them, or simply tolerated them, they seemed to be setting the tone for daily life in public places, especially in New York. Critics complained and claimed that dogs had never belonged in cities in the first place. Some suggested they be rounded up and sent back to the country. Dog owners grew more defensive each year but even the staunchest defenders of the right to keep four-legged friends couldn't deny that the poop situation had gotten out of hand. New York was slowly coming to terms with a canine population larger than any other known in history. Dogs were transforming urban life and causing quite a debate. "They abundantly bring both litter and love, companionship and complaints," read an article in the Real Estate section of the *Times* about the new dog-owning trend. "From hungry strays in the street to diamond-laced poodles on Park Avenue, dogs are among the most controversial tenants in town."[14] Anna Quindlen agreed. "Perhaps it is indeed true," she wrote, "that the world—or at least the city—is divided into two kinds of people: those who carry leashes and those who don't. For it seems that, with the exception of rush-hour traffic and mayoral elections, the subject of dogs can summon up some of the most heated arguments to be had, both from those who are devoted owners and those who think it is cruel, selfish, or just plain unsanitary to keep a dog in the confines of a city apartment and let it relieve itself on the curbing of city streets. Even those knowledgeable on the subject can clash on the specifics of keeping a dog in the city. Companionship or protection? Purebred or mixed breed? Big dog, little dog?"[15]

A popular book called *The Dog Crisis* questioned the idea that dogs were a welcome addition to urban life, or that keeping them in the city was in the animals' own best interests. "Dogs are lovable and trainable creatures," wrote Alan Beck in his introduction to out-line a very real social problem that had yet to be solved. "However, their 'culture' is different from ours. They use their teeth for play and to assert dominance; they use feces and urine to mark their territories and to communicate with other dogs."[16] How would these foreigners be assimilated into urban cultures? Animal welfare was a major con-cern. By the mid-seventies, New York had 140 kennels, 750 pet shops, 100 grooming parlors, and 10 animal talent agencies, but very few agreed-upon standards for the care and control of these animals. And what were the duties of dog owners toward the rest of society? Should government share the responsibility? Or should dog owners themselves bear the entire burden? To some people, the answer was so self-evident that no discussion seemed warranted—dog owners, they assumed, should be held responsible. But to others, these questions weren't so easily answered. "For approximately 40,000 years," wrote the author of *The Dog Crisis*, Iris Nowell, "man's relationship with the dog has remained fairly stable. Now it is severely threatened. And until reason quells emotion, and the seriousness of the issue is publicized and ad-dressed, neither man nor dog will survive the situation with dignity."[17] Was the dog really man's best friend?

Why didn't pet owners just agree to pick up, and to keep their dogs on leashes for the duration of their natural lives? Because they didn't think they had to, and they wanted their dogs to have some ex-ercise. But most important, because New Yorkers don't like to be told what to do, least of all by other New Yorkers. People who have never lived here seldom fully appreciate the concept of shared public space, or the kinds of arguments that develop on an overcrowded city side-walk. This sort of direct and constant interaction is quite unlike anything they've encountered in a suburban traffic jam. New Yorkers are a pedes-trian people. They rely upon pubic walkways and, to a lesser extent, subways, cabs, and buses to get to where they're going. But mainly, and more so than residents of other American cities, they are walkers whose daily lives are dominated by what happens on the pavement. Getting from point A to point B in the shortest time possible is the goal.

But the sidewalk is more than a means to an end. The great pedestrian thoroughfares are where New Yorkers learn what new fashions to wear, what constitutes normal body language, what types of people are best avoided. They might even stop to ask "How much?" for that doggy in the window. In so many ways, the sidewalk is where human behavior is shaped and modified. New Yorkers may not like being told what to do but they're eager to imitate each other. Through observation they learn to make themselves socially acceptable based on whatever happens to be in style at a given moment—and then let the rest of the world take their example, though the residents of some cities seldom walk more than a few steps each day.

"Traditionally," said New York's Environmental Protection Agency (EPA) Administrator Jerome Kretchmer, when he first proposed a poop scoop law in 1971, "dog owners have been allowed to let their pets relieve themselves in city streets and parks. It is a custom that dates from an era of many open spaces, little congestion, and a small populace."[18] But city life was changing and many New Yorkers felt that the rules had to be rewritten. Dog owners, they complained, were claiming more than their fair share of the sidewalk. Pets had been thrust into the daily lives of everyone, whether or not people liked having these animals underfoot. Perhaps their greatest crime, in the opinion of critics, was to have taken up space, namely *public* space, which was already at a premium. Leashes stretched across the pavements, backing up the mass conduits of daily life. A growing anti-dog lobby complained that pet owners thought nothing of letting their animals soil the walkways, or the public green that was covered with free-ranging canines and their feces. In apartment buildings, dogs shared the same elevators and lobbies as humans. Many of them barked all day in tiny apartments for all to hear. Horrible.

At some point, unpleasant altercations began to offset the beneficial effects of canine companionship in the city. "As a recent transplant to New York from the West Coast," wrote one disappointed new arrival in the seventies, "I find the single most disagreeable thing about New York to be dogs and their effect on the city. It's almost as though there were a civil ordinance requiring apartment dwellers to keep a dog (the larger the better) locked in an apartment all day and then let it defecate in the street at least once a day. And what's this mess going to smell like this summer? I like dogs as much as the next person, but they don't belong in the city. It's inhuman for both people and dogs."[19] New York was unprepared, physically and psychologically, to accommodate so many animals. Like those pesky automobiles that visited daily from the suburbs, running over pedestrians and choking them with carbon monoxide, dogs were viewed as four-wheeled nuisances that fouled the air and competed with people for safe walking space. If public transportation and fuel emission standards were to be the solutions to traffic jams and smog, then an all-encompassing plan to deal with the city's dog problem—to control the population, to regulate the behavior of the owners, and to keep the poop at the other side of the curb—was still forthcoming.

The problem only escalated. The more dogs found homes in New York, the more it seemed the time-honored practice of leaving animal waste in public places, and perhaps the idea of keeping dogs in the city at all, were outdated. "It is a fact," wrote one New Yorker who was mad as hell and not going to take this anymore, "that there are sufficient laws on the books empowering the police to give out summonses and the courts to levy fines against these arrogant dog owners. If the city will only give some serious attention to this problem, it could be solved simply and quickly. Have policemen give tickets and have the courts give maximum fines for a week, with full publicity, and this disgusting practice will stop very soon."[20] But the solution wasn't so simple. Politicians shied away from drastic reforms. Police hesitated whenever they were asked to harass dog owners. Neighbors got angry and dog owners grew resentful over being pushed around—and there it sat, this feculent refuse, in fresh piles to steam in the winter air before freezing, only to thaw in the spring and come back with a vengeance. During the rainless months of summer, when stifling heat and humidity enhanced all of the city's unpleasant aromas, the smell of poop was all the more pronounced. New Yorkers speak of those dismal, pre-scooping days as though they were the Great Depression. Many people did, in fact, end up in the gutter, the place where the dogs were *supposed* to be going—sometimes this was the only place left for walking. Long stretches of public thoroughfare were entirely off-limits to humans, to the point that it isn't clear where, exactly, people could possibly have been promenading their pets. Often they allowed them to walk, sniff, and do their business on pedestrian walkways while they themselves followed alongside them, precipitously off the curb and precariously in the street where they held the other end of a leash—exactly the opposite of what the "curbing" interpretation of the law demanded! Whenever it rained, walking conditions worsened as individual mounds of feces dissolved, turning entire sidewalks a deep shade of brown. Again, it was preferable to step off the curb and into the gutter and take one's chances against the rapid currents, and the taxicabs that flew by wildly, ringing manhole covers and slowing for neither man nor beast.

The canine waste problem might have seemed inconsequential in a global context, but the practical effects that it had on the daily lives of New Yorkers could not be ignored. Children brought the stuff to school. Businessmen dragged it into board meetings. Little old ladies took it to lunch. "One night I met a friend for dinner at the Rainbow Room," recalls one woman. "I'd gotten all dressed up. As soon as I smelled it I knew exactly what it was. I was so humiliated."[21] After a few years of carrying this added burden around with them, many irate pedestrians were looking at dogs and seeing only one thing: their waste products. "An English bulldog may do nothing but snort and sleep," wrote one of the more militant anti-dog leaders, "but it also relieves itself on the sidewalk in an amount proportionate to its size. No amount of laws or enforcement can clean up New York's unwholesome mess, unless the majority of the city's citizens realize it's just plain anti-social to own a dog."[22] Increasingly, dog owners came to be regarded as anti-social misfits, renegades who were said to think only of themselves and to care nothing for the rules designed to enable people to live together in crowded cities.

Integrating dogs, and their owners, into the mainstream would be no easy task. The idea proposed as a panacea for all of the city's dog-related problems—a poop scoop law—was met with tremendous opposition at first and was short-lived. Pet owners were insulted. Animal rights activists were alarmed. The ASPCA predicted that such a law would lead to the mass abandonment of dogs across the city. But as pressure mounted, leaders were no longer able to dodge the problem, though it would take them years to find a peaceful and lawful solution. Slowly but surely, legislators and a handful of other City officials grew bolder in their approach toward animal lovers. The EPA Administrator, Jerome Kretchmer, was the first to present a bill to New York's City Council in 1971. But both Mayor John V. Lindsay and City Council avoided what seemed like a radical idea at the time. A year later, in 1972, feeling increasing pressure from anti-poop lobbyists and with the hesitant approval of Lindsay, the Council discussed the possibility of a poop scoop law. The hearings dragged on for several months, leading several City commissioners to unite in official support of the idea, but to no avail. Like the deposits that covered the sidewalks, it never got off the ground.

While elected leaders tried to sweep under the rug an issue that appeared too dangerous politically, the man on the street was in no position to overlook the massive quantities of feces underfoot. Finally, in 1977, after years of fighting and after numerous alternatives were exhausted, another attempt was made to impose a poop scoop law upon dog owners. By this time, resentment had grown to explosive levels on both sides of the battle. The simple question of what to do with a dog's leavings had become a major political issue that divided the city. Dog crap had made the cover of the *New York Times*.

Present-day pedestrians can probably appreciate what New Yorkers were going through in the seventies. Typically, even trace amounts of canine waste are enough to push some people over the edge. But whenever considering an issue that draws so much attention and that summons such fierce, gut-level emotions, it is sometimes healthy to step back and play devil's advocate—if only for a brief moment to better gauge a situation. In the broader context of the 1970s, was New York's poop problem as serious as all that? Was it possible that people were making too much ado about dog doo? And was this law that a few New Yorkers were endorsing the best solution to the city's pet problem? Dog lovers had their doubts. In fact, considering all the other animal-related issues that still needed to be addressed, poop was the least of their concerns. However unfair it might have been for them to expect others to live in these foul conditions, if one considers the overall predicament of domestic animals at the time, the extreme attention paid to Lassie's little doo-doos does begin to seem a bit far-flung. Many dogs, it seems, were no longer benefiting from the trickle-down effects of post-war prosperity. New York had tens of thousands of additional stray dogs each year (not to mention the countless stray cats). These animals roamed the streets and parks, often in packs, and they naturally pooped along the way. The ASPCA, the organization contracted to handle the bulk of the stray population, was, like the City of New York, on the brink of bankruptcy, and would soon begin closing its shelters. Taking care of pets was difficult enough in the city. Who was going to make sure that the strays were treated humanely?

Certainly not the author of *The Dog Crisis*, who complained not that animals were being mistreated, but rather that they were being pampered to the point of obscenity. Protein-rich food, she argued, was being wasted on dogs and cats while humans starved.[‡] As though to rectify this situation, pressure was placed on the United Nations to consider using dog and cat meat as alternative sources of protein in the fight against world hunger. Meanwhile, Saks Fifth Avenue was coming under

---

[‡]Animal rights advocates have long questioned the assumption that by giving to one cause we are somehow robbing another. If we took this "zero-sum" model seriously then we should have told our mothers that leaving food on our plates was actually helping all those children starving in China because there would be more food available globally. Some people grow fat while others starve because of misplaced priorities and misused resources, not pet ownership.

fire for selling rugs made of coyote hair. South Africa was raising dogs, like some Cruella de Vil, to be slaughtered and skinned to make fur coats. Protecting man's best friend in such an unfriendly environment was difficult enough, pro-dog people argued. Now they were being told to pick up feces?

Despite misguided concerns over giving dogs the food that might have been wasted on American overconsumption, objections against the new dog-owning trend revolved almost entirely around not what went into dogs, but what came out at the other end.[§] So focused was the debate on Lassie's little doo-doos that pro-dog people might have had a reason to believe that the poop scoop idea was really no more than a first step toward getting rid of dogs altogether. Indeed, the unshakeable opinion that dogs, if not their owners, were essentially *dirty* animals led many New Yorkers to conclude that the city was simply not a place for either of them, with or without a poop scoop law.

The most popular alternative solution to the dog problem in New York was to dispose of the dogs themselves. From the very beginning, animal rights activist Cleveland Amory had assailed the poop scoop idea as "a carefully planned first step toward banning dogs from New York City."[23] An outright purge—however absurd this may seem in retrospect—was considered by many to be a viable option to a poop scoop law. If not a matter of official government policy, the threat of a ban remained a constant fear in the hearts of dog lovers. Why else, they wondered, would anyone want to make them pick up feces except to punish them for having pets in the first place? When it was announced

---

[§]On the other hand, some dog owners tried to blame the pet food manufacturers—not commercial breeders or the failure of government to encourage spaying and neutering—for the soaring pet population. But wasn't this putting the cart before the horse? Having gotten the whole problem "ass-backwards," they suggested that manufacturers be taxed, and that the money be used to hire someone to pick up after their dogs! The pet food industry wasn't entirely innocent. Companies had encouraged, through irresponsible advertising, the city's overpopulation of pets, and then done little to educate consumers on proper animal care, except to try and make them feel guilty for not buying the most expensive brands.

that a new housing development on Roosevelt Island known as "the city of the future" would exclude dogs of all shapes and sizes, dog owners were alarmed over what they viewed as a dangerous precedent. "The dog droppings won't blend in with it,"[24] said the developer. Would this callous attitude spread to the rest of the city? "Dogs are a problem in New York," an administrator for the ASPCA admitted, "but I would not want to see the city ban them. If you took animals away from people in this city of 8 million, I think you'd see the biggest bunch of psychopaths you ever ran into."[25] Some 200 tenants had already gone to court with their landlords over dogs by the mid-seventies. And though this was a small percentage of the dog-owning population, the mere possibility that people would be forced to choose between their beloved pets and their homes was enough to send shock waves throughout the city. Roger Caras, a television commentator on wildlife and environmental issues (and later head of the ASPCA), only reinforced the belief that certain evil parties wanted to do away with New York's dogs. When Caras spoke at a gathering of the Humane Society and the Dog Fanciers Club in New York in 1972, he reminded listeners that it was, indeed, possible to ban dogs from a city. Reykjavik, the capital of Iceland, did not allow dogs except as service animals for livestock owners.¶ Deeply concerned that America's dog population was growing at an astounding rate, he reported that 15,000 feral (i.e., wild) dogs and cats were being born in the United States every hour, and that $200 million was being spent each year to do away with these poor, unwanted animals. Caras warned that, unless the dog population was controlled, in 30 years there would be no dogs permitted by law in New York City. Instituting a program of mandatory spaying and neutering of stray animals, he insisted, was the only practical way to avoid a ban on dogs. As for that nutty "poop scoop" idea, Caras thought it was absurd and totally impractical, an

---

¶More recently, China banned large dogs from much of the country in 2006 and restricted the number of small dogs to one per person following a rabies epidemic. In response to hundreds of human deaths, mobs approached dog owners, ripping their dogs away and clubbing them to death. In just one province, 54,429 dogs were massacred.

option advocated only by a lunatic fringe of dog haters. What were the owners supposed to do with these droppings once they'd been collected? "I want to give you an all-American scenario," Caras laughed. "Do I bring it as a hostess gift?"[26]

The result was a gigantic mess that would take years to clean up. If this was a joke, then no one was laughing. Dog owners were routinely harassed, not only for their pets' waste products but for any other inconveniences they were said to be causing. Meanwhile, their continual resistance to a poop scoop law only reinforced the belief that their animals should no longer be allowed in New York City. This in turn heightened their suspicions that dog haters wanted to take their pets away from them. Getting beyond this loop would be extremely difficult. And scooping was so radically new that pro-dog and anti-dog people alike were often unwilling to discuss what seemed an impractical idea. Adding to the confusion, the few leaders who were arrogant enough to speak up in favor of such a law tended to view it as the solution to all of the city's dog-related problems (this became the traditional cop-out of New York politicians). Some people took the side of the dog owners. Others kept silent. A few lost patience and joined the anti-poop lobby. Frustrated New Yorkers in favor of passing this law grew so furious over sidewalk conditions that it's not entirely unlikely that many of them did, in fact, begin to see it as the first step in some broader anti-dog agenda. People would never comply with a poop scoop law, they predicted, and it would only be a matter of time before lawmakers took that next step by decreeing an official ban on these animals.

For many years, there were but two sides from which to choose: pro-dog and anti-dog. This was how the issue became laid out politically, and how the battle was fought on the pavement. Though no one was exactly *for* having crap on the sidewalks, being in favor of a poop scoop law meant taking the side of the anti-dog lobby. So being in favor of allowing dogs in New York City meant standing up *against* a poop scoop law! "Legislation asking people to respect one another by requiring dog owners to pick up after their pets is not anti-dog," said EPA

Administrator Jerome Kretchmer in defense of his piece of legislation before City Council. "It's pro-people."[27] The spokesperson for New York's Dog Owners Guild was quick to respond: "Kretchmer said last week in his office that he is not anti-dog [but] pro-people. I read this to mean he is anti–pro-dog people."[28] These pro-dog people had Lassie on their side.

CHAPTER 2

ENVIRONMENTALISM AND GRASS ROOTS

> "Imagine if a big corporation executive steps off a sidewalk into some of this. It could be the last straw if he was considering moving his company out of New York City. People are leaving New York for the dirt and grime and noise and the [excreta]."
>
> —EPA Spokesman, 1971[1]

Whatever complaints people had about pets, New York probably had bigger fish to fry. The City was on the brink of bankruptcy and verging on an all-out crisis by the 1970s. Basic services, including police protection, street cleaning, trash collection, building inspection, subway repair, and park maintenance, were scaled back dramatically during these years. Businesses were relocating, taking with them jobs and much-needed tax revenues. Government plunged deeper into debt but spending skyrocketed as leaders struggled to maintain a crumbling infrastructure. Money problems only heightened social tensions. Poverty and unrest threatened to push certain neighborhoods over the edge and riots, though Mayor Lindsay would always maintain that New York never had any, were a constant concern. Soon the city's violent crime rate was rivaled only by Detroit's. This overall deterioration meant that average wage-earning citizens had to learn to live in filth and fear for their lives. When they weren't dodging the landmines that lined the sidewalks, they were preyed upon night and day by muggers, gangs, rapists, and the occasional serial killer. As the optimism of the early Lindsay years and hopes for "Fun City" gave way to darker visions of the future, even die-hard native New Yorkers chose to get out. The city's birth rate had dropped to an alarmingly low level by the mid-seventies.[*]

New York was not alone. Its perilous predicament was due to a larger and seemingly irreversible trend that transformed American life. The nationwide urban crisis was dragging down Washington, Chicago, Los Angeles, and Detroit, among other cities where the flight of manufacturing jobs and the reduction of tax bases caused living conditions to be degraded in humiliating ways. Yet the personal concerns and daily complaints of New Yorkers got the lion's share of attention. After all, theirs was older and more densely populated than most cities. And whether or not their fiscal predicament was really so unique, or their problems more serious than anyone else's, they could always fall back on those hefty reserves of self-reliance, not to mention self-importance, for which they were famous. New Yorkers were able to summon extra courage from the knowledge that all the media were parked permanently at their doorsteps. Going out, whether to walk the dog or to get some ice cream, they found cameras and headlines ready and waiting to record their every reaction to these trying times. Here was their chance, as they faced obstacles that would have intimidated just about anybody, to show the world just how tough they really were.

"Listen you fuckers, you screwheads," mused the lone vigilante in the 1975 film *Taxi Driver*. "Here's a man who would not take

---

[*]It might also be argued that the 1970s, while remembered mainly for their unpleasantness, became one of New York's most vibrant and creative decades. A new wave of immigrants, mostly young, educated, and of middle-class origins, many of them with artistic aspirations, helped to fill the void left by the mass exodus called "white flight." These new New Yorkers found inspiration in urban decay, and were eager to take advantage of the unusual freedoms to be found in a more chaotic setting.

"Goddam Dogs!"

it anymore, a man who stood up against the scum, the cunts, the dogs, the filth, the shit." Like so many of his kind, this alienated, kicked-around average Joe felt he had an individual responsibility to help save his beloved city from a kind of sickness that he believed had infected it on all levels. From the smoggy skyline to the crime-ridden streets and the rat-infested subway system, New York seemed threatened by unhealthy influences. "Thank God for the rain," wrote the disturbed cabbie in his diary while planning a killing spree. "Just help wash away the garbage and the trash off the sidewalks. . . . Some day a *real* rain will come along and wash all the scum off the streets. This city's like an open sewer."[2]

A fine line separated community spirit from downright vigilantism during these troubled times. Not all New Yorkers felt that taking matters into their own hands necessarily meant strapping themselves with six or eight guns. Still, the purification idea was very tempting when no other plan seemed to be working. The hope that all of the city's problems could somehow be reduced to a matter of hygiene—and solved with a sort of hearty, grassroots cleanup and some elbow grease—was very popular at the time. In fact, the optimistic belief that people still had some basic control over the quality of their lives and the future of their city was what kept the situation in New York from becoming worse than it eventually did. Excitement over sprucing up and weeding out seemed to permeate every aspect of daily life. Countless tulip bulbs were sown during these years, and John Lindsay is still remembered, if for nothing else, because "He planted a lot of trees." But not all improvements were cosmetic. Many a purse-snatcher was knocked down and beaten to a pulp by witnesses who finally decided "to get involved." With the machinery of government approaching a standstill, volunteers or vigilantes took it upon themselves to do the jobs that it no longer could. Leaders made unpaid private citizens bolder with new laws that they themselves were asked to enforce. Surely, it was widely believed, civil unrest and gang activity could be crushed simply by scrubbing the graffiti from Grant's Tomb, and then waiting around to catch anyone from the ghetto who tried to break the new anti-graffiti law a second time. The same sort of reasoning led many people to believe that maybe the streets could be made safer if only the sidewalks were kept clear of dog doo. As a population ran scared and government ran out of ideas, solutions to the urban crisis grew increasingly desperate and ill-conceived. While the NYPD greeted tourists at airports with flyers calling New York "Fear City" and warning them away, and Abe Beame, the Mayor-Accountant, cooked the books to keep things solvent, his wife Mary was doing her part by leading an angry mob though a public park in search of littering pet owners. A few months later, Son of Sam would claim that a Rottweiler had told him to kill all those people.

Despite the best efforts to preserve law and order, confusion was often the only order of the day. Surely no sane person could honestly have believed that dogs were at all to blame for New York's present predicament? On the contrary, filth and violence were the fault of a city that could no longer keep itself either clean or safe. And yet the tendency to confuse the causes with the effects of urban decay was widespread. New Yorkers were, despite opinions to the contrary, only human. They were under tremendous stress. As the quality of their lives worsened, they focused not on the high-minded theories of socioeconomics or recent historical trends, but on the mundane problems and annoyances they confronted daily. Many gave into a kind of creeping cynicism. They either moved out or simply threw their arms in the air and tried to get used to the nastiness of urban life. Others refused to give in or to be forced out of their beloved city. An allegorical painting of these apocalyptic times might depict self-styled heroes struggling, knee-deep in trash and with muggers breathing down their necks, to uphold the columns of Civilization while packs of scrawny mutts nip at their shit-caked heels. New Yorkers labored on, trying their hardest to keep the sidewalk clean and Central Park green, even though neither one was very safe.

*   *   *

It was against this sad backdrop that New York's Environmental Protection Agency was first conceived. No matter how successfully government tapped into the city's reserves of self-reliance, private citizens alone couldn't be expected to do everything. What better way to show an overworked population, and a world that looked on in disgust, that New York was cleaning up its act than to create a vast City "superagency" devoted to this superhuman task?

Cities everywhere owe a great debt to Mayor John Lindsay's EPA, one of the very first of its kind in the world. The advances made in these early years would help to improve living conditions in New York and set precedents that would influence generations to come. Before dogs became the focus and programs started running off track, much of substance was accomplished. The belief that basic quality-of-life issues were as important as all the rest led Lindsay to press on with plans as far-reaching as they were inspirational to the general public. This was no "Broken Window" campaign. Unlike Rudolph Giuliani's attempts decades later to fix the city's big problems by first cleaning up the small ones, Lindsay's move came in response to threats far more serious than drunk and disorderly behavior. Recent studies, and increased awareness of the human impact on ecosystems, were cause for alarm. People were dying from air pollution. The water surrounding Manhattan was toxic. Folk singer Pete Seeger had led a famous protest over a power plant planned for construction on the Hudson River, an event that only hastened the decision of New York leaders to tap into the growing concern over the safety of nuclear power. Public interest was also heightened by best-selling books like *Silent Spring* and *The Doomsday Book* (billed as "a terrifying roll call of man's sins against the earth as she plunges toward a future of sterility and filth"). Suddenly, New Yorkers wanted to transform the environment. "Returning the ecology of certain areas to wilderness state is a faint, contemporary retro-fashion echo of the entire New York social fabric a generation ago,"[3] writes P. J. O'Rourke on the spirit of the times that animated New York as much as it impacted the rest of the world. Citizens were gripped by a sense of urgency and compelled their leaders to take a stand. There could be no delay. Stringent measures had to be taken to prevent New York—and, of course, the rest of the world—from becoming uninhabitable.

Lindsay used environmentalism wisely. To be for "the environment" was to be for New York.[†] The thrilling new movement gave his city the brief burst of optimism it so desperately needed, at least until someone could find a way of rebuilding the economy. Environmentalism, though it came in response to problems quite real and pressing, also served as a temporary distraction from the ones for which there were no solutions at the moment. This new shift of focus renewed New York's energies, however briefly, and restored its faith in the future. It gave people a cause that no one could deny, and had a unifying effect on a population divided over how to solve its problems and still unclear about what, exactly, those problems even were. The appeal of environmentalism transcended class, race, political affiliations, even the

---

[†]The tendency to equate the urban crisis with environmental problems was clearly stated by one of Lindsay's aides who said, regarding the proposed expansion of a Con Edison plant in Astoria: "It's the urban crisis boiled down to the needs of power and the needs of the environment."[4]

generation gap. The drive to make the place cleaner, greener, and more wholesome overall hit an almost messianic note when Lindsay hosted the world's first "Earth Day" in 1970. The following year, he helped to expand the successful event into "Earth Week." Both holidays are still honored across the globe. In response to events in New York, even President Nixon, attacked by Lindsay on many occasions for the war in Vietnam, was forced to admit: "The 1970s absolutely must be the years when America pays its debt to the past by reclaiming the purity of its air, its waters, and our living environment. It is literally now or never."[5] After first trying to sabotage the new movement, Nixon created an EPA in Washington, signed amendments to the Clean Air Act and the Clean Water Act, and instituted other major reforms. Before long, newspapers and magazines across the nation were adding special "Environment" sections for their readers, building a greater awareness of its effects on health and happiness. Like those fearless and industrious New Yorkers, Americans everywhere were taking matters into their own hands by keeping their eyes peeled for "litterbugs" on the highways and reminding themselves that only *they* could prevent forest fires.

    In so many ways, this was a period of experimental change, both in terms of how cities might be run and in the broader realm of political expression. While a group of wealthy matrons from nearby Connecticut's chapter of Women's Liberation filed suit against that state for making dog license tags in the shape of fire hydrants—the tags, they claimed, were "sexist" because only male dogs lifted their legs to urinate—New York leaders were busy experimenting with new ways of handling waste products. They were innovative because they had to be. The city produced an estimated 10 pounds of solid waste per capita daily. The bulk of the money spent in these early years went to constructing new, more environmentally sound waste disposal and water filtration plants, facilities considered indispensable today. Air pollution, too, was reduced significantly by 1970, when the sulfur dioxide content of New York air had been reduced by 60 percent. Though little could be done locally about the fossil-fueled automobile, the number one source of air pollution in cities, new guidelines forcing landlords to upgrade incineration facilities in apartment buildings meant that future generations could breathe more easily.

Yet with each small step toward a more livable city, the public's appetite for environmental improvements only grew stronger. As New York (and the world) suddenly awoke from centuries of guilt-free pollution, leaders were placed in the awkward position of having to find quick solutions to complex problems. By creating a new awareness of the harmful effects of the environment, and by encouraging hope for the future, Lindsay had created a monster.

Even without a fiscal crisis, New York leaders would have had trouble meeting the high standards they had set. According to Merrill Eisenbud, New York's first EPA Administrator and a world-renowned scientist,[‡] taking effective action on environmental problems was difficult from the start. He would later recall that "the public was impatient" with its leaders' efforts and that "politicians vying for public office began to outdo each other in their statements about what should be accomplished."[6] As a result, according to Eisenbud, improving the environment became a complicated and terribly inefficient business. For example, public fervor and the myth of "zero pollution" in 1970 caused a sewage treatment plant on Manhattan's West Side to be redesigned unnecessarily, he said, increasing the cost from $250,000,000 to an enormous $1 billion. According to Eisenbud, this was but one instance of massive overkill by the City's EPA. Most important, he said, legitimate environmental concerns received far less money and attention than they deserved. Though air pollution was significantly reduced during Eisenbud's two years in office, levels of contaminants in New York's atmosphere would surpass national guidelines for decades to come, despite the many efforts made to ban private automobiles from

---

[‡]Eisenbud was actually New York's second EPA Administrator. The brief tenure of James Marcus had ended just a few weeks after his appointment by Lindsay when it was learned that Marcus, a close family friend of the Lindsays, had arranged for mob kickbacks while Commissioner of Water Supply, Gas & Electricity. Marcus was arrested and served prison time. But Lindsay's EPA survived the scandal, becoming a crown jewel in his newly reorganized and gargantuan government.

Manhattan. The success of environmental reform was, at best, partial in these early years, and when it came time for Eisenbud to step down he was already growing disillusioned. The EPA was feeling the heat of controversy over nuclear power, in its early stages of acceptance at the time, when thousands of dead fish were found floating near a new power plant on the Hudson River. This only heightened "misguided opposition to nuclear reactors,"[7] said Eisenbud, insisting that the fish kill was an unrelated and isolated event.[§]

If the greater mission of saving the environment became entangled in politics, Lindsay's appointment of Jerome Kretchmer as the new EPA Administrator was purely political. Kretchmer was a lawyer and a former member of the New York State Assembly. He had no prior training or experience in scientific or environmental matters. When it became known that Lindsay had selected Kretchmer to run the EPA, three commissioners from that agency decided to retire. One dismayed environmentalist said: "Jerry knows about air pollution because he breathes, he knows about solid waste because he takes out the garbage, but he doesn't know about the pollution of water because he probably doesn't drink much of the stuff."[8] Eisenbud, who had planned to leave anyway, was the least happy about his replacement. "Who the hell is he?"[9] he remembers asking the *Times*,[¶] astonished, as were other officials, that the mayor would make a political appointment to an agency that demanded, in their opinion, a technical expertise. Soon Eisenbud and others would learn what a flashy, professional politician could do with New York's environmental fad.

Before Jerome Kretchmer could package canine waste into a legitimate environmental concern, he first had to style himself as a dazzling, fast-track defender of the environment. Unlike his predecessor, he didn't spend time in laboratories or white coats. There were no dull clipboards in sight. The new EPA Administrator stepped into the limelight as one

---

[§]The Indian Point power plant hasn't ceased being controversial. In recent years, however, efforts to close it down are due mainly to its possible strategic use by terrorists.

[¶]What the *Times* printed in 1970 was "I've never heard of this guy."[10]

of the bright, young, hip movers-and-shakers downtown, just the kind of updated politician with whom Lindsay preferred to surround himself. An attention-grabber from the get-go, Kretchmer had arrived, he himself admitted, "to make noise"[11] over the environment. He wore fat, loud, garish ties in swirling psychedelic patterns. No stodgy bureaucrat would have been caught wearing Kretchmer's style of wide-lapelled suits with bell-bottomed trousers. Nor did the cowboy boots endear him to more conservative colleagues. His long, bushy hair and swinging sideburns invited comparisons to Elliott Gould. Visibly ensconced high in the Municipal Building, the lower-Broadway hipster played Elton John records for official visitors, and his staff dressed and acted casually at the workplace long before the yuppies arrived to take credit for these inventions.

Laid back though he might have been, the public defender of all that was green had no illusions about power. For all the young idealism that permeated the Lindsay administration, Kretchmer showed a stark pragmatism despite his upstart age. Here was a hard-edged, scrappy politician risen from the ranks of the working class. Once, in the City Hall rotunda, he had a bloody fistfight with Councilman Michael De-Marco, who had called him a liar. Behind all the artsy, late-sixties cool was an earthy, no-nonsense approach to the new politics of environmentalism and a keen insight into its possible uses. This meant redefining goals. The Lindsay administration had suffered tremendous damage for failing to handle not the "big things," as causes of that era were called, but a recent snowstorm. Kretchmer planned to respond to the public's true concerns. "The guy on the street doesn't want to hear about air pollution," he declared in an interview. "He wants his garbage picked up."[12] This was a new take on the global movement. "When the President talks about the environment," he explained, "he's talking about streams, you know, and fish kills, and all that stuff. When I talk about the environment, I'm talking about the subways."[13] So focused was the new EPA on the day-to-day functions of government that some of Kretchmer's aides, who'd signed up with high-minded hopes for contributing to a greater cause, were disappointed. "We didn't come here to work on street litter,"[14] complained one of them. "It all proves," said an environmentalist, "that Jerry is just a politician on the make who'd have us believe that the environment is everything from a hangnail up."[15] Even in his less glamorous capacities, Kretchmer was inviting criticism. "I was kind of glad to hear Jerry bragging about the new equipment used during the New Year's snowstorm," Merrill Eisenbud told the *Times*, "because I ordered it."[16]

However broadly and inaccurately Kretchmer might have defined "pollution," this was a perfect cause for career building, he said, "because of its universality." If only he could clean up the city a little, he predicted, "man, I'm in."[17]

Over the next two years New York would be transformed into a stage for the drama that unfolded. The problem was that, just as the City's ability to go on making anything more than superficial improvements was slipping, public demand was growing stronger than ever. Despite Kretchmer's enormous budget projections, most of the major advances to be made in these years had, in fact, already been made by 1970 when he took over the EPA. As New York sank deeper into debt, more money was borrowed to feed the public's appetite for reform and ever more lavish efforts were made to stage the EPA's commitment to the cause. Like the new Metropolitan Opera House in Lincoln Center, where almost as much money seemed to go toward scenery as the music itself, sheer spending became a measure of dramatic effect for Kretchmer's EPA. The new Administrator billed himself as a superhero for Lindsay's new superagency. He sought a fantastic 1971–72 capital budget of $1.2 billion, and though he received less than he had requested, it was four times the amount Eisenbud had received. By 1972, EPA projects received 71 cents of every construction dollar, and accounted for 29 percent of the City's capital budget. "Maintaining and improving the environment is very expensive,"[18] Kretchmer explained to the press. And no matter how lavish the expense, the political currency to be reaped from giving such a hearty embrace to the environment could hardly be measured. Kretchmer's job, during this brief fervor for all matters environmental, was second in importance to none other than the mayor's.

Only John Lindsay had more invested in the shiny new cause. Turning back and reversing the course of the movement, however difficult it was becoming to fund it, was not an attractive option. As leaders would soon learn about welfare, it was unpopular to make a gift and then ask for it back. Facing a growing deficit and fiscal instability, Lindsay renewed his appeals to civic duty and "community participation." As he had done in his famous pedestrian travels among the urban poor, he descended to the pavements, this time in a wave of environmental public relations.

Taking back the streets was a major theme of "Earth Day." For Lindsay, this meant using the crowds to help push aside all the automobiles, proven to be the number one source of air pollution in cities. "Alternative means of transportation" became New York's best hope as Lindsay was shown peddling a bicycle up and down the avenues that had been cleared for him. Not far behind, thousands of eager followers also pumped past the barricades thrown up along the way, if only for a day. The following year when "Earth Day" was expanded into "Earth Week," the stage unfolded more elaborately. Not only were streets closed to automobile traffic, much of the city's pavement was transformed into a kind of nature reserve for an entire week. To prove his unwavering commitment to making New York cleaner and greener, Lindsay had his Parks Department install temporary benches, and potted flowers and trees, on paved surfaces everywhere. Once again, Lindsay and a crowd took to the streets on velocipedes.

Lindsay's fierce opposition to automobile transportation tied into not only public demands for a more wholesome environment, but an ongoing debate over whether cars should be allowed in New York at all. "The philosophy of the new administration was, at the time, militantly pro-mass transit, anti-automobile,"[19] Robert Caro recalls of Lindsay's war against these fouling machines, which led to confrontations with Robert Moses, the powerful head of the Triborough Bridge and Tunnel Authority who wanted to build a superhighway across lower Manhattan. Riding against the grain of progress through the makeshift gardens of Earth Week, Lindsay drew as much attention as he had with his impromptu walks among the urban poor. "Lindsay Leads Pack,"[20] said the *Times* after thousands of New Yorkers followed the peddling mayor up and down city streets lined with potted plants. Surrounded by television crews and reporters, Lindsay climbed off his bicycle and made a symbolic inspection of the pavement for cleanliness, publicly upbraiding Jerome Kretchmer for a street that hadn't been properly swept. Then he gave a speech on the virtues of "non-engine-driven means of locomotion"[21] and took a walk for the March of Dimes. The *Times* reported: "Mayor Lindsay took part in the 16-mile walk, loping for ten blocks through Central Park with several hundred squealing teenagers. The Mayor, dressed in jeans and sneakers and a checked shirt, seemed to enjoy the day despite the city's budget problems."[22]

The idea of banning private cars from the city, however likely this was to improve New York's air supply, seems rather quaint today when few people outside California would dare to question the sanctity of the SUV. But the idea was taken quite seriously at the time. And while Lindsay's concerns weren't without some factual basis in recent studies on air pollution, they tied into an age-old debate begun when automobiles had first arrived in cities. The administration shared many of the assumptions of urbanist Lewis Mumford. "The motorcar," said Mumford, "shapes and forms—mutilates and *de*forms might be better words—not only the city but whole city regions."[23] According to Mumford, automobiles had once served a positive purpose by giving urban populations greater access to unspoiled rural areas. But in providing freedom of movement, they caused surrounding areas to be wracked with endless entanglements of highways and the sterile, lifeless suburban towns that sprouted up along the way. In the end, the private car had made the country more distant than ever. In cities, its effects were disastrous. Not only did automobiles become the number one source of air pollution, older cities like New York were simply not designed to accommodate them. "Automobiles and people," Mumford warned, "compete for vanishing space. It is a battle in which all are losers. . . . No form of movement is more greedy of space."[24] As the toxic effects and daily irritants became intolerable, advocates of public transportation like Mumford and Lindsay called for not only fewer cars, but "pedestrian malls" to replace the congested streets. Jerome Kretchmer did his part by endorsing the electric car, and he tried to use the City's large shareholder status with General Motors to help Ralph Nader force the company to reduce emissions. He also had a booth installed at the 1971 Auto Show where brochures were distributed reading "The Car Is Anti-City" and a slide projector showed clouds of auto exhaust and lines of abandoned vehicles. But even the best intentions were proving almost futile. As city sidewalks were narrowed to make ever-wider paths for automobiles, and New York sank deeper into a phase of urban decay, the streets themselves eroded into a network of potholes—the number two complaint in American cities, second only to dog feces by the mid-1970s—leaving the pavements looking like the surface of the moon. Just how was government supposed to keep up with repairs, even if it had the money to do so? "On any given day," Lindsay wrote in his 1970 book *The City*, "some of the thousands of miles of road will be in disrepair—but in a city as densely populated and traffic-choked as New York the closing of a single midtown lane can snarl traffic for hours and send new waves of frustration coursing through the veins of the city."[25]

Not everyone agreed that all the blame should be placed on the automobile. And as living conditions worsened in New York, Lindsay's best efforts to improve the environment were losing steam. Even his more popular PR stunts, it seemed, were beginning to backfire. "The theatricals of riding bikes for a few hours on Madison Avenue is a safe one-shot gimmick," remarked Representative Mario Biaggi, an upcoming mayoral candidate. "The real test between promise and performance would be for the city fathers to jump in and swim in both the Hudson and East Rivers, where 325 million gallons of totally untreated filthy raw sewage is discharged each day by the city."[26] Increasingly, Lindsay followed the path of Jerome Kretchmer, shifting his attention from the grander schemes to smaller, more manageable problems. He tried to open "Little City Halls," places where citizens would be given a greater role in the task of saving their city, or at least be given the illusion that such a thing was possible. Funded not by taxpayers but by private donations, these were to be forums for New Yorkers demanding action on issues like street lights, smoke abatement, vandalism, landlord–tenant disputes, and noncompliance with dog leash laws.

The agenda only lengthened as New York's predicament grew graver. So closely did the city's future seem tied to tiny improvements that the definition of what needed improving became broader by the day. Soon "noise pollution" was added to the long list of impurities that threatened the city's very fragile peace of mind. A "Noise Abatement Bureau" was created in Kretchmer's EPA to cleanse the air of sound waves. "Quiet Week" was celebrated with one minute of enforced silence each day in Central Park. Meanwhile, Mrs. Lindsay rode around the outer boroughs with a fashion designer and handed out cash awards to people using natural-gas lamps in their front yards. In a few years, the editors of the *New York Times* would include under "the environment" such a wide array of problems as "high crime rates, dirt and congestion, weak public schools, and high living costs."[27] As the fiscal crisis worsened and the list of complaints lengthened, leaders were forced to rely more heavily than ever upon "community participation" to do the cleanup jobs that government no longer could. But for John Lindsay, public enthusiasm was fading fast.

CHAPTER 3

CAUTIONARY TALES: DOGGY POLITICS 101

"People who run for public office should not throw rocks at dogs."

—Ed Koch[1]

New York confronted a situation that was unprecedented in the 1970s. In less than a decade, the city had acquired the largest canine population known in history. At the same time, streets had been gradually widened over the years to accommodate more cars, leaving sidewalks narrower than ever. The little concrete left for pedestrians was often covered in feces. Just where were people supposed to walk? Recent writings by urbanist Jane Jacobs on the importance of shared spaces to the life of cities were also drawing attention to these areas. Serious fiscal constraints, combined with the public's newly found and acute awareness of the effects of the overall "environment" on health and happiness, pointed to the conclusion that a solution, as radically new as the problem, was in order. Meanwhile, the mounting tensions of urban life, most of these in response to problems that had nothing whatsoever to do with dogs, added to a mix of circumstances that was bound to be toxic.

But were dog emissions as dangerous as car exhaust? While the shortage of walking space and breathable air became critical, and the war against automobiles began to seem like a pipe dream, many New Yorkers—however absurd this may seem in retrospect—shifted the blame for their problems away from automobiles and onto dogs! Perhaps the greatest excess from this golden age of environmentalism was a continual tendency to compare dogs, and the effects they were said to be having on city life, to automobiles, which had already been proven the number one source of air pollution. Fido was billed as a foe of the ecology and added to the long list of forms of "pollution" thought to be jeopardizing New York's recovery from the urban crisis. What had started as a daily annoyance became one of the hottest political issues of the day. Because of the *social* problems that dogs were causing, New York leaders were forced to respond not only to unwarranted fears of contagion and contamination, but to this strange tendency to cast canines in the shape of a big, gas-guzzling Ford station wagon. Dogs, like automobiles, were viewed as four-wheeled nuisances that belonged on the other side of the curb—if, indeed, they belonged in the city at all.

Comparisons ranged from subtle and understandable to blatant and absurd. This was the language of the times. "Because dogs serve a psychological function for some," said the Director of the Bureau of Animal Affairs, "do we all have to put up with their filth? That's nonsense. Cars are important, too, but that does not mean we shouldn't have emission controls."[2] The *New York Times* received a plethora of letters from concerned citizens offering their own personal solutions to this two-pronged problem. Typically, letters about dogs appeared alongside similar complaints about automobiles, questions on where taxicabs should be allowed to pick up passengers, even suggestions on how to prevent those terrible New York traffic jams known as gridlock. "An auto owner pays for licensing and maintenance," reads one such letter, "whereas dog owners do not and expect the rest of us to pay the freight in filthy cities and high costs . . . Up the license fee, substantially. Fine them for the mess."[3] Then, just next to the letter about dogs appears another that reads: "The reduction in traffic when owners of private cars had less gas was a revelation. Buses, trucks, and taxis moved quickly and efficiently. It would make much more sense to ban private cars and increase the number of buses, subways, and cruising taxis to move people throughout the city."[4] In another example, a letter suggesting a single-car-per-family law for the greater metropolitan area is followed by a letter demanding a "limited dog density per gutter block"[5] and a ceiling of two dogs per household. These comparisons come up repeatedly throughout the seventies and represent not only a lack of clarity in defining legitimate environmental and safety concerns, but often an insensitivity toward man's best friend. Even dog lovers couldn't resist making the comparison, if only to defend their right to keep their pets. "Less unhealthful but nevertheless more disgusting," wrote one of them, "is the mess left behind by those who selfishly do major automobile repair work in city streets, leaving oil and grease and the litter of discarded auto parts."[6] New York was on the brink of bankruptcy and fiscal worries also entered the discussion. "One solution to the problem," reads yet another solution to the problem, "involves looking on each of these canine deposits as a tax on New Yorkers levied by the dogs and their owners. Each time a dog does his thing he simultaneously reduces (that is, taxes) the quality of life of all the city's inhabitants. It is a particularly insidious form of tax in that we never get anything in return. Recognizing that a complete ban on dog ownership is, unfortunately, an unreasonable thing to expect politicians to support, I suggest an equitable compromise. Let each dog owner be required to pay a stiff levy, perhaps $100 per year, for the privilege of owning one of these street-fouling machines!"[7]

Lindsay's position on automobiles was quite clear. His travels on foot and on bicycle for Earth Day and Earth Week were incontrovertible proof of his firm pro-mass transit, anti-automobile stand. His Parks Administrator had Central Park closed to cars on Sundays. Lindsay himself tried to have Madison Avenue converted into a permanent pedestrian mall. But he was careful not to say, at least not in so many words, that dogs, like automobiles, should be banned from the city altogether. For if environmentalism served to unite New Yorkers briefly toward a common cause, dogs were another matter. Rather than unifying, dogs were

"We breed them for aggressiveness."

having a divisive effect and became a dangerous topic of conversation. This placed leaders in a very awkward position without robbing dogs of their political usefulness. Just as excessive environmental politics had to do with more than protecting the environment per se, so did this debate have to do with so much more than preventing pollution. However creatively certain parties tried to compare dogs to automobiles in their quest for a cleaner, safer city, deeper beliefs often came into play.

The fact is that with or without environmentalism, dogs would have been a problem for New York City. Environmentalism just provided the vocabulary to express those deep-set emotions that even a poop scoop law couldn't hope to calm. People tend toward two extremes. They either love dogs beyond containing themselves—or they hate them beyond control. Seldom does someone "kind of like" or "not really care for" dogs. Early childhood experiences with these animals, or lack thereof, tend to lock extreme feelings of love and hatred, like any prejudice, firmly into place. As a result, dog lovers have been known to defend their pets absolutely and without the slightest regard for other people. They react like proud parents who are blind to the annoyances their rotten children might be causing for the rest of society. So fierce is this devotion, however much one loves other animals, it can hardly be denied that something very much like a cult has developed around dogs—a cult of innocence.

Anti-dog people have been no more impartial than dog people. Though New York has always had people who could claim, truthfully, to like dogs "just as much as the next person" but to hate wading through piles of their excrement, underestimating the legions of bona fide dog haters would be naïve. The city's anti-dog lobby has, over the years, been characterized by the most extreme militancy. Dog haters have misused science to justify their every paranoia about the so-called "health" effects of pets when these are marginal and almost nonexistent. All too often, cultural and psychological factors have overshadowed the possibility for sensible dialogue. Unbased fears have caused dogs to be banned from supermarkets, cafés, and even Federal post offices in the United States. The fact that dogs happen to have teeth has provided further fuel to arguments for banning them from New York. No matter what dog haters are told about these animals, for some mysterious reasons that lie deep in their formative years or evolutionary past, they continue to fear canines, especially when they have families to protect. Dogs and children, many parents believe, simply cannot coexist in the city, a belief that has caused endless social problems. Superstitious adults, by instilling irrational fears in their offspring, have assured that the next generation will be no less emotionally disturbed and will cringe at the sight of the tiniest lapdog rounding a corner.

Given the overwhelming emotions on both sides of the argument, finding some middle ground for constructive dialogue over dogs has been extremely difficult. Their lovers are said to be defensive and arrogant. "Cynophobists"—people who fear canines—tend to resist therapy, the best cure for what ails them. Yet it would be inaccurate to conclude that nothing's changed in recent years. A few decades ago, not only was standing up against dog owners socially acceptable, dog-bashing was becoming a hobby for many New Yorkers. Social critic Fran Lebowitz, for example, had no qualms about expressing her hatred for dogs and disdain for their owners, and she stated her views in ways that no writer would dare today. Not only did Lebowitz believe that New York's poop scoop law was destined to fail, she represented a solid constituency who felt that no law could make living with dogs tolerable in cities. "Therefore," she concluded in 1981, three years into the new canine waste law, "I might more accurately state that I do not like animals, with two exceptions. The first being in the past tense, at which point I like them just fine, in the form of nice crispy spareribs and Bass Weejun penny loafers. And the second being outside, by which I mean not merely outside, as in outside the house, but genuinely outside, as in outside in the woods, or preferably outside in the South American jungle. This is, after all, only fair. I don't go there; why should they come here? The above being the case, it should then come as no surprise that I do not approve of the practice of keeping animals as pets. 'Not approve' is too mild: pets should be disallowed by law. Especially dogs. Especially in New York City. I have not infrequently verbalized this sentiment in what now passes for polite society, and have invariably been the recipient of the information that even if dogs should be withheld from the frivolous, there would still be the blind and the pathologically lonely to think of. I am not totally devoid of compassion, and after much thought I believe that I have hit upon the perfect solution to this problem—let the lonely lead the blind."[8]

If writers were able to vent their frustrations, politicians weren't quite so free to express their true feelings in public. For elected leaders, taking either side meant taking a risk they might be better off avoiding. In fact, saying anything at all about dogs could unleash an emotional tsunami, and perhaps even fighting in the streets. Breaching the gulf between dog lovers and dog haters would be no easy task for the Lindsay administration. Was it possible to convince the pro-dog lobby that being in favor of a poop scoop law didn't necessarily mean being against dogs altogether? And how could leaders show sympathy for dogs without being accused of showing favoritism toward their owners? In the either/or atmosphere of doggy politics, it would be extremely difficult to convince most people of the possibility for some middle ground, one that would be feces-free, and upon which people with and without dogs might walk together in peace. Just mentioning the idea brought extreme reactions from both sides of the curb. Over the years, most politicians have chosen, perhaps wisely, to sit on the sidelines rather than take on such a volatile topic. Others have, with varying degrees of success and failure, tried to harness the fervor surrounding pets and use it to their advantage. Even Ed Koch, the mayor who would push hardest for a poop scoop law, had to admit that no elected leader could afford to approach dogs without caution. "People who run for public office should not throw rocks at dogs,"[9] he observed in later years. Rudolph Giuliani, who later managed to revive anti-poop vigilantism on New York pavements while keeping a dog of his own for photo opportunities, would echo these words of wisdom. "It's very bad to run against a dog,"[10] he remarked during his own run as mayor.

Back in 1971, John Lindsay was preparing for a presidential campaign. The Democratic primary of 1972 would soon decide whether or not he would have a shot at the White House. When first pressed into service on dogs, Lindsay avoided getting too involved in issues concerning them—he left this to his EPA Administrator, Jerome Kretchmer. For while elected leaders and presidential hopefuls must use extreme caution when handling the more delicate issues, appointed officials have greater freedom to take stands on the more volatile topics. In fact, an important role of appointed officials is to deflect some of the political heat away from elected leaders and to do some of the dirty work that their bosses cannot do themselves. Jerome Kretchmer might have been in a very good position to take on the city's dog owners. But even Kretchmer had greater political ambitions that could be thwarted were he to be labeled a "dog hater." While Lindsay was planning to run for President of the United States, Kretchmer was considering running for Mayor of New York City.

Pushing for a poop scoop law in New York meant walking on some very slippery pavement. The media only made the walk more hazardous. Dozens of stories appeared in the early seventies describing, in gory detail, how small children and infants had been mauled and killed by dogs, those very pets many people believed to be a vital part of the all-American family. At the other extremity, when dogs weren't portrayed as bloodthirsty killers, they were shown as saints. One heart-wrenching "humane interest" story, for example, appeared in the *Times* in 1971, the year Kretchmer first proposed his poop scoop law to City Council and began asking for Mayor Lindsay's support. This was the story of an 11-year-old boy in Dayton, Ohio, whose dog had been hit by a car. It seemed the dog was in great pain, and that his leg would soon have to be amputated. The little boy was heartbroken, and this was a tale guaranteed to move anyone but a cold-hearted scoundrel. President Nixon took it upon himself to write a letter saying how badly he felt for the boy and his beloved companion. "I can well understand why this cruelty to Chopper is as painful to you as it most certainly is to him," Nixon told the child. "Sometimes in life we have to make bad things work for good, and I think the best tribute you can pay to Chopper is to resolve firmly that you will always be especially kind to those who cannot help themselves. In a positive way, you can help balance the scale of justice, but in a way that could make Chopper proud of you. Animals always need our protection, but I have a feeling that more than ever Chopper needs to have a cheerful friend. I know he will be able to count on you."[11] Nixon's letter received national attention.

Now, feeling or showing sympathy for a dog in distress does not make a person naïve. But the overflow of emotion brought on by the mere mention of dogs has served to make any issue even vaguely related to them very muddy, indeed. And it can scarcely be denied that the very chaos surrounding the subject does present leaders with oppor-tunities for self-promotion. For Nixon, a kind letter to a boy with a sick dog managed to deflect, somewhat, from an unpopular war in Vietnam. And although John Lindsay was a fierce opponent of the war and of Richard Nixon, he could not ignore the lesson to be learned. Nixon had demonstrated early on in his career the effective and even brilliant use of pets in politics. His famous "Checkers Speech" of 1952—Checkers was a black-and-white cocker spaniel—had saved him the nomination for Vice President on the Eisenhower ticket. One of the most noted oratories in American history, the Checkers Speech was about the family dog and determined Nixon's future in politics.

It all began when Nixon was accused of receiving inappropriate funds from supporters while he was a California senator in 1951. A scandal broke and he was forced to defend himself publicly. Whether or not the accusation was true didn't matter once the press had run the story. Eisenhower, who had been considering Nixon as a vice-presidential candidate, was changing his mind about the Senator's usefulness. He decided to cut his losses and ordered Nixon to confess to the American public, however damaging this might be. At this point, any further association could have been damaging to Eisenhower, or to anyone else for that matter. Nixon's entire political career was in the balance.

Nixon rallied, however, with one of the landmark media ploys of all time. He hired a staff of advertising executives to help him work on a new kind of strategy, a televised speech. For several weeks, Nixon was coached by the team he had hired to perfect the poses and smiles for a live performance scheduled to clear his name. He even had the transmission delayed by two days in order to build a larger viewing audience. When the fateful evening finally arrived, Nixon appeared in living rooms across the nation as a common, hard-working American with a wife and two daughters—and a little dog named "Checkers." He flatly denied having received inappropriate gifts from supporters but admitted that one present, the baby cocker spaniel that his young daughter had named, did, in fact, come from a supporter in Texas. "And you know," Nixon said to millions of viewers, "the kids, like all kids, loved the dog. And I just want to say this, right now, that regardless of what they say about it, we are going to keep it." The speech was a huge success. Months after his heart-to-heart talk with the American people, Nixon and his family were still receiving gifts for Checkers, including hundreds of leashes, handwoven dog blankets, and enough Purina to feed their dog for a lifetime. They received nearly 4 million telegrams and the speech made Nixon into a folk hero. It also got him into the White House. As for

Checker's gravesite at Bide-A-Wee Pet Cemetery, Wantagh, NY. The first of two final resting places for Richard Nixon's very public pet.

Source: Alan M. Beck

the legendary spaniel, he lived in the limelight until he was laid to rest in New York's Bide-a-Wee Cemetery. Checkers was exhumed in 1997 and given a final resting place with Richard and Patricia Nixon on the grounds of the Nixon Library in Yorba Linda, California.

Going back further into the history of presidential dogs, there was Franklin D. Roosevelt's personal but public pet, the famous black Scottie named "Fala." When FDR's political enemies tried to attack him for spending taxpayers' money on his dog, he, too, was given an opportunity to take a potentially negative point and turn it into a positive one. It seemed a rumor had been floated that the President's staff had inadvertently "forgotten" Fala on a visit to the Aleutian Islands in 1944. This in itself might have been damaging enough. But Roosevelt's Republican opponents claimed not only that he had allowed his dog to be left behind, but that he had sent a destroyer back to fetch the animal, at an enormous cost to taxpayers! Roosevelt was quick to respond by accusing his enemies of preying upon the easiest victims. "These

Republican leaders have not been content with attacks on me, my wife, or my sons," he replied in what became another famous speech. "No, not content with that, they now include my little dog, Fala." The American public sided with Fala and forgave the President.

And then there was the more recent example of Lyndon B. Johnson, who hadn't been so fortunate in his public ties with dogs— proof that it's sometimes wiser to have no association with these animals than to have a potentially negative one. It was common knowledge that Johnson kept two beagles, named "Him" and "Her," as family pets in the White House, a fact that earned him points with the American people. But near the end of his term in 1969 when the press featured a photograph of Johnson lifting both "Him" and "Her" up by the ears, this brutal schoolboy prank proved to be very damaging. Johnson was besieged with thousands of letters from outraged citizens across the nation. If the simple fact of having dogs had made Johnson a "good" person in the public's opinion, then having it known that he had "kicked" his dogs greatly outweighed any of the possible benefits. And so just two years later, when John Lindsay was asked to confront New York dog owners with a very unpopular law, one which was assumed by animal rights activists to be a first step toward banishing dogs altogether, he was understandably cautious in deciding what his next move should be. Lindsay had no dog of his own, at least not since the family pooch, "Jet," had moved "out West"[12] with his daughter. Lindsay's known pet affiliations were minimal. He seems to have cared very little about dog matters personally, and at first to have thought them totally irrelevant to the governing of New York City. But dogs seemed to be drawing as many complainers as there were defenders, and it's more likely that Lindsay was being cautious.* Why should he have taken a stand that

---

*A survey conducted by the National League of Cities in 1974 would reveal that 1,031 mayors and council members across the nation ranked dog and pet problems above all others. But assessing the situation by guessing at the number of complaints made to City Halls could be misleading. Persistent calls very likely came in from the usual complainers, overstating the importance of a few whiners and amplifying their often petty concerns. In fact, New Jersey's Chief Health Officer Walter

might upset dog lovers unless there was some political benefit to be gained? He was a visionary but he wasn't naïve. Certainly, many voters were unhappy about the condition of New York's sidewalks and parks. But the friends of Lassie were a growing coalition with some very vocal leaders of their own. Hadn't the *New York Post* told Jerome Kretchmer that it had received more letters, both for and against his controversial poop scoop idea, than any preceding issue? Lindsay balanced "environmental" benefits with a possible backlash from the dog-owning community. He approached this political animal very slowly. "Jet" stayed "out West" and out of the picture. In 1971, when his EPA Administrator asked him to present a bill before City Council that would force people to pick up after their pets, the official response from City Hall was that the law would be controversial and difficult to enforce. As for City Council, no members could be found to back Kretchmer's bill officially, though many of these elected officials were just as sick and tired of stepping into crap as anyone else in town.

In retrospect, the EPA's approach to the dog problem seems to be a matter of common sense—of course New York needed a poop scoop law! But Kretchmer's first official mention of the idea was enough to alarm the city's dog owners and create as much turmoil as Lindsay's advisors had predicted it would. "The city's Environmental Protection Administration is considering several methods to alleviate the problem of dog leavings on city streets and sidewalks," read an article appearing in the *Times* in 1971, the first of a long series that would span over three decades on the subject of dog crap. "Among the alternatives suggested in a report to the agency's Administrator, Jerome Kretchmer, is legislation for making it a violation for owners not to clean up after

---

Lezynski blamed that state's poop problem on "complete apathy of citizens." A more inclusive local survey had already been taken for New York City in 1972 and with similar results. The study conducted by the Ad Hoc Committee for Clean Streets suggested that, although canine waste was annoying and unpopular, most New Yorkers did not rank this as a top priority for government. Instead, poop seems to have been first introduced by special interest groups and then packaged and circulated by a few politicians.

dogs. The owners would be required to take the offal home and either flush it down the toilet or dispose of it with the garbage. Another alternative would involve raising the license fee for dogs to the point where 'a lot of them simply would not be there,' according to an agency spokesman."[13] From the very beginning, the discussion was framed in terms of two alternatives: Either dog owners would be made to carry their pets' waste home with them or they would be discouraged from having dogs in the first place. "The authorities might even consider revoking dog licenses like driving licenses after a certain number of offenses," was a typical response. By encouraging the opinion that the dog population should be limited, Kretchmer was confirming dog owners' greatest fear that someone was looking for an excuse to take their pets away from them.[†]

Much to his favor, Kretchmer resisted the temptation to cast canines in the shape of a big, gas-guzzling Ford station wagon. But the

---

[†]New York dog owners thought that Kretchmer was asking too much when he suggested they pick up, but they could have done a lot worse. The idea for a poop scoop law was not, it seemed, first conceived in the 20th century but much earlier and had harsher terms of compliance. As René Merlen explains, "The Senchus Mor," a body of Irish laws based on Roman laws and translated by St. Patrick in the 5th century, included elaborate instructions for whenever hounds did their business: "If a dog strayed on to another man's land no action for damages of any kind could be brought against its owner, but if in so straying it left ordure behind it then it was regarded as having committed a trespass of the same magnitude as man trespass, the mangling of cattle or the breaking of dwellings. When ordure had been left behind the law prescribed two methods of making good the damage which had been done, and in the first of these the ordure was carefully removed and a rod was placed upon the spot where it had been and was covered with cow-dung which was left over it until the end of the month. The second procedure was far more elaborate and here three times the bulk of the ordure measured in butter, curds and dough had to be paid to the owner of the land on to which the dog had strayed. In addition, the ordure had to be removed and the earth dug up from underneath the place where it had lain until no smell could any longer be perceived, and when this had been done the hole which had been made had to be filled up with fine clay and pressed down with the heel. Finally, two horses in a cart had to be grazed over the place, and if no roots of the newly-sown grass could be found sticking in their teeth, thus proving that the grass had well and truly struck, the law was satisfied at last that the damage done had been properly made good."[14]

EPA's take on the dog licensing question was ill-considered. As a result, the question of raising the fee would be debated for even longer than the poop scoop law. Over the decades, the most controversial question was always: What to do with the extra money? Dog owners said on many occasions that they were not opposed to a license fee increase, provided the extra money be used to help the ailing APSCA, which survived almost entirely on license fees. But the EPA, and much of New York, felt that any increases should be used not to treat animals more humanely, but to get the feces off the sidewalks! Even Jerome Kretchmer seemed to have doubts about the effectiveness of a poop scoop law to solve the problem. Instead, the most popular alternative was to increase the license fee so that "a lot of them simply would not be there"—as though the economic laws of pricing and supply-and-demand, and the prospect of paying a couple dollars more each year (when about half of the city's dogs weren't even licensed), would force New Yorkers to give up dear old Spot.‡ The ASPCA and the dog license fee will be discussed further in following chapters.

Jerome Kretchmer, whose children had two turtles and a white mouse but no dogs, was already beginning to feel the political backlash of confronting city dog owners. When word got out, his apartment was picketed. "The dog problem"—that is, the poop problem in many minds—was generating more controversy than any single issue confronting the EPA during his years in office, more so than the trash in the streets, smog, or even nuclear power. Not only did Kretchmer not have a dog, he took a potentially neutral point and made it a liability. But there would always be voters who disliked dogs. And fortunately in the long run, another thread ran through the debate, a voice of reason that said that it was, indeed, possible to like dogs "just as much as the next

---

‡Though the dog crisis could not be reversed with the tools of the trade, its causes had been partly economic. Disposable income in the post-war years made it less difficult to buy and care for animals. During the urban crisis, fiscal constraints made dogs necessary for protection. Much of the inspiration behind dog ownership had also come from the profit-driven pet food manufacturers who had encouraged consumers to go out and purchase dogs without thinking about the responsibilities attached.

person" but to hate wading through piles of their excrement. Despite the EPA's suggestion that dog ownership be discouraged altogether, Kretchmer defended his position as a "centrist"[15] one, explaining that he advocated a midpoint between two extremes, the first being the demand for a ban on dogs, and the second being the belief that dogs should simply be allowed to overrun New York City. Appealing to the new idea of a "rational center" in American politics—finding a midpoint between the revolutionary radicalism and reactionary conservatism that were tearing the nation apart—Kretchmer said that non-dog people and dog people could coexist peacefully. His plan even included a campaign aimed at pressuring New York landlords into providing "special dog runs on roofs or in back gardens" to limit canine use of public spaces.[16]

Behind Kretchmer's "centrist" position on dogs was another high-minded ideal and an unrealistic goal, at least for the time being. A poop scoop law was meant to solve one of those perennial problems that become the focus of politics every few years in New York City. Sidewalk litter has long been a favorite pet peeve among New Yorkers, and some of the more die-hard advocates of the prospect of pristine pavement never seem to tire of pursuing this distant dream. While others eventually decide to give up on dirt and get on with their lives, others keep insisting that city surfaces should be at least as clean as they are in the suburbs. Even dog owners have not been entirely immune to the notion, however utopian, of having tidy walkways in New York City. But in these early years, they believed that their animals should be accommodated by the City regardless of the cost to taxpayers, and that in any event, the problems that dogs created were minor compared to the many others that pedestrians were facing. There were, after all, far more threatening forms of "pollution." New York's EPA Administrator, on the other hand, chose to combat this "particularly obnoxious form"[17] of littering. Taking this position came with a political price: Dog lovers and animal rights activists, almost universally opposed to having a poop scoop law, made up a very vocal part of the environmental movement. But although leading environmentalists were flatly against the idea, the cost-benefit analysis for Kretchmer seemed to favor the law. For one, dog owners were still a minority. On the whole, they didn't appear to be very well organized (in this respect, Kretchmer underestimated the pro-dog lobby). Even if they chose unanimously to disobey a poop scoop law, the simple fact of having one might be beneficial to government: With the law in place, the official blame for dirty walkways could be shifted away from the ailing Department of Sanitation (now part of the EPA) and onto dog owners. Any fines collected from resisters (surely, a few of them could be caught leaving the scene of their crime) would, like other fines levied, add to the City's dwindling supply of cash (fines for traffic offenses, littering, dog-related offenses, and various other infractions continue to the present day to be a vital source of revenue—in other words, it's very much in government's interest to have people breaking laws). Most important, a canine waste law would show the world that New Yorkers still cared about "the environment," even if theirs was made up almost entirely of concrete. Corporations might be convinced not to move their offices to Danbury, Connecticut. The tax-paying middle class might decide that New York was once again a nice place to raise a family. And there was an added benefit to pinning the hope for New York's future on dogs: A growing anti-smoking lobby wanted the poop scoop law, with its reliance upon peer pressure, to serve as a model for an eventual ban on smoking in public places.

Or maybe all Kretchmer really wanted was to get the crap off the sidewalks.

In the final analysis, Kretchmer was considering running for mayor and so all of his decisions were crucial. Overall, confronting the city's dog people seemed to be a wise move. But no one else stood to gain—or lose—as much as he was gambling on the politics of poop.

"The first thing that has to be done is to sensitize people to the fact that this is a problem that has to be addressed,"[18] said an EPA spokesman. The events following the announcement of his plan suggest that Kretchmer had no idea what he was up against when he proposed something as simple and reasonable, or so it seemed, as asking people to pick up after their pets. Having no dog of his own, he was completely out of touch with dog owners and their most intimate concerns. For example, while attending a meeting of animal advocates in Greenwich Village, he learned that one woman was especially fond of her pets. "You got *five* cats?" he cried in disbelief. "And a *dog*? Christ. What you need is a good man."[19] Animal lovers failed to see the humor. Nor did Kretchmer's creation of New York's first environmental court help him to win their hearts. The city didn't have a poop scoop law yet. But it had a leash law and a curb-your-dog law, neither of which was being followed. Explaining that the normal courts currently had a backlog of over 70,000 summonses, many of them dog related, Kretchmer said: "We can't get the judges to pay attention so we have a bill in the legislature to create an environmental court and clean up these cases with $100 and $200 fines."[20] Dog owners were getting tired of reducing the City's deficit.

Within a few days of the announcement of the poop scoop bill, an emergency meeting was called in Brooklyn Heights to nip Kretchmer's idea in the bud. "Mr. Kretchmer has aligned himself with professional dog haters,"[21] said Max Schnapp, the outspoken leader of the city's largest pro-dog group, the Pet Owners Protective Association (POPA). Schnapp had no cause for alarm, at least not yet. Not a single City Council member was willing to take an official stand on canine waste. On the contrary, Councilman Carter Burden actually charged Kretchmer with "discriminating"[22] against dog owners! Cleveland Amory, the social historian, animal rights activist, founder of the Fund for Animals, and an active member of POPA, was also at the meeting to declare in no uncertain terms: "Kretchmer's law is a carefully planned first step toward banning dogs from New York City."[23] Max Schnapp agreed. "It's pet hysteria!" he shouted. "Sure the dog dirt is a problem," he admitted. "But you don't solve a problem by passing a law."[24] When the Committee's chairwoman, Nancy Wolf, stood up and tried to explain that all anyone wanted to do was to "clarify an existing statute,"[25] dog owners returned the favor by heckling her mercilessly. Robert Angus, founder of the Dog Owners Guild (DOG), claimed that City Council's Cleanliness Committee was deliberately spreading "anti-excrement vigilantism."[26] Dog owners were, in fact, reporting a marked increase in harassment throughout the city. Assemblyman Joseph Martuscello took the stand and called Kretchmer's proposal "another one of his zany ideas."[27]

Just who were these "professional dog haters" that Schnapp and Amory warned against in their speeches? The harshest criticism of Kretchmer's poop scoop bill came not from a dog lover at all, but from that most militant of anti-dog voices, Fran Lee, the founder and leader of a militant pro-child group called Children Before Dogs. Ms. Lee, more so than any individual, would be responsible for making canine waste into a public health issue in years to come. Lee's organization was the largest anti-poop group in the city and the nation, with paying members who believed that dogs and children were probably incompatible. Lee attended the meeting in Brooklyn Heights accompanied, as was her custom, by pregnant women and toddlers. For the safety of the city's young ones, she said, dogs should be trained to go "in the owner's bathroom," perhaps on newspaper, but in any event *not* in public places. Her solution to the pet problem in New York City was inspired, oddly enough, by smaller towns and suburbs where dogs were being made by local lawmakers to go "in their own backyard." But were the two pet-owning situations comparable? Since most New York dog owners didn't have backyards, Lee said that their dogs would have to use the bathroom floor, that is, if anyone wanted to keep dogs in the city. She believed that Kretchmer's bizarre idea would never work, and soon emerged as a leading opponent to the poop scoop law. Kretchmer was backing the wrong idea, Lee thought, and she would stand firmly on this opinion for years to come. "You cannot walk away from it—the stench, the mess,"[28] she cried against whistles, jeers, and gibes. Her life was threatened on several occasions.

Chapter 4

Keep off the Grass

"Personally, I'm of the view that the dog ought to go in the owner's bathroom."

—John V. Lindsay, Spring 1972[1]

The mayor openly agreed with Fran Lee, New York's "foremost fighter against dog dirt,"[2] and was willing to endorse her homespun cure for the city's pet problem.

A year had passed since the EPA's failed attempt to coerce City Hall into backing a piece of legislation widely thought to be political suicide. City Council members, too, were hesitant, having been warned by some voters that if they changed their minds about the poop scoop bill then they had better not seek reelection. Jerome Kretchmer was back on the scene again, campaigning for his law and making everyone uneasy. Complaints had been pouring in about the shameful condition of sidewalks and parks. But convincing leaders to take on such a radical new proposal would be difficult. So controversial was the idea that they'd have to spread the blame for it as evenly as possible. Politically speaking, poop had become a hot potato. Most New Yorkers agreed there was a problem. But few of their leaders would commit to anything stronger than speculation on what *should* be done. There were so

many factions with conflicting opinions. Should dog owners be forced to carry their pets' waste products home with them—or should the dogs be made to go in their owners' bathrooms, as Lindsay and a group of concerned parents suggested? Maybe dogs should be "curbed," perhaps even banned? Should restrictions be placed on ownership? Could the licensing fee be increased—and if so, then what should be done with the extra money? Whatever decision was made, no new legislation would stand a chance without City Hall's blessing. When Kretchmer announced confidently that he would unveil, within two weeks, a comprehensive plan that would make city streets "livable" once more, there was no turning back for the EPA. City Hall kept silent. Kretchmer waited patiently for two weeks, then brought up the unspeakable once again. Dwight MacDonald, the mayor's aide for environmental matters, continued to stall for time by saying that City Hall would have to wait and see what City Council thought before taking an official position on canine waste. Within a few days, Kretchmer announced that he had the support of two, or perhaps three, City Council members. If only Lindsay would present the bill, then Council would proceed. The ball was finally in City Hall's court. For the first time, Lindsay felt compelled to take a firmer stand on the dog problem. But a poop scoop law still seemed a bit extreme.

Lindsay's campaign for President of the United States ended almost before it had begun. It didn't help that one of his campaign managers had been thrown out of a Florida hotel for parading his standard poodle around the front lobby—another arrogant New Yorker, they all thought. Lindsay's own reputation had suffered greatly in recent years, though mainly because of what a morass his hometown was becoming. The disastrous defeat at the Democratic primary only weakened his campaign to save American cities and soiled his image in New York. "In 1972," writes Vincent Cannato, "Lindsay grasped for a prize that was beyond his reach. He returned to the city as a beaten man."[3] Seeing Lindsay weakened, one Democratic boss couldn't resist making a sly-dog allusion and said: "Little Sheeba better come home." But when the stray dog returned he wasn't so badly mauled that he'd given up on New York. Lindsay spent his last year in office trying to maintain the public's hopes for the city he'd struggled to rescue from one of its most difficult passages. New York was on the very brink of bankruptcy and was, despite the many well-intentioned reforms, a sinking ship. Lindsay forged on with his elaborate PR events aimed at keeping the faith at a time when City bond ratings were inflated and banks might have reeled in their lines of credit. How long could he keep this ship afloat? Basic services, from street cleaning to trash collection, and from park maintenance to police protection, were curtailed. The public was feeling the effects. Increasingly, leaders felt pressure to find short-term solutions to problems that were too daunting to face head-on. "In the midst of all this," wrote Lindsay's Parks Administrator August Heckscher in his book *Alive in the City*, "the idea was propagated that New York City was dying. The more optimistic would say that, if New York was dying, it was certainly dying with a flourish. The pessimists added that it was dying visibly, its rot a way of life."[4] Considering the city's many ills, superficial cleanliness was probably a petty concern. But outward appearances became especially worrisome as New York began to look like a third-world capital. Against the dark backdrop of the 1970s—the many crime films shot on city streets needed few special effects—the smallest problems were magnified and the pettiest annoyances were viewed as symptoms of a broader decay. Stepping into dog crap took on new meaning to someone who had just been mugged.

Lindsay's endorsement of the bathroom alternative came at the opening of City Parks Week, a time when New Yorkers managed to set aside their complaints about dirty sidewalks for seven days, and shifted the focus of their lament to the shameful state of public parks. "He brought people into the streets," recalled his Parks Administrator, "as he went into the streets himself. He also brought them into the parks."[5] Rallying citizens in the name of public spaces naturally made them more acutely aware of what these areas had become. Not unlike other newly created holidays such as Earth Week and Quiet Week, with their focus on quality-of-life issues, City Parks Week tapped into the public's outrage over everything else that was wrong with New York. Dog owners found themselves on the receiving end. When not fending off their curbside critics, they came under sharpened scrutiny for letting their animals run off-leash in parks where they frightened the elderly, chased joggers, and sometimes bit children. Strays that roamed the parks in packs of six to eight were enough to inspire a panic. No less frightening was the fact that dogs, whether or not they had owners, were urinating and defecating along the way. Contrary to popular opinion, dog feces were not fertilizer. High concentrations of nitrogen, and the ammonia content in urine, were harmful to plant life. Dogs were killing the grass.

The new pet culture could thus be viewed as working directly against efforts to make the city, and the world, cleaner and greener, a cause in which so much of New York's identity had been invested. Mass layoffs of park workers and wildcat strikes, it was widely believed, weren't as much to blame as dogs were for the sad state of public parks. These areas had become not only the natural battlegrounds for dog-related problems, but the man-made stages for environmental causes and the setting for a turf war that would last to the present day. If pavements were hopelessly lost to defecating curs, then what better way for leaders to show that they were on top of the problem than by finding a place from which these animals might be banned altogether? Parks, conspicuous triumphs over nature, were just the right places, and one park in particular stood out among all the others. "Central Park came to symbolize the increasing shabbiness and deterioration of the city at large,"[6] recalls Cannato. "Now that spring is upon us," wrote one concerned citizen to the *Times*, "and the warm walking weather has begun, I would suggest that we all stop for a moment to take a look at what has become one of New York's greatest treasures—Central Park. It has become a dumping ground for defecating dogs whose feces despoil the paths, grass, and air of the park. The crisp green grass, the smell of blossoming cherry trees, the playing fields are all being taken from us by the hordes of dogs that romp freely, off-leash, in Central Park. Can nothing be done? Are we all to be slaves to people who find pleasure in keeping Great Danes in three-room apartments?"[7] A mother of two bemoaned the city's treatment of its little ones who could no longer, she claimed, use the parks safely. "The toddling child," she testified bitterly, "too young to enjoy the asphalted playground, can no longer be set down on the grass to play. He is too likely to crawl in—and pick up—dogs' ordure. The young baseball player soon learns that this is no sport for the butterfingered. If he fails the catch the ball, he hesitates to pick it up. He knows what it has landed in. Climb trees? Most of them serve as urine posts for the city's dogs. The picture is no brighter in winter. When snow blankets the city, splotches of brown quickly speckle the white. Sledders not only have to avoid trees as they swoop downhill, but dog feces as well. Today's city children are taught to look down. In times past, parents would chide youngsters, 'Head up, shoulders back when you walk.' That rule went out with the trolley cars."[8] Another concerned parent suggested "that one better keep the children on a leash."

The state of the public green wasn't the concern of parents alone. Yellow patches impacted New Yorkers from all walks of life strolling in search of relaxation and an unbroken expanse of that soothing shade. *Times* columnist Marya Mannes, in her now-famous lament on the public disgrace that was Central Park, only stiffened the resolve of lawmakers. "Natural beauty?" she asked sarcastically. "In the last few years, vast areas of trodden earth have spread like *mange* [italics mine] across the hills and hollows of the listless grass. The edges of lakes and ponds are garlands of scum and bottles and wrappers and paper cups. Litter overflows the baskets near the foodstands, lies under benches, catches on twigs. Broken glass glints in the rocks where mica once glittered."[9]

Dogs were no doubt causing problems in public parks. But only because government had found no intelligent way to accommodate them. It was almost as though their presence alongside all the unsightliness made them guilty by association. "City Will Restrict Dogs' Use of Parks," read the *Times* headline announcing City Parks Week with its overwhelming focus on dogs. The official statement from Administrator August Heckscher demanded an end, once and for all, to the "fouling"[10] of public parks. Since a poop scoop law seemed impractical at the time, the existing leash law enacted after much discussion in 1969 but seldom obeyed by dog owners was called upon to restore Central Park's past splendor—and so, it seemed, to solve New York's countless other problems.

One of many such campaigns to be waged in years to come, Lindsay's leash drive started innocently enough. Over the course of City Parks Week, rangers and police officers watched patiently over Central Park, especially in the early morning and late evening hours when most dog owners were out running their beasts. Of course, the leash drive would have no impact on the number of strays that roamed free. But there was hope that the presence of law enforcement officers would be a gentle reminder that dog owners should think twice about giving their animals any exercise off-leash. Police and rangers distributed flyers listing park rules and regulations: Dogs were to be kept on leashes of no more than six feet in length; they were not to be brought into playgrounds or zoos; they were not to do their business anywhere but off a curb; etc. The leash drive was accompanied by a ticketing drive. The fine for letting a dog off-leash was $50 (a large sum at the time) with an optional 15-day prison term. Despite all the other problems faced in parks, the whole point of City Parks Week, it seemed, was to convince dog owners not to let their pets detract from the public green, a precious commodity growing scarcer by the day.* If dogs could not be made to go in their owners' bathrooms, then Heckscher said they would have to be "curbed" on leash before entering a park, as the municipal animal waste law had already been interpreted but was seldom followed. Under no circumstances were dogs to be allowed to do their business in public parks. Once inside one of these, the owners were forbidden by the leash law from letting their animals run free for even a moment. But was it realistic to expect the dogs to run home to their owners' bathrooms whenever the need to evacuate overcame them? What if the animals still needed to poop or pee once inside a park? And could they be made to resist the temptation to "mark" public property as their own? According to Heckscher, they would simply have to hold it.

Anyone who knew anything about dogs knew that this latest attempt at controlling them was tantamount to banning them from parks altogether. But unlike the similar ban on automobiles from Central Park on certain days of the week, attempts to exclude dogs were futile. The owners kept running them off-leash for years to come on the wild assumption that lawns were meant to be used, not admired from afar. They met clandestinely in the off-hours of early morning and late evening and kept a constant vigil for ticketing rangers and police officers. Because their dogs preferred grassy areas to dusty ones, they had to keep moving. Once a lawn was destroyed, they'd pick up like a wandering tribe in search of greener pastures, continuing the cycle of destruction and earning themselves many enemies. In all fairness, it should be noted

---

*One should not underestimate the effectiveness of the color green on the public imagination. Studies have shown the color to have a natural soothing effect, relieving stress and fatigue. From the formative years, human responses to green suggest that even its metaphorical uses can have the most dramatic psychological effects. Infants are less agitated when teething if the ceilings of their nurseries are green. Along the same lines, governments have long been using the color to calm their subjects, planting lawns and trees and painting trash cans as often as possible. London's suicide rate is said to have dropped by 34 percent when Blackfriar Bridge was painted green.

that dogs were not really as much of a problem in Central Park, with its endless expanses of arable land, as they were in the smaller parks around the city. In no time at all these tiny doormats became enormous bald spots on the Parks Department's reputation, which was, after all, measured in square feet of public green.[†]

* * *

Interestingly enough, Lindsay's crackdown on dogs came at the tail end of an era known not for regulations, but for rule-bending and perhaps unprecedented tolerance. Much of this new spirit of the times had found its best expression in public parks. "In the middle and late sixties in New York City," Heckscher recalled fondly, "a curious thing happened. People in great numbers and of all varieties came out into parks and squares and streets, and there they professed the values they lived by, exhibited the latest fads and fashions, paraded, demonstrated, acted out their emotions, walked, bicycled, made love, just sat. It was quite a spectacle. It was a source of alarm for politicians who raised the slogan of 'Law and Order' to the level of Holy Writ, for bureaucrats charged with keeping the grass green, and for some people scared by the abundance of life. But millions—young and middle-aged and old—enjoyed being part of the scene, and breathed with fresh delight the airs of the city, which were still polluted but, according to the reports of the newly established Environmental Protection Administration, were getting less so."[11]

So popular were these new social and cultural forces, and so strong the demands of a society in flux, that Lindsay went out of his way to encourage certain groups to take over entire areas of parks as often as possible. He had little choice in the matter. New York's growing insolvency, and its inability to police itself, had led to a new kind of

---

[†]I recently had the rare pleasure of viewing the film *Barefoot in the Park* on a big screen. Seen up close in 1967, Washington Square Park already seems to have very little grass left. Robert Redford is running barefoot in the dirt.

freedom. Lindsay's first Parks Administrator and Heckscher's own role model, Thomas Hoving, is best remembered for his famous "Hoving Happenings" in Central Park. The idea behind these popular events, Hoving said, was "to take the 'no' out of parks." Much to the dismay of conservative New Yorkers, Central Park became the setting for free concerts, performances of Shakespeare, "love-ins," "be-ins," and even "fat-ins." Central Park's rolling lawns were stages for hippies, flower children, Hare Krishnas, hashish smokers, anti-war demonstrators, flag burners, bra burners, ethnic demonstrators, and even pro-war demonstrators. The belief that parks should be used for something other than strolling with parasols on Sunday afternoons—although this eccentric behavior, too, surely would have been tolerated—gave way to the wide array of "happenings," some of which would become traditions in years to come, while others would fall by the wayside. The same populism and environmentalism that favored public transportation over private automobiles in New York City led to the closing of Central Park to automobile traffic on Sundays (a custom that survives to the present day). This brief respite from the noise, smell, and dangers of automobiles allowed New Yorkers to reclaim the park on foot and on bicycle, in the same way that they took back the streets during Earth Week. "It was a picture of outward harmony,"[12] Heckscher recalled of another park in Tompkins Square. "Children and dogs . . . ran around freely, chasing each other around trees and up the huge boulders."[13] Everywhere, New Yorkers were learning to accept each other's differences. "Even the drunks and winos seemed to have their place. Young and old moved within respective spheres with a nice adjustment, and the dogs, if not all leashed, seemed better behaved than in other places. Not far from these peaceful scenes, in the shadowed side streets around the park, a heavy contingent of police kept watch."[14] The "outward harmony" was, in fact, a fragile balance.

However appealing the new, nontraditional uses of public parks, taking the "no" out of parks meant taking the grass as well. Hippies were probably the most controversial newcomers, after dogs. The long-haired youths were no less guilty than the canine population of trampling the lawns that they occupied endlessly, seated in the lotus position, playing bongos, doing drugs—and trying carefully not to pass out in a pile of dog feces. Hippies were often allowed to camp out overnight in parks, even though they were officially closed to the public after midnight. They danced all night, tearing up the lawns beyond repair. And though they were known to be meticulous about cleaning up their litter, the hippies built bonfires that scorched the earth and left large black patches where they encamped. "Blame the people who go to the Sheep Meadow for their pot parties and rock concerts," wrote an angry New Yorker who was not amused with that other "movement" that was destroying the lawns, "the drunks and derelicts benched both inside and on the perimeter of the park and, finally, the graffiti-prone, barefooted, half-dressed youths frequenting that area. They are befouling Central Park, not the canine population."[15] Another wrote: "It is about time to stop depriving the taxpaying citizens of this city of the enjoyment of the once-beautiful Central Park because all the 'freaks' and 'humanity polluters' from all over the country choose to use it as a campsite, garbage dump, and site for all their anti-cultural behavior. They especially scream for Earth Day and anti-pollution causes while they in their appearance and behavior are pure pollution."[16]

The Parks Department found itself between a rock and a hard place. "To keep liveliness and the sense of life," Heckscher noted, "even when the grass got trampled and Monday morning showed a flood of litter, was an essential task, to which we in Parks were dedicated. We did try to replace the grass with sod, and to become efficient in getting the outdoor scenes cleaned up more quickly. But to put tidiness as the first and only consideration, and to be blind to the big things that were happening, seemed a betrayal of the city's best hope."[17] Despite the many "big things" that were happening in parks, maintaining "the outdoor scenes" like a stage set was a priority for the Parks Department. In fact, keeping public areas as neat and green as humanly possible became a kind of crusade during the last months of the Lindsay administration. Heckscher struggled with a dilemma that no parks administrator would fully resolve in years to come: How were parks to be used and, at the same time, maintained? The crowded lawns might have been, as Heckscher believed, indicative of "liveliness and the sense of life." But a finely manicured and unbroken expanse of green was also a sign of "law and order." Was it possible for both ideals to be represented simultaneously in the same public square, especially when the City's treasury was running dangerously low and there wasn't enough money around to maintain much of anything?

As the openness of the sixties gave way to the paranoia of the seventies, the times demanded a new approach to public spaces and a new sense of urgency was attached to their upkeep. Hippies and dog owners weren't the only newcomers to parks. Behind the bucolic settings so artificially laid out in Central Park, new dangers awaited. Parks had become sanctuaries to untold numbers of violent criminals. Beyond the bushes and trees, and underneath those once-scenic bridges now covered in graffiti, lurked muggers, rapists, drug dealers, and gangs of angry young men. Not only were parks becoming unpleasant to the eyes and nostrils, they were downright life-threatening. It was already assumed by 1972 that treading upon the city's green spots, especially at nighttime, meant placing one's life in someone else's hands. At all hours of the day and night, the graffiti that hung from bridges and monuments was a constant reminder that others, not dogs but gangs, had "marked" this territory as their own. City parks, designed to relieve the tensions of urban life, were having the opposite effect.

Despite his best intentions to remain as open-minded about parks as his predecessor, and however fond he was, like both Hoving and Lindsay, of the new counterculture, when push came to shove, August Heckscher was another one of those "bureaucrats charged with keeping the grass green." And dog owners were treated no differently from the muggers, rapists, and drug dealers who also frequented public parks. "Dogs constitute our largest group of lawbreakers," wrote one of many New Yorkers who believed that destroying a lawn was as serious an offense as any other. But Lindsay's leash drive would have no impact on the city's dog problem, with one possible exception. It served to further alienate dog owners, a growing segment of the population. In fact, enforcers were encouraged to harass, bully, and illegally detain them for decades to come. Although Lindsay admitted that enforcing park rules would be "very, very hard" to do without public cooperation, it was in the early seventies that park rangers first acquired a taste for venting their frustrations at the expense of a minority of citizens who were only trying to be responsible pet owners by letting their dogs take daily exercise.

The very opinion that American cities needed leash laws at all was far from unanimous at the time. Considering events in Boston, New York's solution seemed a bit extreme. Mayor Kevin White had just vetoed leash legislation passed by his own City Council. White said that he had serious doubts about the effectiveness of such a law. He predicted that dog owners would choose to disobey, gladly risking fines and imprisonment to give their dogs the pleasure of romping freely across the Emerald Necklace. If a leash law were enforced properly, White predicted, Boston's prisons and animal shelters would soon be filled beyond capacity. How would belligerent New Yorkers—"dog terrorists," as Parks Commissioner Henry Stern would one day call them—be made to keep their pets on leashes when even their more compliant neighbors to the north refused?[‡]

Daily migrations made New York dog owners—whether they were liberal or conservative, draft dodgers or flag wavers, poor or middle class, single or married with children—a radicalized counterculture for years to come. Simply having a dog in New York meant being

---

[‡]"Dog runs" begin to sound like the obvious solution to the many problems dogs were said to be causing in public parks. The dog run idea, however, was as controversial as the poop scoop proposal. Local communities, Parks officials, and other leaders would fight against it for decades to come, long after owners had agreed to start picking up after their pets. People were not about to hand over parcels of public land permanently to dogs, and it would be many years before dog runs would be "happening" in most New York parks.

permanently marginalized, at least in public parks, and all because the poor animals needed to take exercise.§

---

§While Central Park's importance seemed to grow, so did those tiny gestures to the Great Outdoors planted on side streets seem all the more dear. To a person immune to its allure, a tiny piece of ivy growing from a crack in the concrete was just that. But to the soul who planted it, this was Paradise. New Yorkers are so desperate for green that they've been known to chain themselves to trees before allowing developers to build on vacant lots. But it's always been a losing battle. So long as people believe they can transform their bleak sidewalks into lush woodlands, they're bound to be disappointed. This hasn't stopped angry block associations from chasing down leg-lifting canines. These nature-starved New Yorkers would be vital in the enforcement of the poop scoop law in years to come. But no single law could resolve all disputes over ornamental greenery in a town where trees, despite the heavy symbolism, were really nothing more than potted plants.

One of the most dramatic examples of an argument over green spots, and of the kind of extremism that characterizes doggy politics, comes as recently as 1993 when a little bichon frise named "Pepsi" was allegedly assaulted on Manhattan's West Side for doing his business on a man's plants. "Bruised Dog Frays Nerves on 33rd Street" read the headline in the *Times*.[18] Pepsi's owner, Helen Graue, claimed that her dog was savagely attacked by a man named Heung Tam when he saw the dog was urinating on the little garden he'd planted in front of his building. According to Ms. Graue, Pepsi had been kicked in the head and was bleeding from the eye and nose. The dog was hospitalized and Mr. Tam received a summons from the ASPCA. Barely a day after the incident, before the matter could even be investigated, Pepsi's owner and a friend said to have witnessed an appalling act of animal cruelty mobilized over 100 of their fellow dog owners to stage a march in front of Mr. Tam's home on West 33rd Street. Graue told the *Times* that she'd been minding her own business when Tam came out and kicked little Pepsi, sending him flying into the man's iron fence and onto the sidewalk. "I think he's angry at all the dogs in the neighborhood and took it out on Pepsi," she said. The mob of dog owners paraded for a full day in front of Tam's home chanting "Shame, shame on you. Beating dogs is what you do." They carried signs with an enlarged photograph of Pepsi (pre-kick) and the message, "PUNISH ANIMAL ABUSE."

Mr. Tam had another version of what happened that day. He said that the two women had been deliberately provoking him for several weeks by allowing both of their dogs, despite his many complaints, to destroy his plants with their urinating and defecating. On the day in question, he said, he came out and "lightly tapped" little Pepsi to stop the dog from doing any further damage. Then, Mr. Tam said, one of the women blinded him with mace and they both began kicking and slapping him. Not one of the over 100 angry dog owners ever stopped to ask what these women were doing in front of Mr. Tam's home in the first place. Nor did anyone consider the women's role in provoking him, or ask why they would expose their pets to potential danger when they had reason to believe that Mr. Tam did not like dogs. Why did these women encourage the situation to escalate? And wasn't it possible that little Pepsi got hurt accidentally in the shuffle? What riled the angry mob to the point of becoming wild with rage was the mere *idea* of something like this happening to a dog. And while protecting a tiny patch of green was no justification for mistreating a dog in any way, the rabble of dog lovers probably should have stopped for a moment to decide what, exactly, it was that they were fighting for.

"The dog is an innocent tool," Mr. Tam said in his defense, "that the owner uses to vent her dislike for a neighbor."

CHAPTER 5

... AND DON'T EAT THE DAISIES

"Show business is dog-eat-dog. It's worse than dog-eat-dog. It's dog doesn't return other dog's phone calls."

—Woody Allen, *Crimes and Misdemeanors*[1]

Strangely enough, the inaugural event for City Parks Week was held not in a park but in front of Bloomingdale's, the elegant department store on East 59th Street. Like Earth Day and Earth Week, "The Greening of Bloomingdale's," as the celebration was called, also took place on pavement. Television crews and newspaper reporters stood along the sidewalk as the city's major political personalities prepared to make their official statements on what, exactly, was wrong with New York. To indicate the temporary shift in focus from the disgusting state of pavements to the deplorable condition of parks, the sidewalk itself was dressed up to look like a park, complete with fake grass and real potted flowers and trees. Shoppers exiting Bloomingdale's suddenly found themselves treading upon a great green carpet, a verdant pasture interspersed with potted pear trees, 15 in all, cloaking this small corner of the concrete jungle and transforming the sidewalk into an idealized version of Central Park. Astroturf, technology's bold new alternative to grass, that modern wonder cropping up in football stadiums across the land, might have lacked the texture and substance of the real thing but the color green carried the vital message of City Parks Week and The Greening of Bloomingdale's. In a town where the most aggressive individuals, if they were lucky, might harvest the world's richest rewards, New Yorkers knew all too well that green was the color of envy. But it could also be a shade of hope. The choice of green as a theme color was made to portray City government as greener than the sum of its parts, as sort of an organic whole, and to dispel the myth that New York's ancient political power structure was no more than a loose pack of fiefdoms, each with a vested interest in competing, one against the other, while the city as a whole fell apart. Gathered on this makeshift lawn in front of Bloomingdale's, standing solemnly under the Parks Department banner of bright white with a green London Plane tree leaf (a logo introduced by August Heckscher in 1970), were "about a dozen politicians,"[2] the *Times* reported, including officials from the departments of Environmental Protection, Parks, Sanitation, Transportation, and Police, united in an impressive show of solidarity against the city's most obnoxious litterers: dog owners. The message of City Parks Week was clear. These irresponsible, inconsiderate renegades were not doing their fair share to make the city as clean and green as possible. In fact, the vast numbers of officials attending the opening didn't reflect the role of government at all. It would be up to "community participation," not salaried civil servants, to whip New York back into shape. Why, after all, wasn't the opening of City Parks Week being celebrated in nearby Central Park? Because it was Monday morning, Lindsay explained, and after every busy weekend the park was left "looking like a pigpen."[3]

Apart from an unsuccessful leash drive in Central Park, the most heavily publicized events for City Parks Week weren't held in parks at all. Instead, this weeklong tribute to the city's besieged green spots extended far beyond their borders and onto concrete surfaces everywhere. A group of concerned citizens calling themselves NEAT (The Neighborhood Action Team) planted 300 begonias on the Upper West Side, transforming sidewalks into lush gardens. Actress Gwen Verdon pushed a vacuum cleaner symbolically across West 73rd Street. Others banded together on streets across the city to sweep the pavement and repaint lampposts and fire hydrants. Behind all the scenery and theatrics was a message: Maybe New York was going through a rough patch, but that was no reason for people to live in filth—in other words: Poverty need not preclude cleanliness. A few blocks downtown, on a small triangular parklet squeezed onto a traffic island in the middle of Broadway and shaded in a mist of car exhaust, a group of vocalists from the New York School of Opera stood around a statue of Giuseppe Verdi ("green" was in the composer's name) to sing a quartette from "Rigoletto." Jerome Kretchmer was on hand to praise citizens supporting the weeklong effort to revitalize neighborhoods with a little elbow grease and sprucing up. A few blocks uptown was another little parklet. Sherman Square had been renamed "Needle Park" in recent years because of the heroin addicts who had taken over this tiny gesture to the Great Outdoors, also in the middle of Broadway.

But the center stage was back at Bloomingdale's where leaders were handing out free kosher hotdogs and great green balloons full of helium to anyone willing to stop and admire the virtual Central Park. Before Lindsay could finish the speech he had prepared, Jerome Kretchmer, eager to rally support for a bizarre piece of legislation that would take New Yorkers a step further than the mayor seemed willing to go, rushed across the platform of resplendent green, zigzagged through the small orchard of pear trees, and jumped up to the podium to be photographed next to Lindsay. "He always does that," Transportation Administrator Constantine Sidamon would later complain to the press. "The Mayor hates that,"[4] he added, hinting that green was still the color of envy.

The *real* Central Park was only three blocks to the west of Bloomingdale's. Lawns were overgrown and littered with every imaginable form of refuse. Fountains were drying up and plumbing rusted. Ponds and lakes had become floating trash dumps. The vast area had been designed in the 19th century as an informal, English-style garden. But in recent years the City had pushed that informality to a new extreme with its own version of picturesque classical ruins: Monuments, fountains, and bridges were dissolving from decades of disrepair. This park and others across the five boroughs now had that weathered, Old World charm of Rome—the Rome that tourists saw and not the one of ancient times. New York rivaled even Egypt with the patina of sulfur dioxide that experts were saying had managed to corrode Cleopatra's Needle more during its brief sojourn in Central Park than the thousands of years it had endured the desert storms of Africa.[*] But New Yorkers were more upset over the graffiti someone had scrawled on the base of the obelisk.

"I'll be very brief because no one can hear me!"[5] Lindsay shouted as the sound system began to falter. It was at this point that he told the press he felt, personally, that dogs ought to go in their owners' bathrooms. These animals, Lindsay and his army of Commissioners tried to assured everyone, would not be allowed to go on destroying the city's precious few remaining square feet of public green, the last oasis in a land with no other hope for the future.

Lindsay turned and stepped away from the podium. He grabbed a tin can and watered one of the fifteen potted pear trees—a symbolic gesture that seemed to say: "New York can be a nicer place, if only we all help it along." He continued his trajectory along East 59th Street, followed by a crowd much smaller than would have been eager to accompany him a few years earlier. To show that public support hadn't dried up entirely, Lindsay stopped to accept a single red rose from a local florist named Joe Mills. Then he turned again, and with the meager crowd continued in the direction of Central Park but stopped, instead, at the northeast corner of Park Avenue and 59th Street. Waiting in front of a newsstand was the man who ran it, Eddie Mack, a 40-year-old blind newspaper dealer featured recently in an advertisement for Dry Dock Savings. Mr. Mack was vigorously sweeping a tiny patch of concrete in front of his place of business, pushing aside the refuse along Park

---

[*]The theory that New York's atmosphere was corroding the obelisk has since been disproved.

Avenue to make way for the mayor. "Mr. Lindsay lauded Mr. Mack for the civic-mindedness he said was necessary to make a cleaner city,"[6] the *Times* reported.[†]

*   *   *

The elaborate events staged during City Parks Week were not enticing enough for Lindsay to regain the faith of New York City. Overall support for government was dwindling as leaders came under more pressure not only to keep the city clean and green, but to maintain some semblance of civil order. Barely a month after an unsuccessful leash drive in Central Park, Lindsay took a radical change of course. The ball was still very much in City Hall's court: Unless Lindsay backed Kretchmer's poop scoop proposal, City Council wouldn't vote on it, and the blame for dirty sidewalks and parks would fall upon City Hall. One of Lindsay's aids had already announced that the mayoral endorsement of the law would depend largely on whether City Council planned to go along with Kretchmer's plan to hold dog owners, with threats of fines and imprisonment, responsible for their pets' mess. But now Kretchmer was able to say he had the support of a few Council members. It was during these dark final days of the Lindsay administration, a time when everyone seemed to be turning on the man who was supposed to save New York City, that the failing mayor finally came around to accepting Kretchmer's idea. Having avoided the issue like a pedestrian on the pavement, having criticized the law for being controversial and unenforceable, Lindsay finally announced his official support of

---

[†]"The Greening of Bloomingdale's" in honor of City Parks Week was organized in 1972, just after John Lindsay was named a vice president and administrative board member of the department store. Later that year, Bloomingdale's would celebrate its 100th anniversary by donating enough money to refurbish the seating area of an outdoor theater in Central Park. But as in the case of City Parks Week, the actual event did not take place in a park at all. Instead, Mrs. John V. Lindsay hosted the event in the offices of Dry Dock Savings. To honor the department store's contribution to the park, Dry Dock's President presented Bloomingdale's with a bicycle rack.

Kretchmer's poop scoop bill. It was almost as though he had nothing more to lose.

Some thought the decision had come better late than never. "Mayor Proposes a Stricter Law on Dog Littering" the *Times* announced on July 1, 1972. "For those of you who find the job of cleaning up after their dog unpleasant," Lindsay explained to hundreds of thousands of dog owners who were no less than stunned by the news, "they might well consider the outraged feelings of other New Yorkers who walk through and in the maze of dog litter that befouls our city."[7] New York, Lindsay said, was being made "unhealthy by dogs and some dog owners who are thoughtless."[8] A new law, he said, would require people to pick up after their pets or face a $100 fine, 30 days in jail, or both. But however hard-nosed his new position might have seemed, Lindsay was extremely careful to stress that he had nothing against dogs per se. On the contrary, he said, dogs were "both useful and loyal,"[9] and his decision to hold the owners responsible for their mess made "one simple judgment: a loyal pet and protector should not be the source of aggravation and filth in its neighborhood."[10] By evoking feelings of loyalty toward their dogs, Lindsay was reaching out to the owners, suggesting that by failing to do their civic duty they were, indirectly, doing their best friends a real disservice by making their neighbors into dog haters. Perhaps in the long run, the dogs themselves might suffer if their owners resisted the proposed law. Lindsay didn't say that a ban on dogs was an option but the message was there, nonetheless, hidden subtly in the reference to what some New Yorkers might do if dog owners didn't take control of themselves. Nor did Lindsay need to explain why pets were not only companions but also protectors in a town where police protection was being scaled back and basic survival on streets, in subways, in parks, and in private homes was becoming more difficult by the day. How could dog owners be so "disloyal" to their own personal bodyguards?

Still, they would need more coaxing. Lindsay's endorsement of Kretchmer's poop scoop bill came with his public acceptance of a new invention that would, in the best of worlds, make this grueling task easier to perform. The design was simple enough, consisting of a piece of cardboard that was folded into a shallow box. A rubber band was attached to one end. This "Pooper-Scooper" came with instructions. The operator was supposed to hold the device firmly in one hand with the thumb on the top cover and two fingers on the bottom, then bend over, "scoop" up a dog's mess neatly from the open end and quickly close and seal the parcel with the rubber band, thus sandwiching the nasty business in between the cardboard like a marshmallow between graham crackers. The odd contraption was invented by a man from New Jersey named Henry Doherty, an office manager between jobs who presented his little gizmo to Mayor Lindsay as a solution to the dog problem in New York City.

Patent No. 3,685,088 had the formal title "Means for Collecting a Dog's Excrement by the Dog's Owner or Walker." The distinction between "owner" and "walker" was an important legal one that would lead to much discussion in future years about a possible loophole in the city's eventual poop scoop law. But in 1972 no one, neither the "owner" nor "walker" of a dog, was technically required by any law to use a "Pooper-Scooper." Jerome Kretchmer had been promoting the device in the hope that it would somehow make the idea of picking up more palatable to dog owners. The lure of new technology might gently seduce them into performing an act the mere thought of which made them retch. If only dog owners could be coaxed into using these contraptions of their own free will, then maybe his controversial law wouldn't be needed.

A host of other governmental projects, begun by Kretchmer before Lindsay's acceptance of the new bill, suggest that the EPA wasn't entirely sure a poop scoop law would even work. An "educational campaign" was already under way on Manhattan's West Side and in Brooklyn Heights, where Kretchmer had quietly arranged for a number of "Curb Your Dog" signs to be painted over with a new message asking—not ordering—"Pick Up After Your Dog—Please." The polite suggestion seemed a more practical solution than forcing dogs off the curb and into oncoming traffic, as the current "curbing" interpretation of the existing law still demanded. Kretchmer's plea was ignored. "Dog

Owners Say City Errs" read the headline when the Pet Owners Protective Association (POPA) and the Dog Owners Guild (DOG) blamed the new signs for actually making the sidewalks "filthier than ever."[11] Now that dog owners weren't at least being asked to take their pets off the curb, it was claimed, they were more likely than ever to let them go on the sidewalk where they rightly refused to pick up! Both organizations demanded the signs be repainted at once so that sidewalks would be cleared for pedestrians.

"Dog Owner's Guide to Scooping" was another pet project under way as part of the EPA's educational campaign. This was an eight-page booklet outlining where dogs could be legally "curbed" ("not on personal property, such as cars or stoops or houses"). Bags and news-papers were recommended for those willing to pick up. "Don't be dis-couraged," read the text, "if your first attempts at scooping are awkward or distasteful. Remember, with practice it becomes easier." The EPA even published its own "newspaper," as Kretchmer called another of his alternate solutions, a 40-page tabloid containing instructions on how to paper-train dogs to go indoors. This throwback to Lindsay's original idea to make dogs go "in the owner's bathroom"[12] seemed to suggest, again, that Kretchmer had serious doubts about the effectiveness of his own law, and that he suspected polite requests and helpful hints on the sidewalk might lead nowhere. Kretchmer seemed to be covering his bases by distributing, free of charge, the "newspaper," which included fully illustrated, step-by-step instructions on paper-training dogs to go indoors. It also included a special centerfold section of 28 blank pages that were be removed and used, one sheet at a time, on the owner's floor. "First read the newspaper," read the front-page headline, "then give it to your dog."

Other alternatives to the poop scoop idea came from sources far and near. Sanitation Commissioner Herbert Elish was insisting that if the poop scoop law didn't make it past City Council, the "curb" inter-pretation of the law would still be very much in force. Even though his department had said it didn't have the funding to flush out the gutters, and would probably leave the mess right where dog owners had left it,

One of several projects tried by New York City's EPA in order to avoid passing a law requiring dog owners to pick up.

Source: Used with permission of Robert Lascaro.

"Dog Owner's Guide to Scooping" gives precise directions on where dogs can go.
Source: Used with permission of Robert Lascaro.

anyone who allowed a dog to go anywhere else would be fined between $25 and $100, as the penalties had already been set. In a warning to dog owners, he told the press the story of one of his Sanitation inspectors who had recently witnessed a well-dressed woman on the Upper East Side letting her dog go right in the middle of the sidewalk, despite the "Curb Your Dog" sign that was clearly posted a few feet away. The woman apparently didn't have a leg to stand on. In fact, she was so distressed at being stopped that, while the officer was writing out the summons, she stepped back into the pungent pile her dog had just left. "Lady, on second thought, I won't give you a summons," the officer said. "I guess that's punishment enough."[13]

Another alternative came from City Councilman Michael DeMarco, who was against the poop scoop law but no less eager to take a leading role in New York's cleanup. DeMarco suggested restricting dogs to doing their business on alternate sides of the street on different days of the week. This, he reasoned, would save the city some money on street cleaning. If the Department of Sanitation still refused to treat dogs as horses and clean up their droppings as they'd done until automobiles took over the streets, then why not treat dogs as cars? "You mean alternate-side-of-the-street dogs?"[14] Kretchmer asked, shaking his head in disbelief.

In the meantime, Abraham Beame, the City Controller who was as eager as anyone to contribute his two cents, masterminded a plan he believed would solve this and many more of the city's sanitation problems. Not long after Jerome Kretchmer had been seen riding a garbage truck to work one morning, Beame also took a leap onto the environmental bandwagon. He said that what New York really needed were "Envirmaids," a special corps of female inspectors who would police the city night and day, "making sure the sidewalks are kept clean, getting after air polluters or litterers, or reporting to the proper agencies the cluttered empty lots, abandoned cars, water leaks, sewer backups, and dirty playgrounds that make life less enjoyable."[15] Why women? Besides the obvious savings—women would work for lower wages than men—Beame said that they were just neater. Tapping into a tradition started at the turn of the century when the Women's Municipal League took a role in keeping streets clean, Beame explained that "women are more conscious of their surroundings," and that "the city might profit from their awareness in the environment."[16] Kretchmer didn't share Beame's enthusiasm for "Envirmaids" and the idea was shelved.[‡]

* * *

So many of the reactions to Lindsay's very late endorsement of the poop scoop bill pointed to the inescapable conclusion that no one was about to make dog owners bend over and handle feces, with or without "Pooper-Scoopers," bags, newspapers, or scoldings from "Envirmaids." Nor should they give into this kind of pressure, their supporters believed. In fact, when word got out about Lindsay's position, Councilman Carter Burden announced that he would be one of many leaders to vote *against* the bill, which he considered unfair and impractical. "Frankly, a lot of other animals contribute to the litter on the streets,"[18] he said at the eventual hearing, referring to those horses still used by policemen and for carriage rides in Central Park, and to the litterers who used the entire city as their wastebasket. Many New Yorkers were on Burden's side. "Where are all your articles calling for closer control of bums who defecate and urinate in public phone booths?" someone asked the *Times*.[§] At least as offensive as any other form of animal waste were (and still are) the *human* feces and urine left reeking in subways and alleys, and often right in the middle of sidewalks. "We wouldn't tolerate people defecating in the street,"[19] said

---

[‡]Later studies on compliance with poop scoop laws, both in the United States and abroad, would confirm the "sexist" belief that women were somehow tidier than men. C. Swann's 1998 findings in a Chesapeake Bay community showed that males were far less likely to pick up than females. "Males between the ages of thirty and fifty most typically disobey the law," Yves Contassot reconfirmed from Paris City Hall in 2007. "This isn't surprising since they don't change diapers."[17]

[§]Public phone booths were eventually removed from New York City largely for this very reason—too many people were using them as toilets. As a result, to the present day, callers without cell phones are forced to stand in the rain.

Alan Beck a few years later. "I invite him to come to Broadway and 93rd Street, where they do so,"[20] came the response. "I'm tired of hearing the monotonous complaints about dog 'litter' week in and week out," cried another angry voice. "Why is nothing said of the mountains of litter stemming from innumerable leaflets being distributed throughout the mid-town area? These advertising efforts run the gamut from announcements of bank openings offering valuable gifts to new depositors through religious groups offering instant salvation and down to massage parlors offering extra pleasures. Why not put a stop to this source of unsightly litter? Perhaps the authorities are hoping that it will bury the dog droppings, thereby silencing that complaint."[21] Another wrote: "People, not animals, pollute the water, the air, and the land to the extent that our world is fast turning into an uninhabitable sewer for man and animal alike."[22] Still another voice was added to the apocalyptic din: "Hordes are spitting on the streets and smoking on the subways with total disregard for the law and humanity. New York's dog litter problem is but a small symptom of the terrifying social decay that is filling our air with a far greater stench than dog feces."[23]

Despite the many good points brought up to suggest that maybe New York had more serious things to worry about than canine waste, the problem refused to be swept under the rug. People were sick and tired of stepping into crap and they pressured their leaders to take a stand. "The dog turd in our region is . . . epidemic!" wrote one very frustrated New Yorker to the *Times*. "Dog owners here feel that anything is good enough for their little darlings (some of which are short the size of a pony)."[24] But being in favor of the new law didn't necessarily mean being anti-dog, as another wrote to reassure pet owners: "It is easy to appreciate the needs dogs satisfy and the pleasure they give their owners. Still, the mess they make in the streets is a very real nuisance and some means should be found to deal with it."[25] Meanwhile, the nation looked on as a very strange drama began to unfold in New York City. Already, there was hope that a successful canine waste law in New York might set a precedent for other cities where attempts at curbing dog owners had failed. But whatever the virtues of this new idea, mixed with the excitement over events in New York was the tempered optimism of those who had dealt with the most militant of dog owners and knew, all too well, that laws alone would probably never change their behavior. A retired Army Colonel in Fairfax, Virginia, wrote to express a distant hope that New Yorkers might set this bold example for the nation. But he was doubtful whether even a military state stood more than a small chance of enforcing a dog law. "The dog litter question in New York City," he wrote skeptically, "brings to mind an order that appeared in the Heidelberg Post (U.S. Army, Europe). Circular No. 210-1 (Instructions to Occupants of Dependent Quarters). It went like this: 'Pet owners will be guided by the slogan, Curb Your Pet; that is, owners will insure that their pet defecates and/or urinates in the street or in the gutter, and not on lawns, plants, shrubbery, sidewalks, or playgrounds.' None of the quadrupeds complied with the order. How do I know? I had to mow the grass in front of my quarters."[26]

Dog owners themselves were almost unanimous in their attitude toward Kretchmer's poop scoop idea. When word got out about Lindsay's formal support of the bill, Max Schnapp, the outspoken leader of POPA, predicted that any attempt to hold humans accountable for their dogs' mess would inspire a mass uprising of the city's estimated 310,000 dog owners! "I can assure you City Hall will echo with protests of pet owners against that bill,"[27] promised Schnapp. Though full-scale rioting was averted, the announcement caused shake-ups on both sides of the question. Within a few days, an already nervous City Hall received dozens of letters from angry animal lovers ready to unite against the proposal. A group of about eighty of them actually picketed Gracie Mansion, the mayoral residence, but spent most of the time chasing dogs. "Rabbit Diverts Dogs at Protest," read the headline.

"To Scoop or Not To Scoop?" asked the *Times*. "Dog Owners Protest Bill To Force Street Cleanup," read another headline. "Dog Litter: A New Augean Headache,"¶ announced yet another as special

---

¶The *Times* made frequent use of this colorful reference to classical mythology. According to legend, the "Augean stables" were owned by King Augeas, who apparently kept some 3,000 oxen in his extensive stables but never, not once, did he arrange to

committees were formed and New Yorkers of many different minds stood up to be heard. Lindsay's go-ahead may not have led to the mass uprising that Max Schnapp had predicted. But the matter was forcing people to choose sides. And the battle would be a fierce one. Suddenly, an entire cast of characters came from out of the woodwork to influence City Council's decision. A group called SCOOP ("Stop Crapping on Our Premises") followed Kretchmer wherever he went, sitting by his side and fending off the insults. One meeting held by Community Board 8 on Manhattan's Upper East Side was called "Dogs-Health-Environment." Various groups attended, including PAWS ("Pets Are Worth Safeguarding), and a very small minority that called itself "Dog Owners for a Cleaner New York." The latter was made up of dog owners who were actually in favor of a poop scoop law. Their iconoclastic leader, Paula Weiss, explained, "I compare it to mothers who let their children run around without diapers. Why mess with commercial scoopers?" she added with a nonchalance that was uncommon in a person facing the dreaded parcel. "It really isn't that terrible,"[28] she insisted before a group of mortified dog owners. Robert Angus, head of the Dog Owners Guild ("DOG"), didn't believe her and asked a *Times* reporter, "Look, if you know anyone who's tried it, would you ask them how they manage?"[29] Angus' fear of scooping was shared by the many dog owners who felt that Kretchmer's law was absurd and humiliating. Cleveland Amory only heightened their concern when he called the poop scoop law, once again, a first step in a plan to ban dogs from New York City.

Meetings like the one on the Upper East Side were characterized by shouting, merciless heckling of speakers, and borderline violence. Passions flared at the mere mention of dogs, and it seemed unlikely that either side would back down. The largest and most vocal group of dog owners was POPA with its over 800 official members. Formed by

---

have these facilities cleaned. The gods—cleanliness being next to godliness—were very unhappy about the odor. This shameless disregard went on for an unhygienic 30 years. In the end, Hercules himself is said to have swooped down from the heavens and taken matters into his own hands, diverting the river Alpheus through the king's raunchy stables and flushing them miraculously in a single day.

Max Schnapp, a former labor union organizer for the CIO, POPA was known to rely heavily on labor-organizing tactics. Schnapp, who led his group in this latest battle, was no newcomer to animal politics. His commitment to animals was beyond suspicion. He'd fought with the Sierra Club to save endangered species and he'd been rescuing strays for many years. At home he had two Great Danes (named "Tiger" and "Sampson"), a pet crow ("Mitzvah"), three rabbits ("Pinkie," "Dutchie," and a third without a name), a white mouse ("Piggy"), a baby squirrel ("Elmer Wiggley"), an anonymous gerbil, and six alley cats ("Mau Mau," "Nebisch," "Sister," "Freddy the Freeloader," "Monty Wooley," and "the cat who came to dinner"). Schnapp founded the Jewish Humane Society, and in 1970 he started POPA in response to the growing number of complaints from New York tenants who had been evicted by their landlords for having pets. Schnapp's opposition to Kretchmer's law, like Cleveland Amory's, was based on the assumption that it would set a dangerous precedent that could lead to further restrictions on animal ownership, and perhaps a ban on dogs. Schnapp gladly admitted, with his heavy Austrian accent, that poop was a problem in New York. But he encouraged stronger enforcement of the existing "curbing" law, not a poop scoop law. He even suggested, half-heartedly, allowing the dog-owning community to police itself for scooping. How he proposed to coax anyone into believing that picking up was a good thing to do remained unclear. But passing a new law, he maintained, was no solution to the dog problem in New York City.

Schnapps' most formidable foe was Fran Lee, the founder and spokesperson for Children Before Dogs, the largest and most influential of the anti-dog groups. Lee stood firm in her belief that Jerome Kretchmer was backing the wrong law and was determined to fight him *and* Max Schnapp to the finish if necessary to prove her point. Lee maintained that the current law disallowing the depositing of any "offensive animal matter" on public property was the only one that made any sense. The "curbing" interpretation of that law was wrong, she believed. Dogs should not, she said, be encouraged to use the city as their bathroom. Lee assumed that Kretchmer's law, even if it were to be passed, would soon be forgotten and New York would still be facing feces and the dangers they supposedly posed to children. Unlike Schnapp, Lee had no pets at home, although she did try to distance herself from her more extremist followers who insisted that poisoning all of New York's dogs was the only solution to the canine waste problem. Still, her pro-dog claims were suspect. She often told the press about the dog she and her husband briefly had but abandoned, like so many people did, because they didn't think the city was a good place for pets—or was it that having pets in the city was an inconvenience for some people? When confronted by a dog owner trying to defend his right to let his dog run off-leash in parks based on the precedent of Lassie never having been leashed on television, Lee responded: "But Lassie never litters."[30]

Like Max Schnapp, Fran Lee had a somewhat illustrious career. Before she founded the most visible of organizations in favor of dog control, she had been an actress and then a consumer expert on WNEW-TV. She was among the first media personalities to talk about the harmful effects of cyclamates in food, and she helped to expose the unsanitary standards of the spice importation industry. Lee was already a major player in public health politics when she went on to found Children Before Dogs. She attracted thousands of followers and became known as "New York's foremost fighter against dog dirt,"[31] as the *Times* liked to refer to her. The emphasis on health issues, particularly on the safety of innocent children, made her platform especially potent. Lee claimed that the presence of dog feces on sidewalks and public lawns was endangering the lives of children who played in the same areas where dogs defecated. "If you are lucky," she warned in one of her circulars, "you'll come home with only the stench and the mess of scrubbing it off. If you're not lucky, you'll come away with a lot more than you bargained for." *Toxocara canis*, the common roundworm found in dogs, was known to have possible but extremely rare health effects upon children in frequent contact with their feces. Most illnesses associated with exposure—with symptoms like asthma, stomach upsets, and sore throats—were not serious and were easily diagnosed and treated. Ms. Lee begged to disagree. She carried around a folder full of "research" showing, she claimed, that pet feces had caused blindness in 300 children across the nation, though she didn't like to share the results of her study. Dr. Howard Zweighaft, former president of the Veterinary Medicine Association of New York City, said vaguely that "one or two"[32] children each year in the metropolitan area suffered from loss of vision from infection. Despite the secretiveness and the lack of hard evidence, Lee was able to attract followers both here and abroad who were understandably alarmed by her claims—although, oddly enough, documented cases of serious illnesses contracted from *Toxocara canis* were almost nonexistent in New York City, poop capital of the world. In fact, more formal studies than Ms. Lee's would reveal that children were in the greatest danger in private households, not on sidewalks, in parks or playground sandboxes, or in any other public places for that matter. On the contrary, it seemed that having dogs do their business indoors—exactly where Fran Lee said they should—was the most likely way to make children sick. The most common carriers of *Toxocara canis* were the puppies brought home for youngsters. Veterinarians encouraged owners to keep these dogs indoors until they were old enough for their shots.[33] But by the time they were out walking the sidewalks, or running leashless in city parks, they were no longer a significant threat. A canine waste law could not be enforced in someone's bathroom. And the only way for dog feces to become a serious health risk outdoors was to leave them in moist places for long periods of time—exactly what the Department of Sanitation was doing after demanding that owners "curb" dogs in the gutters and then failing to clean these as often as it should have. A poop scoop law probably would have been a good solution. But Lee maintained that the mere presence of feces in public places—even if dog owners were to pick up as much of it as they could—would endanger children. "All I want is to help make this a better world,"[34] she pleaded.

Was canine waste a legitimate public health problem? Later studies would reveal that *Toxocara canis,* the ultimate justification for having a poop scoop law in New York City, was not typically an urban problem, except possibly in parks where roundworms flourished because of the grass and dirt in which moisture collected. Feces could, in theory, encourage flies to breed on any type of surface. They could attract more rats than were already scurrying along the gutters, though the banquet of rotting food left uncollected by the Department of Sanitation in the 1970s was probably a rodent's first choice. *Toxocara canis* was found to be far more prevalent not in crowded cities but in wide-open rural areas[35] where the risk of contracting serious illnesses was still so rare that even country folk weren't alarmed in the least. "Fran Lee's claims were not supported by prevalence rates," recalls Pascal James Imperato, former NYC Health Commissioner and one of several officials harangued by Ms. Lee and her followers. Illnesses contracted from exposure to *Toxocara canis* were "very rare." What was Lee's mass appeal? "She presented anecdotal cases which were powerful. She was able to elevate an esthetic issue into a public health issue."[36]

Lee spent years bringing fecal samples for testing to the Board of Health, or to anyone else who might be forced to listen, in the hope of finding trace amounts of dangerous bacteria and worms. She paraded through New York parks accompanied by young mothers carrying infants. She wore a wide straw hat and a big poster board tied around her neck that read: "CAUTION. DO NOT SIT ON THIS GROUND. DOG and PIGEON DROPPINGS make this a potentially DANGEROUS AREA. *TOXOCARA-CANIS* (Roundworm) EGGS COULD BE SWALLOWED. ORNITHOSIS COULD BE INHALED FROM PIGEON MANURE. WATCH YOUR TODDLER." Lee also carried posters with enlarged photographs of dogs doing their business. She sowed an early seed of fear in the minds of urban parents with her vision of a world with dirty, dangerous predators on the one side, and innocent, germ-free toddlers on the other. In this mythical place, children and canines were mutually exclusive and there was no room for a peaceful co-existence. Evoking the same fears of contagion and contamination that fueled environmental politics, Lee's crusade ran on some high octane. The perceived threat to children would be her legacy, dividing the city along lines that offered little hope for a mutual understanding between people with dogs and people with children—or for the peace of mind of those who just happened to have both.

In the weeks to come, while the EPA tried to gently persuade dog owners with tracts and pamphlets that picking up was the right thing to do, animosity continued to spread like wildfire among the various factions. Gatherings degenerated into shouting matches, with speakers on both sides heckled and issues left unresolved. As the first clues to the Watergate Affair were coming to light in the media, meetings of Children Before Dogs were routinely invaded by POPA members who heckled speakers and forced enemies to disband. Max Schnapp was notorious for following Fran Lee to her speaking engagements in the five boroughs, then directing his followers to break up the meetings with heckling and chanting. After one highly publicized event, Lee was struck in the face by a plastic bag full of dog feces! Lee picked it up and hurled it back as she quickly ducked out the door. She later expressed some relief that the mess had been contained securely in a plastic bag when it hit her. Schnapp apologized officially for the act of a lone dog owner, and a few days later he told the press he had searched high and low for the guilty party but without success. Still he couldn't hide his true feelings about Ms. Lee. "I told her that meeting would be loaded with dynamite," he said, as though Lee had asked for a bag of feces in the face. "*Toxocara, Toxocara*. It's a scare campaign,"[37] Schnapp insisted, adding that he could see through to Ms. Lee's real intention of having dogs banned from New York City. Lee eventually filed harassment charges and a judge warned Schnapp to leave her alone. Schnapp, in turn, accused both Fran Lee and Jerome Kretchmer of using "divisive action"[38] on the dog-owning community, causing dog owners to fight amongst themselves over poop so that further steps could be taken against their animals. Only time would show that New York City's policies on pets could, in fact, do precisely this by bringing out the very worst in people.

Fran Lee's followers were no angels. Though a bit less rough around the edges than the dog people, they were ready to defend their young ones against any perceived threats to their safety. They gladly attended Lee's often-dicey speaking engagements, usually adding children for dramatic effect. Parents failed, however, to take note of the extreme rarity of *Toxocara canis*, and of the unlikelihood of contracting illnesses in public places, surprising details given the enormous quantities of feces around town. Was it true that Ms. Lee had built her entire platform upon rather soft foundations? In time, she would even convince the city's Bureau of Infectious Disease Control, which had no experience whatsoever with *T. canis*, to include this among the list of *possible* health hazards posed by canines. But before Ms. Lee took an interest, practically no one in New York had even heard of it. Lee herself, the woman solely responsible for introducing *T. canis* and forming one of the nation's largest dog control lobbies in order to fight it, hadn't even been aware of roundworm, as she herself admitted, until a doctor happened to mention to her in passing that it might be something to get involved in. Fran Lee, the media personality, seemed to be shopping for a new crusade during a dry spell in her career. Her solution to the canine waste problem would not help matters: Dogs, she maintained for several years, should be made to go in their owners' bathrooms. When the EPA announced that City Council would soon be considering a poop scoop law, Lee stormed the Municipal Building, accompanied by mothers carrying infants. She carried a large placard reading: "You cannot walk away from it—the stench, the mess." When she burst into Kretchmer's 23rd-floor office to find on display seven patented cleaning devices, she rallied her followers into denouncing the law as "a commercial venture to sell pooper-scoopers."[39] Fran Lee's crusade only confused the real issues, helping to put off a practical solution to New York's canine waste problem for years to come.

Was it possible that trying to find a solution was causing more bedlam and mass hysteria than simply leaving the mess right there on the pavement? Taking a position, any position, meant taking part in the fight. Politicians were no strangers to the fact that being associated with an issue as emotionally charged as this one could be very dangerous for their careers, if not their own personal safety. John Lindsay, the man who had risked his life by appearing on the streets of Harlem after

Martin Luther King was shot, was a bit more cautious when confronting dog owners on the sidewalks. In fact, behind his hesitant nod of approval for Kretchmer's law was one small but important detail: The whole idea had been Jerome Kretchmer's. Lindsay's brief show of support was probably not supportive at all. When the announcement was made by City Hall, Kretchmer was quoted in the *Times* as calling this "a welcome move."[40] On the contrary, an anonymous member of the EPA was quoted that same day as saying that Lindsay's imprimatur was not a blessing but "the kiss of death"[41] for Jerome Kretchmer.

CHAPTER 6

A SHOWDOWN

"Public dog litter is the subject of more local anger and frustration than the Presidential Election, War and Peace, Minority Rights, and even Landlord–Tenant relations."

—a lawyer writing to City Council on the poop scoop bill[1]

These very strange final months of the Lindsay administration were marked by a growing panic and a further confusion of issues that no one, neither government nor citizens, seemed prepared to handle. Amidst all the finger-pointing and running for cover, a final battle was waged, and another diversion created, showing just how far the city had drifted from a bright and optimistic era into the decade of dark despair.

Nowhere does the tendency to confuse the causes with the effects of the urban crisis, to turn into political issues problems that were social and economic in origin, to view psychological and esthetic concerns as matters of public health appear more blatantly than in the successful attempt at linking, however briefly, the canine waste problem to another issue at the forefront of public concern: graffiti.

From a distance, pet feces and graffiti don't seem to have much in common. But New York's "graffiti problem" was the one issue that shared the limelight with "the dog problem" during these surreal closing moments of the Lindsay era. While the various factions of the dog debate fought tooth-and-claw over their apparently irreconcilable differences, a photograph appeared in the *Times* showing a series of concrete posts in Central Park that had been entirely defaced by spray paint. Readers were outraged. Lindsay himself took an active role in decrying this other blight upon public surfaces that had been spreading for years, covering New York's fountains and pavilions, lampposts and street signs, buildings and bridges, and monuments like Grant's Tomb with stylized scrawl emblazoned in multicolored spray paint and felt-tipped pens. When graffiti defiled the subway stations and trains—the populist symbols of mass transit—this was more than Lindsay would stand for. "Graffiti in the Seventh Avenue IRT subway have taken on dimensions that linger like an all-devouring threat over one's journey," wrote one concerned citizen to the *Times* with the sort of reference to vicious canines that was all to common at the time.[2]

Unlike the politically charged debate over dogs, the graffiti problem appeared, at least on the surface, to be cut-and-dry. Public opinion was almost universally opposed to graffiti, which made this a safer cause for Lindsay to back. Graffiti was said to be the handiwork of juvenile delinquents, plain and simple, kids who deserved, most people agreed, to be punished for their wanton acts of vandalism. But graffiti begged to be viewed in a broader spectrum. After all, it was hardly a novelty but an ancient form of communication that took its name from the Romans. In the present context of New York City in the 1970s, when graffiti wasn't seen as yet another symptom of the moral decay of western civilization, it was viewed as the sign of broad discontent within society that could, many people worried, lead to something much worse. Modern urban graffiti, mainly the work of rival gangs of ghetto youths, was seen by sociologists as the indelible mark of society's deeper socioeconomic problems. A disenfranchised people, some said, were defacing public property in a desperate attempt to be seen by a society to which they were otherwise invisible.

If "the dog law" was to be the solution to dirty pavements at a time when street cleaners were being laid off by the thousands, then "the graffiti law" was proposed as the answer to urban poverty when welfare abuse and reform—read: welfare reduction—were destroying Lindsay's dream of a new kind of society. Both laws were, in fact, band-aids for deeper problems that New York leaders were in no position to solve anytime soon. Meanwhile, it wasn't only ghetto kids who were responsible for graffiti. White, middle-class students at Columbia University were transforming the elegant, neoclassical facades of campus buildings into open books of war protest. Graffiti was clearly more than a sign of disrespect for public property, or an untidy habit. In fact, many people felt a pressing need to have it wiped clean, swiftly and permanently.

Both "the dog problem" and "the graffiti problem" were considered simultaneously by New York's City Council. Both issues were given top priority due to their highly political nature. "The dog bill" and "the graffiti bill" were assigned to the Council's Cleanliness Committee. As the two highly unpopular "pollutants" were discussed by legislators, similarities were pointed out and dog feces and graffiti became linked in the public mind. Graffiti was framed in very much the same health language as feces, with Mayor Lindsay announcing a massive campaign in 1972, including a special task force, to control "the graffiti epidemic." Meanwhile, City Council announced it was working on a monthly "Anti-Graffiti Day" to be modeled after Earth Day, Earth Week, Quiet Week, and City Parks Week. Both graffiti and poop were assigned to the Environmental Protection Administration, even though graffiti wasn't one of Jerome Kretchmer's own pet projects. And both of these issues were covered concurrently by the press and were often used in the same sentence, as in the headline, "Action on Dog Litter and Graffiti Put Off for Months by Council." Neither issue was, it seemed, as straightforward as anyone had imagined.

Could New York afford to wait yet another summer until City Council reconvened in the fall to vote on these two very pressing urban problems? If it was true that behind the written messages there was, indeed, a cry for revolution, then the dog days of August might lead to riots just as they had in so many other American cities. Everyone knew that summer was the worst time for poop, what with the heat and humidity that encouraged bacteria and amplified the stench. But social unrest threatened any attempt at curbing dog owners. When Lindsay first announced his support of legislation banning graffiti on the city's vertical surfaces and dog excrement on the horizontal ones, dog owners had been quick to storm Gracie Mansion in protest. Graffiti producers never showed this kind of solidarity, which made confronting them a lot safer.

What, more than anything else, made canine waste so deplorable? Like graffiti, poop was a blatant form of territory marking. But while the many similarities between these two major concerns might have seemed uncanny, a number of differences emerged. Both were viewed as attacks upon public spaces but poop could strike people where they lived, which made it far more controversial. Rioters, on the other hand, weren't following people home, at least not yet. "I'm tired of trekking that stuff through the house,"[3] complained Councilman Monroe Cohen, Chairman of the Public Safety Committee. Leonard Scholnick, Chairman of the Buildings Committee, noted that the dog bill would nonetheless be the "rougher"[4] of the two to decide on when City Council met again in the fall. The aim of the graffiti bill, for example, was to prohibit persons from carrying open aerosol paint cans or broad-tipped markers in public places. The dog bill stopped short of requiring dog owners to carry "pooper-scoopers" on them at all times (this would be tried in Chicago, only to fail miserably). How would offenders be punished, in the unlikely event that either dog owners or graffiti artists were even caught? Originally, the same penalties were set for graffiti and poop at $100, up to 30 days in jail, or a combination of the two. But a few weeks after New York's graffiti law was passed, the maximum fine for defacing structures would rise to $1,000, and the jail term would increase to a full year. Still, catching offenders at all would be the biggest problem. Lindsay suggested hiring members of rival gangs to inform on graffiti artists. But no one knew how to spot dog owners before they left the scene of their crime. One letter to the *Times* suggested killing two birds with one stone: Why not make the graffiti artists clean up all the dog crap?

Graffiti did, however, manage to win a few supporters. While most people saw it as a form of pollution or vandalism, others embraced it as the work of bona fide artists, and as a vibrant form of expression that had to be protected and preserved. "Slop Art," as it was called in the early seventies—suggesting a basic untidiness—would later be renamed "Graffiti Art." Works on canvas in the "slop" style would one day fetch high prices on New York's art market. The bold designs, once painted on the outsides of buildings, would soon find places *inside* galleries and museums. Saying that one liked graffiti art would become the hallmark of a politically progressive connoisseur. While the few graffiti artists caught defacing public property were made to take back their words with elbow grease, works on canvas in the graffiti style were collected and preserved like strange artifacts from a brief period of decadence before New York's renaissance in the eighties, a time when buildings and monuments were sandblasted and subway cars were armed with new, nonstick surfaces. Dog feces, for whatever reasons, never attained the same level of respectability. Unlike graffiti, and despite the extensive use of both human and other animal waste products in subsequent works of art—and the enormous controversies these caused at the National Endowment and at New York's City Hall—dog excreta were never actively sought after by collectors. That was the whole problem.

*   *   *

The summer of 1972 was about as hot and miserable as it can be in New York. On most days, and until some sea breeze arrived to flush it all out, the atmosphere encircling the city was dense with ozone and a host of impurities. It was as though a vast bubble, a stadium roof, arched over the skyline, trapping inside the noxious gases and particulates. Bad air only worsened the already unstable relations at ground level. With pressure rising and no end in sight, large-scale rioting was kept at bay in the city's trouble spots. Even in the nicer neighborhoods civil unrest always seemed just around the corner. As temperatures increased, so did tension over pet feces smoldering on the torrid pavement, graffiti that baked onto the scorching vertical surfaces, and the countless other hellish irritants that government seemed unable or unwilling to wash away. Some New Yorkers worried that the two debates in City Council might end in stalemates. When lawmakers adjourned for their summer recess, they'd left a glimmer of hope for making the city a better place. September would soon arrive, bringing with it a major victory: the graffiti law was passed. But the dog bill was dying a slow death.

Councilman Alvin Frankenberg of Queens got the debate off on the wrong foot before it officially began. By early September, he'd already grown so tired of hearing dog owners' excuses, and impatient with his colleagues on City Council for always stopping short of confronting them directly, that he lost his cool and resorted to threats. Frankenberg wrote to the *Times* promoting his own piece of legislation for a measure far more extreme and intolerant than the EPA's poop scoop solution.

"Much of the furor re: 'To scoop or not to scoop,'" he wrote in response to the recent exposé, "emanated from the bill I introduced into the City Council which would ban dogs from multiple dwellings in the City of New York. Like it or not, in a city of 8,000,000, this, in the long run, would be the only effective legislation to keep our city clean."[5]

Frankenberg confirmed the greatest fear of dog lovers. The threat of a ban had always been present, looming behind various approaches to the problem. Many pro-dog people had assumed all along that a poop law, vicious, absurd, and impractical in their eyes, was a smokescreen for taking further punitive action against them and their animals. Frankenberg couldn't have stated their case more clearly. Since practically all New Yorkers lived in "multiple dwellings," this measure, unlike any other proposed in the past, was truly aimed at putting the city's dogs not only out on the street (where so many of them already were), but eventually out of New York altogether. Reactions to the Councilman's irresponsible threat were a bit overblown. It should have been obvious that the government was in no position to ban dogs, even if it had wanted to. Attempting to do so would have caused the fighting in the streets that Lindsay had been trying to avoid. But just in case, Frankenberg's fellow lawmakers were careful not to be associated with a self-proclaimed dog hater. His rash proposal, for apparent reasons, failed to win the support he had hoped for, and the Councilman from Queens had wedged the first nail into a coffin for Kretchmer's own legislation. Max Schnapp, the gritty commandant of the Pet Owners Protective Association, responded with a plan for several protests aimed at blocking what was by now being called "the Kretchmer-Lindsay bill." Rather than give into the "divisive action" of the politicians, Schnapp's followers were more unified than ever to fight this measure. "Don't help the dog haters!" urged one of the dozens of letters received by City Council in the weeks prior to the hearing. Another letter warned that, by passing the poop scoop law, government would not only fail to make the city a better place, but "further encourage the exodus from their city of a substantial number of people you want to keep here." Despite the sense of urgency attached to it by a number of citizens, the poop problem would not have a public hearing until November.

"I didn't even go out to eat that day," recalls former Councilwoman Carol Greitzer of the moment of truth that leaders had long been dreading. Greitzer was head of the Committee on Solid Waste and, along with Ted Weiss, one of the very few members of Council willing to take an official stand on dog doo. For an entire day, Greitzer and the rest were trapped in a long and grueling session. "I ordered a sandwich and someone complained that I was eating during a hearing," she says. "That was the sort of atmosphere that day." The meeting of November 10th was "a wild hearing. Raucous. It was difficult to keep order. You rarely attract this kind of attention in City Council. We had dog owners arriving hysterical. Fran Lee was there to talk about diseases. We gave up because we couldn't get anything done."[6]

Dog lovers and their most-hated enemy weren't the only warring factions to squeeze uncomfortably into the Council Chamber that day. Over a hundred speakers were expected, from both sides of the argument, to represent pet owner groups, humane organizations, civic and block associations, medical professions, government, even pooper-scooper manufacturers. Each was scheduled to give testimony, and they all would have, if only there'd been more hours to a day. Emotions ran high as they began taking their stands, one by one, trying to push their causes to Council, and to an audience overflowing into a hallway that echoed with cries from inside. The mood was already intense when Jerome Kretchmer, the man behind it all, stepped up to state his case. The EPA Administrator was booed and taunted by people he could safely assume were dog owners opposed to his measure.

Kretchmer's stand on the dog problem wasn't as dastardly as some had made it out to be. "People have a right to have dogs in the city, for whatever reason,"[7] he began, trying to open the proceedings on a sane and friendly note, and perhaps to undo some of the damage already done by Councilman Frankenberg.

"But just as surely," he continued against the jeers from people not interested in anything he had to say, "the rest of the public has a right not to have dog feces imposed on them throughout their neighborhoods. The bill before you would go a long way toward balancing these two rights."

So far, Kretchmer's assessment sounded fair enough to at least a few members of the audience. Against the backdrop of whistles and howls, Kretchmer's words seemed calming and reassuring, carefully reasoned and a far cry from some of his inflammatory comments to the press. "What's the difference," he had asked only weeks before, "between a guy whose dog is shitting on the sidewalk and a guy throwing his cigarette pack on the sidewalk?" He had also said: "I hereby invite the next person who steps in dog shit on Sunday morning when he goes out for the paper wearing sandals to let me know how it feels."[8] Kretchmer seemed to be speaking from personal experience about a matter that impacted him directly. Like most New Yorkers, he had strong feelings on the subject. Putting these aside, and struggling to maintain the respectful tone befitting a legislative hearing, he outlined a problem he said was not only destroying the city's outward appearance but corrupting its very sense of identity. Poop, he claimed, was having harmful effects on New York's morale at a time when people needed it more than ever.

"Dog litter seems to be all around us in this city," he said, determined to forge ahead. "It is a demoralizing example of how some New Yorkers impose themselves on each other. We work hard to clean our neighborhoods, yet the primitive practice of allowing feces and urine on our streets and in our parks goes on and on. . . . In response to local requests, we have designated parts of several neighborhoods as experimental areas to test public attitudes, willingness of residents to clean up after their dogs, and willingness to use scooping devices. . . . While the results from these areas are not yet in final form, I think it can be said that there is very substantial interest in the idea of promoting cleaning up after their dogs and a surprisingly easy acceptance of the use of scoopers, which many had predicted would produce self-consciousness and embarrassment, at least at first. . . . Many manufacturers have indicated to us that they would move into the market rapidly, if this bill before you is passed. . . . We haven't the manpower to guarantee that every violator, or even most violators would be summonsed. And we will never have that much manpower. But there is more to any law, and its function in society, than simply total ability to enforce it." Kretchmer reached high, trying to end on a resonant note. "As Martin Luther King reminded us on a far more pressing matter, the law is an educational instrument. It has the ability to shape and guide behavior even without total enforcement capacity. And, of course, that enforcement capacity, however limited, does have an effect. The prospect of drawing a heavy fine . . ."

Appealing to dog owners' sense of duty, Kretchmer had tried to avoid resorting to threats. But if that failed, then the constant scrutiny of law enforcement officers, backed up by a shameful appearance in his new environmental court, he predicted, should be enough to make any lawbreakers see reason. As an aside, Kretchmer noted that he was all for making the spaying and neutering of pets more accessible, and for solving the city's enormous stray problem so that responsible dog owners would no longer be blamed, as they currently and unjustly were, for the city's tens of thousands of abandoned animals and the horrific problems they were causing. Kretchmer praised the efforts of Councilman Carter

Burden to open low-cost clinics throughout the city. But in the context of the heated public debate, controlling the dog population in some humane way was widely viewed as an *alternative* solution to the problem, an idea backed by Burden who stood firmly opposed to Kretchmer's poop scoop idea. The two bills, in fact, were considered mutually exclusive. To focus on broader humane issues, rather than on sanitation or public health concerns, was to take a pro-dog stand. On the other hand, imposing a poop scoop law was still largely viewed as distinctly anti-dog. Whether he supported Burden or not, Kretchmer had taken no personal role in trying to solve the stray problem. That wasn't his department. Did he stand a chance of winning over dog owners and legislators when the best he could offer were fines, prison terms, peer pressure, shame, and the barely believable promise of a cleaner city?

The question of whether dog owners even had a responsibility to pick up after their pets simply would not be reduced to notions of civic duty or community pride. Rather than inspiring dog owners, Kretchmer's words only made them more defensive. The mere mention of dogs tapped into deep-rooted feelings about pets, sentiments not shared by all New Yorkers and utterly unexplainable to those who weren't partial to them. Dogs provided companionship to the aged, the lonely, and the alienated. They offered protection from violent criminals. And though pet fanciers could often be marginal and a bit odd, even the more mainstream New Yorkers were finding good reasons for having dogs. Other people just didn't like dogs and never would. Any issue touching upon something so multifaceted was bound to become immensely complex and problematic. Kretchmer presented the law as a fair and simple compromise. Dog owners would finally be allowed to let their pets relieve themselves on public sidewalks, in all legality and harassment-free, provided the dogs stray no further than a respectful three feet from a curb while performing the dirty deed, and that their escorts then immediately collect the results and take these home with them. They weren't taking the bait.

Adding to the melee that day was a basic fact of life in New York City. Seldom does the slightest worry escape from becoming an "issue" and avoid taking on some nightmarishly political spin. Another extreme in a town of extremities, this small concern had become "the hottest and most volatile issue in the administration,"[9] said Joyce Selig, Kretchmer's community liaison worker at the EPA's Office of Citizen Involvement. Canine waste was generally acknowledged in the press to be attracting more attention than any other environmental matter, including air pollution, water pollution, or that other albatross around the EPA's neck, garbage collection. "Public dog litter is the subject of more local anger and frustration than the Presidential Election, War and Peace, Minority Rights, and even Landlord–Tenant relations," wrote a lawyer perplexed over all the attention such a minor issue was drawing.

This solid waste problem, however insoluble it appeared, could not be ignored. The flood of letters, telegrams, and mailgrams—City Council stopped taking phone calls after the first few days—must have alerted Tom Cuite, the Vice Chairman to whom all of these were addressed, to the possibility of the hearing going out of control. Each message added to the confusion as its author tried to sway the decision in one direction or the other. From the most carefully reasoned argument to the nuttiest raving, each writer wrote categorically and showed no signs of backing down. One of the more colorful missives, entitled "Dung City," came from Edward Eisenberg, Vice President of the Manhattan Beach Community Group, Inc., who tried to dispel the myth that the fecal concern was yet another personal obsession of self-indulgent Manhattanites. "Walking down Brighton Beach Avenue or Ocean Parkway," he wrote, "one sees enough urine to float a good-sized ship and enough fecal waste to fertilize the Ukraine."[10] Similar opinions came from representatives of block associations around the metropolitan area, and from parent groups, environmental groups, civic groups, the Kiwanis Club, even the Boy Scouts of America. All were included on the Council's official roster of "Community Leaders in the Campaign Against Dog Litter." One of these, Joseph Santangelo of the Mill Basin Civic Association, wrote to express the horrors of having feces underfoot. "How many times," he asked, "has one walked down the street and stepped on dog excrement? Maybe it is on your property!

Near your gate! Your children's shoes! Near your car so that you carry it into the car!" The mere thought was mortifying.

Individual citizens, unaffiliated with organizations, also wrote in to voice their concerns and to convey their sense of urgency. Mrs. Winifred Wakerly told Councilman Cuite about how she had slipped on feces one day and hurt herself. Robert Barron, another plaintiff, had no sympathy for dog owners because he had seen a blind man slide into a pile and fall on the sidewalk. "For every dog-owning voter who 'coos and goos' over his hound," he warned, "there are ten of us who would prefer a crowded city to be dog free." A certain Thomas O'Connor wrote with both clarity and passion: "Please pass the dog litter bill as soon as possible. The streets are terrible."

On the other side of the argument, the mountains of letters Cuite received from individuals and groups opposed to the bill rivaled the number of those supporting it. Were they from a bunch of crazies? Overall, these letters expressed the sentiment that having a poop scoop law was unimportant, and that its intention was unfair and its aim impractical. "Forcing a person who curbs their dog to pick it up with new contraptions that will be put out on the market seems another new beginning of 1984," wrote Adele Bender. "It is also a strange paradox that the constant breeding of animals is allowed to go on and that a push and advertising campaign for neutering one's pet has not been forthcoming in view of the problem which seems to be taking up so much of the City Council's time." The Interfaith Conference Against Cruelty echoed the sentiments of virtually all animal advocates when it said that the City should focus on controlling the population in some humane way instead of passing a poop scoop law. The Jewish Humane Society agreed. The New York Animal Adoption Society expressed a solid agreement among rescue organizations by calling the measure "repressive and coercive in its intent" and demanding "that Mayor Lindsay declare an embargo on the importation of new dogs to the city." Not only did the proposed law distract from more pressing problems, many said, it was simply cruel to people who had taken on the already difficult task of caring for a dog in New York. Mrs. Hedwig Willimetz called the law "a method for pet haters to harass pet owners." Even the Brooklyn Cat Club was sternly opposed. Curbing was fine, wrote Mrs. Thomas Kelly. But "to actually pick it up is really stretching the rubber band. I saw a woman let her child urinate and poop in Woolworth's last week. An insane, ridiculous bill." Susan James sent a Mailgram reading: "I urge opposition of 956 as anti-people." The National Conservation Recycling Corps was also opposed and suggested instead that building owners be required to provide "dog walks" on their property. The Chelsea Committee for Canine Calm proclaimed that it was decidedly against the "punitive legislation" of the EPA. "Avoid passing a dictatorship law!" urged C. Rosenfeld. E. Bosch-Fischer asked a good question. "What is a dog owner supposed to do if his dog has diarrhea?" he wondered. "Bring a mop and pail?"

Another letter, from an elderly woman terrified that her best friend might be taken away by the same government trying to force an oppressive law upon her, deserves to be quoted in full:

Dear Mr. Cuite,

I am opposed to Bill no. 956. I am eighty years old and live alone except for my dear companion, a beautiful female Scottish terrier who keeps me active since I must walk her at least one mile every day. In the early morning of October 17, 1972 (see records of the 50th police precinct), she chased an intruder from my apartment, probably saving my life. You know what the crime situation is in this city and how criminality has been encouraged and even underwritten by the Lindsay Administration. We are not allowed to have firearms or mace and now it is planned to deprive us of our faithful canine defenders.

Yours very truly,
Dorothy Brace Howe

When the time came for leaders to respond by either siding with Kretchmer or standing against him, speakers had to make it brief. The day's hearing dragged on for so long that many were denied the opportunity to speak at all. Parks Administrator August Heckscher, however, was one city official able to state his case in full. Known for his liberal approach to the use of wide open spaces, Heckscher was nonetheless facing a recession in public green, and a shrinking budget for his own department. In order to save his lawns, he suggested picking up as a kind of emergency back-up plan. He seemed to be beating around the bush. All dogs, he insisted, should at least be "curbed" before entering one of his parks. "However," he admitted, "even someone with the best of intentions will undoubtedly be unable to avoid an 'accident' in all cases. Dogs, and a dog owner like myself knows well, can have a will of their own. I, therefore, intend to encourage people who walk their dogs to bring with them the means of properly cleaning up the results of any such accident. . . . I would further point out that effective enforcement of this law would result in a greater police presence in our parks." Heckscher left some important questions unanswered. Who would pay for the extra cops? And was he trying to imply that forcing dog owners to pick up would, because of a greater police presence, somehow help to protect citizens, with or without dogs, from the muggers who had all but taken over the city's green spots?

Fran Lee, a dog owner's worst nightmare, took the stand. Her massive campaign against not only *Toxocara canis* but also Kretchmer's poop scoop bill had left her with far less time to speak than she perhaps would have liked. In a letter of her own to Mr. Cuite a few days earlier she had written: "Due to flying all over the country making TV appearances, I would appreciate being put on the speakers list as early as possible." During her hurried oratory, she managed to paraphrase a few of the pamphlets that her group Children Before Dogs had been disseminating across the continent. "Is your child's eye worth a dog's dung?" asked one of these, referring to the cases of blindness said to have resulted from exposure to pet feces. "Join Children Before Dogs and become educated in the bias of the dog world today. The most endangered species in America today is your child." Lee was still very much opposed to the bill under discussion, and to any measure that would allow dogs to do their business anywhere but "in the owner's bathroom." A poop scoop law, she predicted, would never work, and even if it did, dog owners couldn't possibly remove every speck of the dreaded offal from pavements and parks where children played. She blamed John Lindsay and Jerome Kretchmer for failing to enforce the current law forbidding the deposit of any "offensive animal matter" in public places. Were it not for these weak leaders, she said, "we would not be known as the largest dog toilet in the world."

As far as the dog owners in attendance that day were concerned, un-housebreaking their pets seemed as ridiculous an idea as picking up after them. Lee got her fair share of hisses and booing, and it was nothing short of a miracle that she wasn't struck in the face again with a bag of feces. Mindful to keep to her schedule and catch her next flight, she introduced Dr. Michael Katz, a professor of tropical diseases and pediatrics at Columbia University whom she had brought along to discuss the breeding habits of flies. After Katz had outlined those exceedingly rare cases in which children, or anyone else, had contracted serious illnesses from dogs, Irving Witlin, the Health Department Counsel, tried to turn attention to the growing dog bite epidemic. A number of salesmen from the pet supply industry then stood up to demonstrate their poop-scooping gizmos.

The room resounded with names like Good Neighbor Products, the Canine Toilet, Eco-Scoop, Doggy Tongs, Dogmatic, Pooch Scoop, Scoop'n Bag It, Scoopet, and Scoop de Doo. "How many times have you wished," asked one salesman, "that you could clean up your dog's litter without embarrassment and awkward, conspicuous motions?" Promises were made, such as "Your hands will never come near the litter" and "There are no embarrassing odors in the apartment elevator or in your home." Another claimed: "Very briefly we will prove a method exists enabling dog walkers to clean up with dignity while at the same time containing the droppings in an airtight package without physical contact." A representative of Valcon Associates described his company's "dog toilet," which included tanks of insecticide and an attractive chemical scent guaranteed to seduce dogs into using the facility. Street application, he said, would be as easy as tapping into the city's sewer system and flushing. Next in line was Wetzler Industries of Florissant, Missouri, which sent in a free box of Sani-Scoop Disposable Collectors. Dog owners might have been overwhelmed by all these choices if they'd had any intention of using any of the products. If Fran Lee hadn't rushed out so early, she would have had all the evidence she needed to back her claim that Kretchmer's poop scoop law was no more than "a commercial venture to sell pooper-scoopers."[11]

But dog owners weren't buying the arguments of Fran Lee *or* Jerome Kretchmer, much less the sales pitches of the pooper-scooper companies. The hearing dragged on as criticisms were hurled from all directions. Carter Burden, who was present that day, had already charged Kretchmer with "discriminating"[12] against dog owners. Councilman DeMarco, with whom Kretchmer had had a bloody fistfight, offered a few wacky alternatives to the law but his opponent shot them down as quickly as he launched them. By the time that Cleveland Amory stepped up to speak, the crowd had grown wilder and the mood had degenerated. People, like their insults, were practically bouncing off the Chamber walls. Despite the chaotic tone of the room, Amory was determined to have his allotted time but not opposed to engaging in a sharp exchange with a woman who kept on interrupting him. "In any park in the city I can't put my one-year-old down!" she cried. "Come to Central Park and I'll show you all sorts of places to go!"[13] Amory shouted back. He then spoke of conspiracies and thinly veiled motives, saying that he could see through government's attempt to set in motion an eventual ban on dogs.

In the whirlwind of passionate exhortations and unsubstantiated claims, calm and rational arguments were made and evidence presented, as might have been expected in more humdrum Council hearings. But unfortunately for Kretchmer and his sympathizers, solid cases were presented for *not* passing the law. In fact, reasonable doubt was cast upon whether the matter was even worth discussing. Everyone knew that dog filth existed in New York. But was the problem being blown out of proportion by a few self-promoting alarmists abetted by a press that seemed to be having fun finding acceptable synonyms for "shit"? Signed petitions were produced, suggesting that the current "curbing" law was strong enough. The Ad Hoc Committee for Clean

Streets, obviously as concerned as anyone else in town about the condition of pavements, then appeared to present the results of a survey it had taken to gauge the *true* daily concerns of New Yorkers. Responses to a questionnaire, which covered 29 separate factors that were correlated by a computer, spoke for a more moderate approach to pets. "Only one out of four respondents," said the Committee spokesman, "felt that laws currently on the books relating to the curbing of dogs are at least adequately enforced." Many New Yorkers seemed to feel that enforcing the existing law made more sense than creating a new one. Others didn't even think that poop was a serious problem. According to the survey, "only one out of fifteen interviewees felt that dog feces were the major source of dirt in the streets. Neither of the two above factors are correlated with dog ownership despite the fact that all three factors vary over wide ranges with dog ownership for the city as a whole being just under 40%. . . . The main objective of my testifying before you today is to put the problem of canine offal in our streets in the proper perspective. There are six times as many dog owners as there are residents who consider dogs a major problem despite the current campaign to focus public attention on them. . . . Higher priorities must be given to legislation and/or expenditures to remove paper, varied litter, glass and cans from our streets, all of which were cited with more interviewees than were dog droppings. . . . The city's limited resources should be allocated to these problems at least roughly in the order of importance they are given by her residents." The spokesman provided a detailed breakdown of the numbers leading to this conclusion.

A good many citizens writing to City Council had arrived at the same conclusion on their own. "I think until our streets get the proper attention they should," wrote Marjorie Cap, "we ought to leave dogs and their owners alone." Repeatedly, suggestions were made for better enforcement of "curbing," and for putting more pressure on the Department of Sanitation, which fell under Kretchmer's EPA, to start doing its job. Officials were accused of using the bill as a "smoke screen" for government's failures. Rather than turn dog owners into criminals, wrote Mary Isaacs, Council should focus on the big companies polluting the city. "There are some people," said the ASPCA's Gretchen Wyler, "who would have us believe that dogs in New York City are either concealed weapons or major pollutants. . . . Responsible, taxpaying pet owners do not intend to become unpaid sanitation workers." What was government being paid to do, anyway? Several references were made to high union wages. "What will the street cleaner do?" asked Tanya Rubenstein. "Get a big salary and look at the girls go by." Pointing to the widespread abandoned car epidemic, Laurence Vide wrote that the bill "obviously makes law-abiding dog owners victims of the Sanitation Department's refusal to move illegally parked cars whose wheels cover the dog refuse and prevent pick up." If only salaried workers would use "chemicals in water spray tanks," mused E. Conway. In case all else failed, Carla Cicero made the same suggestion as that crazed cabbie in the film *Taxi Driver*. "A good rain washes away dog litter," she reminded Councilman Cuite.

Were dog owners as open to Kretchmer's idea as he made them out to be? Hadn't he just reported that residents of several experimental neighborhoods were gladly accepting his idea and willingly bending over to pick up after their pets? As a result, he claimed, those areas were noticeably cleaner. Not so, wrote Mary Waldo of the Dog Owners Guild of Brooklyn Heights, the day after the hearing because it had run too late for her to stay and testify in person. "The majority of Heights dog owners stand opposed to scooping," she reported, "and many of these are deeply resentful of Mrs. Wolf's and Mr. Kretchmer's attempts at 'education.' Our gutters are indeed cleaner since we became one of Mr. Kretchmer's 'experimental' districts. This is due to the additional street cleaning service we have been getting. That relic from a bygone era, the *manual street sweeper*, has even put in an appearance in our neighborhood. Dog dirt in Grace Court, cited in another testimony as a 'success in scooping,' is *daily* flushed down from the city hydrant." Some neighborhoods were, indeed, becoming cleaner—but only because the Department of Sanitation was finally doing its job. Not only was a poop scoop law unwelcome and unnecessary, Ms. Waldo added, if it were passed it could actually have harmful effects on the environment.

"From the standpoint of sanitation," she concluded, "it is better to leave the feces in the gutter to be swept or washed away—they are, after all, biodegradable—than to add hundreds of thousands of nonbiodegradable plastic bags to the City's daily refuse."

Finally came the public health angle. Mrs. Yolan R. Guttman, a registered nurse, rose to discuss the study that she herself had conducted of the incidence of *Toxocara canis* in children's hospitals across the country. "I have a strong sense of unreality," she began, "when I contemplate the many sad problems that we face in this community, problems that almost defy all solution. Yet, so much time and energy have to be wasted on discussing the meaningless issue of 'scooping the poop.' This just cannot come to be." Mrs. Guttman submitted to the Council "a study on the incidence of the disease condition that dogs are supposed to spread to many little children. I can say, without hesitation, that this is another item of divisive hearsay, foisted on the people of this city without any supportive medical evidence. Of course, the disease entity does exist, but its frequency is so limited as to be almost nonexistent." Fran Lee's case, she suggested, was only helping to make people paranoid over dogs. "Generally, domestic animals do not spread diseases to humans to the degree that humans spread these to animals. It is a fact that little children catch more diseases from their human contacts than they ever could or would from any of the domestic animals, including any pet animal. . . . No reputable physician would attempt to offer a diagnosis of an infection with *Toxocara canis* based upon the slim circumstantial evidence that the little child entrusted to his care had in the past, or now has, a puppy for a pet."

If Mrs. Guttman's testimony was accurate, then the only way for small children to become seriously ill from exposure to dog feces would be to encourage them to roll around for endless hours in moist and rancid city gutters, and then to let them consume massive quantities of dirty, rotten garbage to their hearts' content. Otherwise, it would be next to impossible for dogs to make them sick.

"An educational campaign, yes," Mrs. Guttman concluded. "Unjust coercion, no." Instead, she and other opponents of the poop scoop idea viewed Carter Burden's own bill for spay/neuter clinics, and a campaign to encourage dog owners to follow the existing "curb" law, as the only fair and sensible solutions to New York's dog problem. Any other decision, it was thought, might only make the situation worse than it already was. Both humans and their beloved pets could suffer greatly. "It is our belief," wrote Charles Haines of the ASPCA, referring to the poop scoop bill, "that if such legislation was enacted, and if it was successfully enforced, the result would be a substantial increase in the inhumane treatment of dogs. Certainly, a large number of families would turn their animals out in the street, rather than risk the fine imposed by this new law. Abandoning an animal is against the law, but it is also an act of extreme cruelty, and therefore, we cannot in good consciousness agree to support any legislation that would adversely affect the animals of our city."

*   *   *

A few days later, another hearing was scheduled to decide whether or not to exempt blind persons with Seeing Eye dogs from a law that showed very few signs of being passed. Hardly anyone attended, though discussions about the dog bill dragged on for much of the following year. By April 1973, in a last-ditch effort to rescue a dying cause, the Commissioners of Sanitation, Police, and Parks appeared before City Council to express their support for a poop scoop law. But City Hall had quietly dropped its own support for a highly controversial piece of legislation that it never really wanted to endorse in the first place. Mayor Lindsay was on his way out, though not without thoughts of salvaging what was left of his political career. In one of the letters written before the raucous hearing in November, a Mr. and Mrs. Joseph Warner had sent a warning that must have chilled him to the bone. "It appears to us," they wrote, "that you are being brainwashed by Jerome Kretchmer and his cohorts. He, Kretchmer, really hates dogs. His ultimate hope is to see dogs completely disappear from the city. Why would he support Fran Lee in her rantings and ravings about the disease that dogs purportedly pass on to children—he has backed her at public meetings and she has appeared with him on television. . . . If the law to enforce pet owners to clean up dog droppings is passed, the city will be more divided than ever, and self-appointed vigilantes will endeavor to enforce it, making the old, women, and the crippled perfect prey for their hatred. And how long can a person endure harassment and even physical violence? So that more strays will occur, and Mr. Kretchmer will have more fodder for the death chambers! What a horrible place to live in this will be, when a child won't be able to love and be loved by an adoring dog; when a lonely person will have no living being to share his home, when the timid person will have no dog to warn him or her of approaching danger. . . . Don't deprive the thousands of people of what psychologists can tell you are a great need and comfort in these tumultuous times!" City Hall, citing mass letter-writing campaigns and the picketing of Gracie Mansion, bailed out. Jerome Kretchmer was left holding the bag.

Was Kretchmer as evil as people were making him out to be? The EPA Administrator tried to approach the matter sanely, keeping respectful of the fears and aversions dog owners seemed to have at the mere mention of handling feces. Despite his vague understanding of the deep emotional attachments that motivated dog lovers, he had been especially careful not to say anything negative about their beloved pets. He even considered the owners' concern over "social embarrassment"[14] but believed, contrary to virtually every canine rights advocate of the time, that it was possible and necessary for people to overcome this aversion to handling feces in public. He also believed, unlike Max Schnapp and his followers, that it was physically possible to bend over and snatch a nasty parcel with one hand and, at the same time, to hold a leash safely and securely in the other to avoid endangering a dog's life. Kretchmer had gone out of his way to court the city's dog owners gingerly, concocting one scheme after another to help render the thought of picking up more palatable, even offering alternatives for those with stomachs too weak for the task. But in his office at the EPA were seven different patented devices for scooping poop that were now collecting dust, and stacks of "newspaper" that no one wanted to read. In the end,

Kretchmer's vision of a feces-free New York was not shared by all New Yorkers, and the notion that scooping was the responsibility of each and every dog owner was far from becoming the assumption it is today. Kretchmer was, indeed, a man before his time. He told New Yorkers they would have to start picking up after their dogs. For daring to say so, he was assailed from all sides. Some dog lovers accused him of being, if not overtly against animals, then "anti-pro-dog."[15] Other, less equivocal critics like Cleveland Amory accused Kretchmer of trying to do away with the city's dogs altogether. On the contrary, the militant pro-child/ anti-dog lobby maintained that Kretchmer's law wasn't harsh enough, and that the EPA Administrator was only trying to profit financially from the sale of poop-scooping devices. Voters and fellow politicians alike decried his arrogance. Kretchmer rose briefly on the wave of environmentalism. But he struck a reef when his poop scoop bill, the single most visible and divisive item of his entire political career, was written off by a State Assemblyman as "another one of his zany ideas."[16]

It was clear to onlookers that Kretchmer's bill, like his political career, was going nowhere. Abraham Beame, the City Controller who had been trying for two years to convince Kretchmer of the merit of his plan for "Envirmaids," still thought the idea was a good one. He went over Kretchmer's head by proposing it directly to Lindsay. For obvious financial reasons, New Yorkers never saw the legion of pert, pleasant ladies Beame thought would enjoy keeping the city clean and tidy. But for the failure of New York to clean up its act, Kretchmer was blamed. One forthright citizen wrote to the *Times* accusing him of using the canine waste issue to further his political career:

> After failing even to put a dent in the city's major ecological problems, Jerome Kretchmer has finally found a publicity vehicle equal to his ambition. Of course it's easier for him to attack the dog, and the dog owner, than to bring about solutions to the problems confronting us, especially when these solutions are balked by well-organized groups and powerful industries. But how else does a poor frustrated Environmental Administrator make himself look like a hot mayoral prospect? Just find a "patsy" like the dog.

What about the droppings of that other beast, the automobile? How about making every commuter in a car collect his car's waste products in a plastic bag? Certainly these are more dangerous than the droppings of the dog. Wouldn't the city be cleaner and healthier if Mr. Kretchmer and others rode to work on large dogs instead of their polluting autos?

Besides being another virtually unenforceable law to be administered by an already overburdened police force, the proposed legislation increases the sense of alienation from their government of many middle-class residents—a feeling of being assailed by the criminal in the streets on one hand and, on the other, by a city administration insensitive to their needs.

No one will pretend that dog leavings in the street are pleasant, but let's put it in its proper place on our list of city priorities. Now let's see—number 7,862 by my count.

Hal Davis
New York, Nov. 10, 1972

Kretchmer had, in his own way, been a "patsy." Despite his continual self-promotion that annoyed Lindsay to no end, he had served as a loyal appointee in a time of uncertainty. He had helped to deflect some of the political heat from City Hall by taking on the issues that most concerned voters—or so he said—however petty they might have seemed in the greater scheme of things. But it could scarcely be denied that Kretchmer was guilty of trying to make a career out of shit. On that issue he had failed to rally the support he needed and that failure was highly visible. Despite this disastrous defeat, Kretchmer was still planning to run for mayor. He stepped down as Administrator for the EPA in February 1973, returning to his law firm, he said, to "create the sense that I take this candidacy seriously."[17] Herbert Elish, the Sanitation Commissioner who was determined to make people at least "curb" their dogs, became the new EPA Administrator.

Kretchmer would never again hold public office in New York City. He withdrew early from the mayoral race of 1973. He also lost a bid for Congress in 1974, then returned to the State legislature in Albany

Cartoon by Charles E. Martin accompanying a 1972
letter to the *New York Times* on Jerome Kretchmer's
brief career in environmental politics.

Source: Charles E. Martin, used with permission.

where he was hired as special counsel to the state Senate Democratic
minority from 1975 to 1977. Oddly enough, Kretchmer eventually made
a career change and became one of New York City's premier real estate
developers. His company, aptly named with an environmental reference "Recycling for Housing Partnership," specialized in converting
large industrial buildings into sleek residential properties as New York
regained the faith of the nation in the 1980s and people began moving
back to the city. Kretchmer also went on to become one of New York's
premier restaurateurs by opening such famous spots as Gotham Bar
& Grill, Mesa Grill, BOLO, and Judson Grill. He received numerous
awards for his culinary accomplishments.

But a scandal broke in 1981 concerning Kretchmer the developer. It was learned that Kretchmer, while serving as counsel in Albany during the seventies, had possibly gained insider knowledge of the state's decision to build a convention center on the West Side of Manhattan. The Jacob Javitz Center was to be built in the West Thirties between 11th and 12th Avenues, an area that included a building only recently purchased by Kretchmer's company. When the state's Urban Development Corporation (UDC) learned that Kretchmer was about to sell a piece of property, an industrial building on 11th Avenue that was in the way of the convention center, and at a huge profit just so the state could tear it down, the president of the UDC, Richard Kahan, moved to block any profit that Kretchmer and his partner stood to gain from the sale of a condemned building. Harold Fisher, a director for the convention center, recalled, "I realize that there are people in the city who try to sharpshoot us. I wanted to stop it."[18] Kretchmer stood firm on his claim that he was innocent of trying to profit from insider knowledge of the construction site, insisting that he could not have known about last-minute alterations in the architect's plan that included the land he just happened to have just purchased. "I got my money,"[19] he recalls. Still, it kind of makes a person wonder. Could Fran Lee have been right all along? Was Kretchmer using his poop scoop law as "a commercial venture to sell pooper-scoopers"?[20]

If Jerome Kretchmer's name would be forever associated with a failed attempt at curbing dog owners, then John Lindsay's would be tied to all of the city's *other* problems. Parks Administrator August Heckscher recalled that Lindsay had to contend with "an accumulation of grievances against him, and with the role as scapegoat that had been formalized and almost institutionalized. Never, it seemed, had so many owed so much in the way of inconvenience or disappointment to one man."[21] In years to come, enemies and former supporters alike would delight in blaming all of their problems, if not on pets, then on the one man who tried to save New York City from going, as the expression goes, to the dogs. Even Jerome Kretchmer, an unknown legislator until Lindsay appointed him as head of a very visible agency, turned on his benefactor by openly blaming him for tolerating corruption in City government. Soon Lindsay found it difficult to go on residing in the town for which he had worked so hard to save from one of its most trying ordeals.

Environmentalism, it was true, had managed to unite the city briefly, putting off the national, post-war trend of abandonment that was driving American cities into bankruptcy. Lindsay had created one of the nation's first environmental protection agencies. As long as New Yorkers believed there was still hope of "cleaning up" the city, Lindsay managed to keep some measure of peace. But as the city's list of pressing problems continued to lengthen and the recession of the 1970s worsened, "the environment" came to mean anything from the crime wave to poor public schools. Lindsay had created a monster. By thrusting New York's many problems into the open, he had made its imperfections seem all the more apparent and intolerable. No one could rightly deny that Lindsay had made the air a lot cleaner. He had set an example for the rest of the nation and the world. State-of-the-art waste disposal plants were under construction. But despite the many advances made, the often lavish spending on environmental improvements played a role not only in making the city cleaner but in hastening its downfall. New York was on the brink of bankruptcy with a deficit approaching $2 billion. Most of the environmental advances had been made by 1970, before Jerome Kretchmer arrived on the scene. What had the Lindsay administration done *lately*? The public's appetite for improvement was no longer being satisfied and the money needed to fuel it ran in ever shorter supply. Big Government was downsized to make way for what Lindsay was calling "greater community participation." But what good were brooms and dustpans, green paint and shrubbery, or even expensive, ultra-modern waste disposal plants, when there was no way to get trash to its destination?

While many New Yorkers put all their money on the environment, others decided cynically that the city simply wasn't worth saving. Some of their predictions might have helped to doom Lindsay's vision before it was put to the test. William F. Buckley, who had lost the mayoral election to Lindsay in 1965, hastened to write a book that following year, as though to try and uproot New York's new optimism before it had a chance to grow. In *The Unmaking of a Mayor* Buckley used all the imagery of the day when he asked, bitterly: "To what extent is New York, for mysterious ecological reasons, a kind of major dumping ground toward which the inertial forces of despair tend to propel the loose and the restless who, having come there, huddle down and will not go away, no matter what the attendant miseries of their new life, because by now they are spiritually exhausted?"[22] With dispiriting remarks such as these, New York's demise was almost inevitable.

While Lindsay waged a war on graffiti during his last months in office, he failed to read the writing on the wall: His political career was over. And New York was in big trouble. Social unrest was to be the predominant theme of this unhappy period the city was entering. Welfare and civil rights, it seemed, didn't automatically end poverty or calm urban violence. Non-white minorities, though they still tended to favor Lindsay in the polls, were losing faith in his ability to solve the socioeconomic problems of the ghetto. Many white voters were radically opposed to Lindsay's social reforms such as desegregation, particularly when this meant building low-income housing in their own neighborhoods. "White flight," despite Lindsay's improvements to the city, continued chipping away at New York's tax base.

Lindsay was no better liked by fellow politicians. Years of hostility with Governor Nelson Rockefeller had culminated in the Scott Commission, by which Albany monitored the city's spending habits. A recent switch from the Republican to the Democratic Party, moreover, left Lindsay without solid backing in either when he tried briefly to run for president. Lindsay's disastrous defeat in the Democratic primaries had only weakened his image at home. He had campaigned mainly for urban issues, evoking the theme of the "crisis" of American cities, assuming that Americans still cared about what happened to their once-great metropolises. But millions had already moved on to less stressful if more vacant lives in the suburbs or newer, smaller cities. As a result, historian Vincent Cannato remarks, Lindsay's defeat in the primaries served to underline the fact that conditions in New York City had actually worsened over the course of his two terms as mayor. In all fairness, New Yorkers should have noted that their predicament came with a national, post-war trend begun long before Lindsay had appeared on the scene. The ruinous financial practices for which Lindsay was blamed had been initiated by Robert Wagner, his predecessor. But such is politics. When shit happens, all that seems to matter is that someone be found to take the blame.

Lindsay would write in 1976 that being mayor was "like being a bitch in heat. You stand still and you get screwed, you start running and you get bit in the ass."[23] A few years later, in 1980, Lindsay tried for the Democratic nomination to the U.S. Senate. But in the midst of a campaign that was going nowhere, he took a fall. Lindsay was riding his bicycle in the Hamptons, as he had done on city streets during environmental campaigns to endorse alternative means of transportation, when he was met with a familiar sight: a leashless dog. "He was bicycling at top speed on a country road," a neighbor told the *Times*, "when a large, brown dog came out at him from a driveway on his left side. He tried to avoid the dog, but it ran out in front of him and he hit the dog. Mr. Lindsay went up in the air over the handlebars and landed on his right shoulder on the pavement." The dog reportedly ran off and was never seen again. But Lindsay had broken his collarbone. "It's not the kind of break that a candidate hopes for,"[24] he said sadly from the hospital.

CHAPTER 7

NEW STRATEGIES, ODD IDEAS

"Ah, precious Environment, how the heavy wheels of government churn in thy name!"

—*New York Times*[1]

The tidal wave of allegations against John Lindsay were not enough to put out the flame. The tone and style of his leadership, if not the substance, survived. Despite Lindsay's decline in popularity, his famous walks without a dog inspired successors to follow in his footsteps. This very effective public relations tool, which consisted of strolling about town and talking to everyday people, became part of the standard repertoire for New York mayors despite their political differences. Even Ed Koch, one of Lindsay's most vicious critics, would follow the path of the perambulating politician, wandering the sidewalks and parks asking "How'm I doin'?" Unlike the man he so hated, Koch wore a blue-collared shirt for a heightened democratic effect, lowering himself more intimately to the pavement.

Koch wasn't the first self-promoter to rise to the opportunity once Lindsay was out of the way. Abraham Beame, who became Lindsay's direct successor in 1974, also tried to ape the style of the tall and handsome figure by making frequent appearances on paved surfaces

This 1975 cartoon is from a series created by Irving Lepselter for *Our Town,*
a local New York paper.

Source: Used with permission of Irving Lepselter.

throughout the city. The former Controller who had pushed so hard for
"Envirmaids" to keep the earth clean began his tenure by descending
among the masses in the hope of reviving the Lindsayan theme of "community participation," becoming more of a practical necessity by the day.
Not long after he took office, Beame was seen in Chinatown pushing
a broom symbolically down Mott Street in honor of his new "Cleaner
Streets Program." But compared to the sudden and unexpected visits of
a citizen-king, Beame's efforts seemed pedestrian. Few of his subjects

were impressed because it was widely known that street cleaning, along with police protection, public transportation, and other basic services, had been slashed by recent austerity measures. Nor were some of them happy that their leaders had failed to take a stand on canine waste. Was government ever going to lift the shroud of pestilence that draped the city? One un-bedazzled New Yorker sent a letter to the *Times* welcoming the new mayor with a no-nonsense warning that he should consider moving forward where City Council had feared to tread. "Sidewalks Are for Walking" read the headline. Then came the warning:

> Now that Mayor Beame has begun walking through the streets of New York, I hope he will take care not to step into the canine feces on the sidewalks. No other city in my experience offers a comparable display of feculent refuse. Other cities here and abroad require dog owners to clean up after their pets, but not New York. Mayors in the past have been fearful of losing the votes of dog lovers. Since Mayor Beame has told us he seeks no second term, he is in an excellent position to do what his predecessors shunned. No civilized city in the world permits human feces on its streets. What's the difference?[2]

This is one of the charming oddities of our recent past, an embarrassment that many locals have chosen to forget. Not long ago, popular opinion held that no New York politician could be in favor of a poop scoop law unless he had no further plans to run for public office. Even in light of this no-win situation, some voters were still angry with City Council for having backed down on the dog bill a few years earlier. The issue, complex and unapproachable as it seemed, had been left in the open air where it would have to sit until someone decided on how to handle it. As for all of those "other cities here and abroad" said to have poop scoop laws at the time, neither Chicago nor Denver had been able to foist these laws on their populations. Paris and London had been struggling for years to convince dog owners to at least "curb" their beasts. Jerusalem had no poop scoop law. The mayor of Pisa, Italy, received a death threat in 1975 for banning dogs from the city center because they were soiling the pavement. "This is not an idle threat," read the anonymous letter, "and therefore I advise you to reverse the mea-sure, otherwise you better start counting the days of life you have left." Short of hiring bodyguards for their mayors, there was not much that most cities could do about dogs. Around the world, efforts to come to terms with this urban problem were proving futile. Closer to home, several towns and smaller cities near New York reported only "limited success"[3] with canine waste laws. The Essex County Court declared its poop scoop law to be arbitrary and capricious. Even in Nutley, New Jersey, the famed birthplace of scooping, enforcement was the biggest problem. One citizen was fined $10 for not scooping but only after a lengthy court battle. A Paramus dog owner was summoned for failing to scoop but the case was dismissed for lack of evidence. Elsewhere, people were doing anything possible to dodge these laws. One town mayor noted that residents, rather than stoop to pick up feces, were loading their dogs into cars and driving to the nearest town without a poop scoop law to let their animals relieve themselves! Some success might have been expected in smaller communities where everyone knew everyone else's business and where peer pressure was usually enough to induce conformity. But residents of even the tiniest burghs were ada-mantly resisting these laws and enforcement was virtually impossible. Short of taking photos of the dogs doing their business, catching the owners as they left the scenes of their crimes was a losing proposition. "You can't enforce that law,"[4] concluded a Paramus dog control officer. Sixty percent of American mayors interviewed by the National League of Cities in 1974 said they had more complaints about dogs than any-thing else, including potholes. And the number one complaint was num-ber two. Still they were unable to take action against a minority of people who insisted they had a right to let their animals roam freely and that picking up their business was someone else's business.

Not long after New York's City Council had backed down on Kretchmer's dog bill, Councilwoman Carol Greitzer was already look-ing for more practical alternatives. Dog owners were breathing a sigh of relief, and their critics still inhaling the rude aromas on the street, when she announced a plan to do the job that dog owners had shunned and leaders were unwilling to impose upon them. But this emergency measure was going to cost the taxpayers money. "$1 Million Urged to Fight Dog Excreta"[5] read the headline in the *Times* on December 28, 1973, just three days after thousands of new Christmas puppies had arrived in homes across the city. The proposal included a plan to provide local block associations with $1,000 each to hire professional pooper-scoopers to scour the sidewalks twice daily for dog leavings. The block associations were thrilled that government shared their passion for poop. In years to come, they'd need little encouragement to defend their tulip bulbs and ivy patches in ways bordering on savagery. According to Greitzer's plan, the hired hands would "disinfect and dispose of it in plastic bags."[6] This sounded simple enough. But where, exactly, was the City going to get the $1 million needed to pay the pooper-scoopers each year? Sanitation Commissioner Herbert Elish, the man who still sided with the "curb" imperative, gave a whiff of encouragement when he managed to find the funding to increase his Sanitation Police Force to 245 patrolmen in order to better enforce the curb and leash laws. But not all New Yorkers agreed that dog problems should be given priority by government. Spending money to go after pet owners, when the city had so many other problems, caused no small controversy. To curtail the costs, Elish encouraged private citizens to help out by reporting infractions on a special form, and to notify the Department of any problem areas where piles had been collecting.

For obvious financial reasons, Greitzer's own plan never got off the ground, and Elish's expanded police force, even with the help of volunteers, was having little effect. What was to be done? When the State Assembly passed a law requiring restaurants in New York City to have restrooms, a letter to the *Times* expressed hope for similar "constructive legislation" relating to dogs. Another suggested levying a special "dog sanitation tax" on dog owners. In theory, the money would be used to hire back some of the sanitation workers that had recently been laid off and at least get the stuff out of the gutters where it sat reeking indefinitely. But was it realistic to expect City Council to vote in favor of a law taxing dog owners when they, like other New Yorkers, were already paying higher taxes than anyone in the nation and getting practically nothing in return?

Expanding the budget and imposing new taxes were extremely unpopular options by the time that Beame took office. In fact, the City of New York nearly went belly-up in April 1975 when banks decided to stop backing the inflated bonds that had been keeping it afloat. Governor Carey was forced to step in and rescue New York from disaster. "Unable to handle the city's finances," writes Vincent Cannato, "Beame effectively lost control of the city to the Municipal Assistance Corporation (MAC). The fiscal crisis ended the brief tenure of the accountant-politician."[7] New York would suffer many casualties in the years of fiscal austerity to follow. Thus began a period of not only trying to rebuild faith in New York, but of dismantling much of the bureaucracy that was standing in the way of the city's recovery. Lindsay's "superagencies," which had already undergone massive cuts, sustained even more. Layoffs, and the elimination of entire agencies, were on the horizon. Average New Yorkers suffered not only from the further reduction in services and the resulting unemployment, but from the psychological effects of a kind of power vacuum that came about in the mid-seventies. Local leaders no longer had ultimate control over how tax dollars were spent. Instead, priorities would be set by the state, which had never been as sympathetic toward New Yorkers and their concerns as some may have liked. Albany did, however, recruit a number of local politicians to run the MAC, including Herbert Elish, the pro-curb man who recently had been promoted to EPA Administrator. Elish, who still insisted dog owners had a duty to force their animals off the sidewalk and into oncoming traffic, took a key position with the MAC at a salary exceeding Mayor Beame's.

"Three cheers for Richard J. Daley, late Mayor of Chicago," wrote one New Yorker with his sights already set on other places, "where more flowers are planted each year in the parks and where the subways are graffiti-free. Companies are moving out of New York and families are, too, not so much because of the high cost of living, as because of the meanness of everyday life."[8] But if the prospect of pristine pavement, graffiti-free surfaces, and flora still captured the popular imagination, the broader

130

appeal of environmentalism would never again reach the high point that it had in the late sixties. Across the nation, the movement that New York once led was running out of steam. Newspapers and magazines discontinued their special "Environment" sections, and with its broad appeal went the movement's brief unifying effect. Initiatives would continue to monitor industry and conserve natural resources, though the public's attention would go mainly to the protection of endangered species, a noble cause without a doubt, and to a maniacally inefficient obsession with separating paper from metal from plastic from glass. Meanwhile, the rainforests were burning. In recent years, global warming has managed to rattle a few people off the sofa, though New Yorkers see no connection between crowding the curbside with SUVs and rising temperatures. Bicycles have lost much of their cachet since the seventies. In fact, they're often considered Public Enemy No. 1. Once a symbol of resistance against big industry and a welcome alternative to air pollution, today the bike is seen as a last resort for losers who can't afford fossil-fueled vehicles, a nuisance to automobilists, and a danger to pedestrians. Being glued to a bottle of spring water is the new sign of spiritual purity.

"Ah, precious Environment, how the heavy wheels of government churn in thy name!"[9] wrote the editors of the *Times* sarcastically as they wouldn't have dared a few years earlier. New York's EPA, one of the very first of its kind in the world, was downsized and mostly dismantled in 1977 when it was suggested that bureaucracy was actually preventing the state and federal funding the City so desperately needed. That same year, Union Carbide moved its corporate offices out of Manhattan because, its spokesman said, of the unpleasant living conditions and unhealthy atmosphere.

If New York's future had once seemed closely tied to environmental improvements, in time those citizens who remained would have to learn to accept pollution as a daily fact of life in the Big City. The myth of "zero pollution" was exposed and perhaps, many people thought, leaders had done all they possibly could. New York's air was, indeed, measurably cleaner than it had been before Lindsay. In years to come, the air might be made even cleaner still, though mainly thanks to new federal exhaust emission standards imposed upon Detroit automakers and not the result of local efforts. New York's air pollution levels would remain above nationally accepted standards for decades to come. City buses would continue running on traditional diesel fuel, the dirtiest way possible. What good were fuel-efficient taxicabs if black soot was pumped into their passenger seats whenever they stopped for traffic lights?

Manhattan's hazy skyline would be a permanent reminder of the end of the environmental craze that once inspired the masses and sent politicians into a frenzy of competition. Citicorp Center, with that strangely slanting roof now a familiar mark upon the landscape, would add a finishing touch to environmentalism's golden age. Citicorp's rooftop, originally designed to include balconies for private apartments, was rethought to provide solar power to the building. But engineers ran into technical difficulties in the mid-seventies and the idea was shelved. The famous apex, which might have been the sign of a progressive new era, eventually became an esthetic oddity on Manhattan's smog-filled skyline.*

Interestingly enough, anti-poop sentiment gained momentum just as commitment to environmentalism was winding down. This could be partly explained by the fact that New Yorkers—as they waded through trash and dog excrement, waited endless hours for buses and subway trains to arrive, and fell prey to muggers along the way—began to succumb to feelings of anger and despair. The weighty importance they attached to dog problems was inversely related to their loss of faith. Complaining about pets became a convenient way of venting frustration

---

*The borough that pressed hardest for a poop scoop law, Manhattan, can now boast that its residents are more likely to acquire cancer from breathing its air than anyone in the outer boroughs. For climate-conscientiousness, environmental advocates rank New York City as a whole below London, Chicago, and Portland, Oregon. The U.S. Department of Health and Human Services recently reported that unborn babies in New York are at a rising risk of suffering DNA damage from air pollution. New York's recycling rate is less than half that of San Francisco. *The Economist* applied "global livability ratings" to cities worldwide in 2005. A list of 50 cities were ranked by politics, culture, medicine, education, public service, recreation, consumer goods, housing, and environment. New York wasn't even included on the list.

because it was comforting, in some perverse way, to walk up to littering pet owners and "go off" on them. Patience approached a boiling point in the fetid, dog days of August 1975, when the layoffs of thousands of street cleaners by the EPA prevented them from even emptying the gutters as infrequently as they'd been. The stench was said to have been maddening. As government was further downsized and the question of how to provide basic services became a topic of daily speculation, New Yorkers were forced to turn increasingly to individual initiatives to achieve some minimal quality of life. Disillusioned with the stale promises of institutional environmentalism and eager for some small control over their lives, they focused, in greater numbers than ever, on what they confronted daily on the pavement and in the parks. This was a time of rebuilding, with whatever tools available, however blunt or brutal. "Community participation" and a massive shake-up were seen as vital to kick-starting the city out of its depressed state and toward its former glory.

Much of the energy was diverted back to the curb. "For a city as financially strapped as New York," wrote the editors of the *Times*, "it is fatuous to suggest additional services that might be undertaken. However, there are certain self-services that residents can perform which will improve the city's livability without burdening the municipal treasury. One very visible and feasible civic duty is that dog owners curb their dogs."[10] This was hardly a new idea, but a very old one that had never worked very well. Police officers and park rangers were, in fact, already overworked and understaffed, and even less able to make people "curb" their dogs than in the past. Sanitation, too, was in serious trouble. Government's inability to help out in any way led to the plea for dog owners to step in, if only until the City got back on its feet financially—the assumption being, of course, that once government recovered it would assume the task of cleaning up after dogs. In the meantime, if dog owners failed to volunteer their services temporarily, then their neighbors could be relied upon to offer their own. All that it took were one or two troublemakers on each block, black sheep who neither "curbed" nor picked up, to give fodder to their neighbors' vigilante rage.

In parks the effects of dogs were being felt more acutely than ever. As was the case with dirty pavement, while government's role in providing services to parks was reduced, all the more onus was placed on dogs and the problems they were said to be causing. New York's Parks Department would never recover fully from the blows it received during these years of fiscal austerity. Parks would lose 70 percent of its workforce and 40 percent of its funding in years to come. As public greens continued to recede before everyone's eyes, and greenbacks ran in ever shorter supply, citizens showed a growing willingness to take matters into their own hands, if not to pick up the poop, then to protect their parks from the ravages of running canines.

Luckily for dog owners, brute force wasn't the only answer offered to fix New York's problems. The Beame administration invested considerable time in a more peaceful project aimed at keeping the parks, and the sidewalks, feces-free. "Sewer Drains to Be Tried as Street Toilets for Dogs," read the headline as a bold new "pilot project"[11] was launched in Carl Schurz Park during the summer of 1975. The idea seemed simple enough. If dog owners would be willing to receive free instruction from a team of dog trainers hired by the city to "sewer train"[12] their pets—to get their animals not only off the curb but directly over a sewer drain before eliminating—then theoretically the Department of Sanitation would find some way to flush these drains twice daily. Seven sewers were selected along East End Avenue. The goal, said a member of Beame's downsized EPA, Richard Napoli (cutbacks were evident in Napoli's job title: "Director of Citizens for Involvement in Environmental Protection"), was to teach dog owners how to "train their dogs to defecate in the sewers."[13]

The sewer-training program stands out in the history of New York's approach to the poop problem as an attempt to meet dog owners halfway: If they would take free instruction in sewer-training their pets, then waste disposal would be left to the City and they'd be left alone. The project attracted much attention, and despite its many ambiguities the idea was popular. Having dogs go directly into drains, rather than on lawns or pavements, was viewed as a way not only to spare New

Yorkers the displeasure of stepping into feces, but to save some money on cleaning up. If the project worked, then it would be used as a model for the rest of the city, and perhaps the world. Most important, New York would finally be feces-free! Even Max Schnapp, the head of the Pet Owners Protective Association who had fought so fiercely against having a poop scoop law, was in favor of this alternative. He pledged the support of his membership and the use of peer pressure within the dog-owning community to keep a constant vigil for anyone who might refuse to sewer-train a pet. Meanwhile, Richard Napoli advised the owners of dogs weighing less than 30 pounds not to bother—these animals, he said, could be trained to go on paper in their owners' bathrooms, as former mayor Lindsay had once suggested. But larger dogs would have to do their business into the sewers—and perhaps into oncoming traffic along East End Avenue.

Excitement was in the air as yet another social experiment was conducted in a public park. But the promising new project had a few bugs. How was the City going to convince the small-dog owners, whose pets had already been housebroken, to tell their pets they'd changed their minds and to start doing their business indoors from now on? As for the larger, sewer-trained dogs, how were the street cleaners, already understaffed and overworked, going to be paid for the overtime they would incur from flushing drains twice daily? And how were the dog trainers to be paid to teach hundreds of thousands of dog owners across the city how to sewer-train their pets? Theodore Weiss, Chairman of City Council's Environmental Protection Committee and a leading proponent of the failed poop scoop bill, said this new program would require "a combination of education, citizen involvement, and enforcement."[14] This was an attempt to modify the behavior not only of dog owners but of the dogs themselves. For dogs refusing to squat over sewer drains—most are actually frightened of walking on or near gratings of any kind—the EPA offered an alternative. The owners of these rebellious mutts would be supplied with paper that they would have to spread out on pavement as near a drain as possible. The dogs would, in theory, be trained to do their business on the paper, which the owner would then pick up, tossing the contents into a nearby drain. But wasn't this a sneaky way of making dog owners pick up, which most had flatly refused to do under any circumstances? Wasn't this a poop scoop law in disguise?

Volunteers distributing pamphlets for "Operation Aware" reported violent reactions from some dog owners. The mere thought of picking up feces made faces drop and stomachs turn. When government and volunteers encountered resistance to the pilot program in Carl Schurz Park, and the enlightening effects of "education" were wanting, then "enforcement," the third item on Councilman Weiss' wish list, was called upon to keep dog owners with the program. For two months, police officers were instructed to be especially vigilant over the park, making sure that pets were kept on leashes and that when they did their business they did so over a sewer drain or onto nearby paper. Dogs were to defecate no more than three feet from a curb and never at crosswalks or bus stops. If they or their owners refused to comply, one of them would be fined $15. If the program proved successful, on the other hand, it would be replicated throughout the city and the fine for noncompliance would be raised to a whopping $100 (a lot of money at the time). The bills before City Council pending the success of the pilot program also included a requirement for the name and address of each owner to be attached to a dog's collar along with license and rabies tags, just in case anyone tried to give fictitious names to law enforcement officers writing summonses.

When the City's budgetary constraints prevented proper enforcement of the new program, then "citizen involvement" (the second, not the third item on Weiss's wish list) was called upon to keep dog owners with the program. Citizens themselves would have to bear much of the burden of enforcement. By this time, there was no shortage of people willing to help out in Carl Schurz Park. The park's proximity to the mayoral residence made the effects of dogs there seem all the more offensive. Carl Schurz Park would rival even that most central of parks as a symbol for the disgraceful morass the entire city had become. This patch of green surrounding Gracie Mansion would be a major battle ground for many dog-related scores to settle in years to come.

The Carl Schurz Park Association, a militant pro-flower, pro-grass group of some 170 local residents, played a key role in shaping attitudes toward dogs and eventually enforcing the law that would one day dictate what, exactly, was to be done with their excrement. While the rest of the neighborhood danced experimentally around sewer drains along the periphery, the Association kept its eyes on the park itself. Dr. Patricia Livingston, a professor of Health at New York University, was a leading member of the Carl Schurz Park Association. Dr. Livingston insisted there was "no blinking an eye at the fact that the depredations of dogs and their owners have in the last few years turned much of Carl Schurz Park, once one of the city's loveliest, into a wasteland of eroded hillsides and burned turf."[15] But even Dr. Livingston had to admit that dogs weren't entirely to blame for the sad state of Carl Schurz Park. A wildcat strike of maintenance workers in effect for several years and the budgetary constraints felt in parks across the city were also to blame. In the absence of a functioning government, the Association was formed to "rehabilitate" the park by planting new grass, keeping the ground tidy, and waging a campaign called "10,000 Flowers." But local dog owners, Livingston said, were working against their efforts. "It hardly seems worth while to do all that if the dogs are going to destroy it again."[16]

Dr. Livingston and the Association set about patrolling the park for leashless dogs. Livingston, a key figure in dog politics in the years to come, was known to be very persistent. "Some of them call me the crazy woman," she said, describing the reactions of people when she tried to make them behave more responsibly. "They think I am enemy No. 1."[17] Livingston was not as confrontational as some of her contemporaries. The virtue of her approach was in her refusal, despite a background in public health, to limit the discussion of dogs to a fixation on the potential but extremely marginal health risks associated with dogs. Instead, she focused on more pragmatic issues such as their proper care and their broader role in society. Being an educator, Livingston began the long and painstaking process of carefully bringing city dog owners around to the conclusion that they had certain duties, not only toward their pets but also toward the rest of society. She distributed literature on canine care and control, and pleaded endlessly with dog owners in the hope of changing their habits. As an academic, Livingston was thorough in her research. She didn't dwell upon exotic diseases like *Toxocara canis*—Fran Lee's personal demon—but instead she tried to paint a picture of a city in which people with dogs and those without would share a happy, healthy coexistence. Livingston herself had been raised on a farm in Wisconsin and was no stranger to the pleasures of canine companionship. And while she tended to agree with the old opinion that the city was really no place for dogs—"almost universally accepted until a comparatively few years ago,"[18] said the *Times*—she knew that banning them from New York was not a viable alternative to a poop scoop law. Livingston went against the grain of public opinion by resisting the temptation to scold dog owners for keeping pets in the city, or to pit parents and dog owners against each other—again, favorite tactics of Fran Lee. Livingston disagreed with popular anti-dog theories of the day. She rejected, the *Times* said, "the opinion held by many of her neighbors that urban dog ownership is more often than not a symptom of a warped personality, providing a socially sanctioned means, at least at the present time, for the expression of alienation and aggression," and that "the ostensibly beloved pet is the chief victim of the owner's neurotic needs, its spirit likely to be destroyed by another affection or harsh treatment, and by being kept locked up alone, as most dogs are, for the greater part of the day."[19] These prejudices against urban dog ownership ran very deep at the time. And while there were no doubt many people who used pets for their own selfish ends, Dr. Livingston failed to see the benefit in continuing the debate along these lines. Instead of dwelling on the negatives, or fixating on feces, Livingston stressed the positive role of dog ownership in the city. Dogs, she said, provided the elderly with companionship, protection, and "a reason for leaving their apartments once or twice a day."[20] The warmth of their presence helped young people "to find their way through the chaos of the cold, angry city."[21] But whatever richness dogs were adding to urban life, it was unfair for their owners to expect others to wade around through piles of excrement, or to be denied the pleasure of smelling flowers and grass in public parks. In time, Livingston managed to convince a number of dog owners to comply with current laws. Some joined the Carl Schurz Park Association. According to Livingston, a few were even learning to "scoop" their dogs' droppings by 1976, "placing them in plastic bags and depositing them in special cans on the margins of the park."[22] The practice was nothing less than revolutionary at the time.

In years to come, Livingston would be instrumental in enforcing New York's eventual poop scoop law. She would help found The Coalition for Dog Control for that purpose. But protecting the parks would be an uphill battle all the way. Even Livingston's gentle request for owners to "curb" their dogs met with fierce opposition. The most common argument was that altering the natural evacuating habits of dogs would somehow be harmful to them. Many dog lovers feared that limiting where dogs did their business—the instinctive marking of territory was, after all, a driving force behind their bowel and urinary activities— would somehow result in "canine neurosis." Dr. Livingston was quick to discount this theory. "Veterinarians have told me," she said, "that the toilet training we routinely give our children is far more stressful."[23] There was nothing dangerous, she said, in "curbing" or even sewer-training dogs. Still, many dog owners resisted her polite suggestions. "A couple of weeks ago," Livingston said, "I asked a group of people with really big dogs that were running all over the hillside in the park at 86th Street to read some of our literature. They wouldn't, and before I left a couple of them were muttering things like, 'You're gonna get it' and 'Something's going to happen to you if you keep this up.'"[24] Livingston's life was threatened on several occasions in the years she spent trying to reach out to dog owners in Carl Schurz Park. Other volunteers from the Association noted that about 25 percent of dog owners had abused, cursed, or threatened them in some way. "It's essentially a re-education job that we are trying to do," Livingston said. "Dog owners have got to learn that they are doing something their peers don't like, that there are more of us than there are of them, and that we won't take it anymore."[25]

Despite the efforts of Dr. Livingston and the Carl Schurz Park Association, the police and park rangers, the dog trainers, and those dog owners not opposed to helping out in these troubled times, the sewer-training program proposed by the Beame administration as an alternative to a poop scoop law ran into serious difficulties. Had this promising program succeeded, present-day dog owners in New York and in cities throughout the world might very likely be taking their dogs to squat over sewer drains—and only picking up if the dogs themselves refused. But the drains placed along city streets were never intended for waste disposal, and using them for this purpose would have polluted the waterways even more than they were already. And just as dog owners were slowly coming around to accepting the new idea, New York's more serious problems returned with a vengeance. A few months after the social experiment began, and while the EPA was making amendments to the City's sanitary code to allow for drainage, high hopes were dashed when the pilot program was canned. The *Times* reported Robert Low, the current Environmental Protection Administrator, as saying the project was being cancelled "because the city had another drain—its budget crisis."[26]

So for the moment it was back to the other side of the curb, the only place in the entire city where a dog was legally allowed to do its business (except in the owner's bathroom). Two important conclusions, however, came out of the failed sewer-training program in Carl Schurz Park. First: Considering New York's present fiscal state, dog owners, not street cleaners or Parks workers, would have to keep the sidewalks and parks free of feces. And second: Since the same budgetary constraints preventing hired hands from picking up also affected government's ability to police pet owners, private citizens would also have to bear the burden of enforcing any new dog laws. At the very least, average New Yorkers would have to make sure that their neighbors "curbed" their beasts. Along these lines, Councilman Weiss proposed using volunteer patrols instead of paid officials to watch for leashless dogs in parks or owners who failed to guide their pets off the nearest curb. The idea had wide appeal. New York had a surplus of people sick and tired of stepping in crap, and with rising unemployment and lots of time on their hands, taking matters into them was not a problem. One Jesuit priest tapped into this enthusiasm with his own plan for citizen patrols. But he lacked the patience of Dr. Livingston and used, instead, all the appeal of fire-and-brimstone to enlist volunteers to help with the crackdown:

> Thank God that New York is not a home where the buffalo roam and the deer and the antelope play. The dogs are quite enough. Where can we find a Hercules to rid us of this Augean mess? The answer—like the problem—may be right under our noses. Since we already have meter monitors to check on thoughtless parkers, why not litter monitors to give fines to thoughtless poopers? Every time some doting mummy or daddy lets Big Duke or Little Fifi do his or her whimsies on the sidewalk, the Pooper Snooper leaps from hiding and slaps them with a $25 citation. It creates jobs which pay for themselves and, while the stuff is still indisputably there, one needn't walk the streets like a commando in a minefield.[27]

Reverend O'Malley came up with his plan in 1975, the year in which Saigon fell and New York's finances went off the deep end. The militancy of his message was appealing to many frustrated New Yorkers who felt strongly enough about crap to sign up, if called upon, as environmental guerrillas. A lot of them could have used the extra cash. A legion of anti-poop mercenaries? Lindsay's ideal of "community participation" was taking a strange new turn as government-backed vigilantism seemed the only solution to New York's poop problem. According to the Reverend's plan, if dog owners refused to use Pooper-Scoopers, then they would have to reckon with Pooper *Snoopers*, a legion of plain-clothed neighbors who would sit by patiently, ready to leap at any moment from behind parked cars or lampposts and ticket anyone who failed to "curb" a dog.

Indeed, freeing New York's sidewalks and parks of feces was beginning to seem a Herculean task. But the metaphor for the dog problem was still a mixed one. Once again, as in so many discussions of dogs, the discourse returned to the automobile, that other four-legged monster that roamed the streets and fouled the air. "Thoughtless parkers" and "thoughtless poopers," the Reverend said, were in the same way monitorable, if only someone would sign up to keep tabs on them like meter maids did with double-parkers. As in the "alternate-side-of-the-street dogs" idea that Jerome Kretchmer had once fended off, the automobile returned yet again as it seemed virtually impossible to stop seeing dogs as pooping machines that belonged on the other side of the curb.

New York would never see the legion of Pooper Snoopers that Reverend O'Malley envisioned. So how were dog owners to be made to get their dogs off the curb and into oncoming traffic? "Curb Those Dogs!"[28] shouted the editors of the *Times*, having lost all patience. As New Yorkers continued sliding around on the sidewalks, frustration mounted and the passion surrounding curbs began to get out of hand. Many people were saying that it was the owners, not the dogs, that needed to be "curbed" and with whatever means necessary. But one letter to the *Times* made a very good point by suggesting it was physically impossible to "curb" a dog in New York City, even if a person wanted to. "As all dog owners know," it read, "it is virtually impossible to walk a dog properly against the obstacle of automobiles parked bumper to bumper throughout suburbia and much of the metropolis. I remember getting a ticket for leaving my car parked overnight on a deserted Brooklyn street in 1937. What oily auto-industry Oliver managed to get the overnight parking ban lifted? Jaywalking (an illegal action) is the only practical alternative to dirtying the sidewalk or grass strip."

The harshest criticism of "curbing" came from a familiar quarter. Fran Lee, "New York's foremost fighter against dog dirt," a self-proclaimed "dog lover and owner hater,"[29] was back on the scene again. She stood firm in her belief that dogs had no business doing their business anywhere but in the owners' bathrooms—not on sidewalks, not in

parks, not into gutters or sewer drains, and in fact not off curbs at all.[†]
In 1976, Lee took her case to New York's Supreme Court where she
filed to have the city's "Curb Your Dog" signs declared illegal. The respondents in the case were four city commissioners and the director of
the new Bureau of Animal Affairs. Much to Lee's frustration, the "Curb
Your Dog" signs stayed.

So did all the mess that average New Yorkers had to endure.
One woman recalls her childhood in Manhattan. "I was always the one
who got to school with crap on my shoes," she says. "The kids used to
tease me terribly." The woman, now a dog owner herself, adds: "I can't
tell you how bad things were back then. It was disgusting."[31]

[†]In a rare concession to the poop scoop idea that most had already abandoned, Lee
sided briefly with its proponents, pulling the debate, once again, in the wrong direction. If this was the only way to keep feces off the ground, then she suggested the
City establish a corps of "poodle maids" to make absolutely certain that everyone
picked up.[30]

CHAPTER 8

POOP PANIC: PINNING NEW YORK'S DOWNFALL ON DOGS

"We have been worrying about the wrong end of the dog."
—Dr. David Harris, Mount Sinai Hospital, on the dog bite epidemic of the mid-seventies[1]

The stalemate in City Council was a symptom of a broader deadlock that had gripped all of New York by the mid-seventies. In so many ways, an era of vast experimentation and well-intentioned reform had given way to a period of disillusionment and confusion. Watergate, the war in Vietnam, widespread corruption in the NYPD, and the virtual castration of City officials by the rule of the MAC—if New Yorkers had long been skeptical of authority figures, now they were even more distrustful. And what of the future of their city? After a period of unbridled optimism, people were perplexed. The old solutions no longer worked, and the new ones were also failing. The dream of socioeconomic equality had passed. Housing projects, once symbols of hope and progress, had become infernal nests of despair. Lindsay had reorganized New York's ancient bureaucracy into slick new "superagencies" so that services might be improved and government might be run more effectively. Funding this new bureaucracy meant that New Yorkers paid 50 percent more in taxes than residents of any other American city. And yet poverty still existed, surfaces were still strewn with trash, the subways were death traps, and the packs of wild dogs counted for but a small minority of the predators that roamed the streets and parks. It is difficult to overstate how very trying daily life had become. For if conditions were bad in the sixties, then they were worse by the mid-seventies. The "crime wave" had continued to rage for over a decade and police were among the first to admit that they were no longer able to protect citizens. The NYPD was scaled back considerably in the Beame years, with massive layoffs making law enforcement all the more difficult. Meanwhile, the crime rate in New York City was roughly 10 times that of London and 7 times that of Tokyo. Almost daily, it seemed, the front pages of newspapers featured stories of average, middle-class people being robbed, beaten, stabbed, and shot in their own neighborhoods and in broad daylight. New York did, however, compare favorably to other cities when it came to burglaries. This was due in large part to the fact that New Yorkers were keeping large watchdogs at home for protection. "Two couples in our building have been robbed lately," wrote a wary neighbor. "One of the couples said that their insurance company refused to renew their theft insurance unless they got a guard dog." Author Joseph Caldwell recalls the use of dogs for protection and intimidation in his neighborhood, which became the setting for one of his novels:

> In the mid-seventies the Lower East Side around Avenues A, B, and C—later to become the gentrified East Village—was what might euphemistically be called a "difficult" neighborhood. Drugs were the recreation of choice and the burglaries and robberies necessary to securing them were wildly rampant. Bob and Vera's liquor store on Tenth and Avenue B was a favored target—until they got a trained Doberman that would pace restlessly behind the counter, ready, if the right word or gesture were given, to attack. The dog never had the opportunity to demonstrate its skills, but it did provide a solution to a different but still intractable problem. Vera was a very attractive woman. On more than one occasion, a male customer would—as Vera put it—"look at me in a way even my husband shouldn't look

at me." With the pacing Doberman's arrival, total respect for Vera's womanhood was restored, never to be challenged again.[2]

But dogs could only be expected to go so far for their humans. Trainers often pointed out that even the most devoted Doberman couldn't stop a bullet. Whom, or what, could citizens ultimately rely upon for safety?*

While dogs were providing a sense of security to some New Yorkers, to others they had come to represent the city's very downfall. During these chaotic years, the sum total of daily pressures mounted, making the smallest problems like their feces seem gigantic. Sometimes it seemed that dogs had all but taken over the city. "I remember the smell was overwhelming the first time I experienced it," says a New Jersey woman recalling her childhood visits to Manhattan for Broadway shows. "We had to roll up the windows as soon as we got across the Holland Tunnel. I learned to associate the stench with New York. I grew up thinking it was just the smell of the city."[4] The mass exodus of taxpayers to more wholesome suburban settings only helped to reinforce the idea that the city was essentially a dirty place to be visited only on weekends, and then with noses plugged. But pedestrians who actually lived in this poop capital didn't have the luxury of rolling up car windows. Unable to shield themselves from the oppressive stench, and rather than get used to it, resident New Yorkers grew more resentful by the day. They wondered how dog owners could be so inconsiderate and irresponsible. And what were leaders going to do to keep them in line? Considering all the other daily sources of stress at the time, poop might have been the very least of their concerns. But use of the word "epidemic," to describe anything from petty annoyances to mor-

---

*"There's an ego thing involved," Arthur Haggerty of Captain Haggerty's School for Dogs told Tom Topor at the *New York Post* in 1976. "Down in the ghetto, it's that old macho thing so you get a lot of Dobermans and shepherds. A male homosexual might buy an Afghan—it gets him attention. A wealthy man might buy a rare giant breed—to show he's got money enough to get something very unusual. They don't understand that a dog's size has nothing to do with his ability to protect you. It depends on the breed."[3]

tal dangers, had reached epidemic proportions. The *Soho Weekly News* reported in 1976: "For many New Yorkers, 'Do dogs shit in the street?' has replaced 'Are Bears Catholic' as a rhetorical response to any obvious/ redundant question. The attitude toward dogs in this city is not unlike the gun lobby—there seem to be an equal number of canine fanatics who feel totally justified in their right to own and sport a dog as there are Rabido-phobes (i.e., citizens having an excessive and constant fear of being bitten by a dog, *any* dog, and/or stepping in their feces . . . either of these factors liable to result in subsequent dementia and, according to Rabidophobe extremists, even death.)"[5] Though New York had no documented cases of rabies on record for decades, to many New Yorkers the fear of it was no less real. Nor was their terror less palpable whenever they encountered canine waste. As overall life on city surfaces worsened, concerns over cleanliness alternated with basic questions of survival. At times, the two seemed inseparable.

Films provide the most vivid record, if not of daily reality, then of the magnified perceptions of all the horrors dogs had supposedly brought to New York. In 1969, Jack Lemmon in *The Out of Towners* played a naïve businessman from Ohio who tries, with his fragile wife (Sandy Dennis), to conquer the city that even native New Yorkers are having trouble enduring. After a disastrous few hours in Manhattan, which include being mugged and having a box of Cracker Jacks stolen by a Great Dane running off-leash in Central Park, the couple retreats to Ohio, only too glad to give up their dream of being New Yorkers. They have lost most of their personal possessions either to muggers or to dogs but manage to escape with their dignity.

Six years later, in 1975, another film, *The Prisoner of Second Avenue*, also starred Lemmon. This time, the businessman is a native New Yorker who, despite his urban upbringing, cannot manage to insu-late himself from the growing tensions of daily life in a city that seems to have gone completely out of control. Typical, middle-class people like himself (those who haven't yet fled to the suburbs) are being driven out. He loses his job (companies are leaving the city in droves, and white-collar unemployment is chipping away at what's left of New York's tax base). To make matters worse, it's summertime and the latest heat wave is becoming unbearable. Meanwhile, the next-door neighbors have been keeping the businessman and his wife awake with their loud music. One night, the husband leaps out of bed and bangs on the wall. Somewhere in the distance, a dog is howling at the moon. The man loses all composure and runs out to the terrace to cry into the torrid, smog-filled night:

> Hey keep that dog quiet down there, eh? There's human bein's sleepin' up here![6]

The angry tenant of Second Avenue leans over the edge of the terrace to find he can actually smell the piles of fetid trash on the street—a full 14 floors down! "The whole country's bein' buried by garbage," he laments. "It keeps pilin' up higher and higher. In three years this apartment's gonna be the second floor!"[7] The man's wife (Anne Bancroft) is concerned about her husband's increasing irritability and insomnia. "It's not just you," she says reassuringly. "Everyone's feeling the tensions these days." After all, he has a choice. "You either learn to live with it or you get out,"[8] she says, referring to the noise, the trash, the muggers, and everything else that's made the city a living hell. They decide to leave for a weekend to visit his brother in the suburbs where they can "look at his pool and learn how to breathe."[9] But when they arrive, the brother's two German shepherds sense the man's fear of dogs and won't let him out of the car until they're called off by their owner. Later that day, Lemmon finds the dogs have "piddled"[10] on his station wagon.

A few days later, back in the city, the couple comes home to find that their apartment has been robbed. This is the last straw. "The junkies"[11] have taken everything they owned. The man is 48 years old and unemployed. He begins a rapid downward spiral into a complete nervous breakdown. It seems the city has beaten the sad, unemployed, middle-aged executive, who's in intensive therapy and taking sedatives. His wife takes a job to help pay some of the bills but their future is uncertain.

Then one day their unhappy situation turns around. Lemmon is walking aimlessly in Central Park as he often does just to pass the time. He reaches inside his coat to find his wallet is missing. He doesn't remember leaving it at home (which he has, in fact, done). He immediately blames the young, suspicious-looking man (Sylvester Stallone) who just bumped into him. He shouts at the young man hysterically, frightening him into running away, and chases the alleged pickpocket across the park, eventually catching up and knocking him to the ground. After a brief struggle, the young man, on his back and terrified, hands over his own wallet to the unshaven, raving stranger, who looks like any other half-crazed mugger in the park. The executive-turned-common-criminal grabs the wallet and marches away triumphantly.

Before long, the unemployed businessman realizes this is not his wallet at all. He's inadvertently mugged an innocent man! But this isn't the point. The surge of self-confidence brought on by the random act of self-assertion, a bold defiance of a world gone out of control, has been enough to snap him out of his depression. In fact, as he heads out of Central Park, he comes upon a man walking a miniature black poodle. The poor thing isn't even pooping but he really *hates* dogs. Feeling the surge of empowerment brought on by mugging an innocent man, he continues his rampage by accosting the dog's owner and shouting: "Curb that dog, will you? People have to walk in these streets!"[12]

New Yorkers are said to be a particularly tough lot of people. But much of that toughness came in response to the decline in living conditions during the troubled sixties and seventies. Many people opted to get out. But for those who chose city life with all of its imperfections, the stripping away of expectations would be a long and painful process. Basic services would be scaled back but taxes would not be decreased significantly. New Yorkers would not only have to learn to accept far less for their tax dollars than the residents of other cities, they would also need to adopt new survival strategies to match their extreme predicament. Harsher living conditions meant that the old rules no longer applied, and in the process New Yorkers would have to redefine what constituted socially acceptable behavior. Dennis Kenney, in his book *Crime, Fear, and the New York City Subways: The Role of Citizen*

Action, describes the trauma experienced in these apprehensive times when vigilante action seemed the only means for survival:

> All of us, particularly those living in urban settings, surrounded by strangers, have the need to assume that our environments are safe. The need to be able to make sense out of our surroundings is so great that most of us tend to interpret unknown and threatening phenomena in terms that are more understandable and secure. When such perceptions are not possible, because either the reality or the perception of crime have grown too substantial to ignore, our lives become intolerable. We become suspicious of every sound and every person, while our routine activities become filled with terror.[13]

Kenney uses the term "environment" as it is used in psychology to mean the set of circumstances affecting mental health. Awareness of this "environment" largely replaced the concern for that other "environment" that had been at the center of New York politics only a few years before. New Yorkers needed desperately to feel they had some measure of control over this new environment, specifically over what might happen to them on the sidewalk or street, in the parks, or on the subway, those mass conduits of daily life. When experience suggested they had little control over their fate, a sense of impotence resulted, thereby increasing their fear and giving rise to social forces that produced Bernard Goetz but also the Guardian Angels. Many of the so-called "knee-jerk liberals" of the sixties were starting to rethink their ideals when their lives were in the balance. Taking action—*any* action—was often the only relief from the tensions and fears of daily life. Lindsay's ideal of "community participation" took unforeseen extremes as New Yorkers began taking matters into their own hands, and the lone gunmen portrayed in films like *Taxi Driver* and *Death Wish* were in this sense symbols for the state of mind of an entire population. Some businessmen were carrying guns in real life. As early as 1964, a group of conservative Jews in Crown Heights banded together to protect their neighborhood when the NYPD could not. For years, the "Maccabees" patrolled their Brooklyn neighborhood in radio cars, alerting the police to suspicious characters and crimes in progress. In time, the rise in vigilante activity of all kinds made New York seem like the Wild West. Gangs of delinquent youths had long been a presence in communities. The brief decline in violent gang activity during the sixties was due in large part to Lindsay's peace-making efforts. His Urban Action Task Force worked during these years to enlist gang members in the city's Youth Council where they earned money and the respect of their peers by contributing positively to their communities. By keeping street fighting to a minimum, Lindsay was able to avert the full-scale riots that raged in other cities.

But by the mid-seventies, New York had lost 340,000 jobs, and the funding for employment and recreational activities for inner city youths had all but vanished. The entire city felt the effects of poverty and despair. Muggings skyrocketed. Drug use soared. Gangs reorganized, returning to the streets with advanced firepower and terrorizing communities as never before. Thus began the now-familiar killings of innocent bystanders walking the same streets and sidewalks as the gangs engaged in bloody turf war. By 1979, the year in which the film *The Warriors* was released and the Guardian Angels set forth their manifesto, many of the gangs that had once guarded their neighborhoods from the "junkies" that robbed Jack Lemmon were now on the streets selling drugs themselves and guarding their turf ferociously with automatic weapons. The only relief for New York's Finest, and for pedestrians, came from the fact that these youngsters tended to be such bad shots.

In other neighborhoods, a different kind of turf war came about in the power vacuum of the mid-seventies. In the absence of any promising vision for the future of their city, average New Yorkers would have to content themselves with the many small victories to be won on the streets and sidewalks, in the subways and in parks. The simplest pleasures, such as taking a stroll through a green area after sunset, could be fatal. But New Yorkers were willing to fight for their public spaces. "Dog Walkers Consider Park Safe at Night,"[14] read one headline referring to a group of dog owners who ran their pets off-leash in Riverside Park. "I carried a sword the first four years I came here,"[15] said one Upper West

Sider of his pre-dog nocturnal strolls in the park. "You carried a fondue fork for a while,"[16] his wife reminded him. Now the couple and many of their neighbors could finally feel safe entering Riverside Park unarmed at night. And it was only because they had dogs. The mere presence of their animals running in circles and chasing balls was enough to frighten away even the most desperate criminals. Dogs, it seemed, were acting as deterrents to crime, not only in apartments where insurance companies wanted them, but in parks where their owners were glad to risk fines and even imprisonment for letting them run off-leash. Police officers tended to look the other way, and when pain-in-the-ass citizens complained and insisted they take action, they often didn't even ask dog owners for I.D. when writing summonses. "Just give me a name, any name and any address,"[17] was a typical order. Many law enforcement officers were, in fact, grateful for the presence of leashless dogs on their beats. The Russian wolfhounds, English mastiffs, Afghans, standard poodles, and golden retrievers that ran about, tearing up grass and making noise, were nonetheless making the park accessible to certain people and off-limits to others. And while no dog could stop a bullet, no mugger would dare to prowl an area patrolled by what became, after a few minutes of playtime, a functioning pack of predators ready to leap upon intruders. The dogs worked out their differences and the owners could finally feel safe and enjoy the fresh air.

Along with security, dogs were adding another benefit to their owners' lives. The open environment was helping humans, like their pets, to develop new social skills. Barriers were coming down as New Yorkers, who'd been conditioned to look upon each other suspiciously, were finally getting to know their neighbors, or at least those who were also pet owners. Dogs were helping to thaw icy relations among New Yorkers who might otherwise have never established eye contact, much less spoken to each other and formed friendships. It seemed as though the age-old belief that pets added something important to human life was true. Wasn't this worth sacrificing a little grass? In fact, recent studies were showing that canines were having the most marvelous effects upon even the most unreachable of people. It was during these years that the first "therapy dogs" were put to work in hospitals to help treat the mentally ill. One cover story of the *Times* in 1974 was devoted to the healing effects of dogs in otherwise untreatable cases of schizophrenia.[18] It seemed the mere presence of dogs—and, according to researchers, the "love"[19] they provided—brought positive responses from schizophrenics who had failed to respond to medication or any of the traditional forms of therapy, including electroshock treatment. If dogs could help the mentally ill, then surely they could help New Yorkers!

Dogs might have had a sane-itizing effect on some people. But for others who didn't include them in their circle of best friends, these animals became yet another source of instability. To chronic "cynophobists"—people afraid of dogs—the sight of the tiniest papillon was enough to terrorize. Studies in cynophobia, also under way in the mid-seventies, showed that traumatic childhood experiences with dogs affected the way in which people viewed these animals later in life. But there was hope for the afflicted. New treatments included desensitization exercises. Patients were shown photographs of dogs, larger and larger each time, and finally images of extremely large dogs lunging at the camera with teeth bared. During the course of these experiments, it was learned that the size of dogs corresponded to the level of fear elicited in patients. Many cynophobists, it was found, could be permanently cured of their illness through desensitization.[20] Still, the real test was in daily life. Cynophobists (and people who just didn't like being chased by big dogs) didn't distinguish between the group of well-fed, groomed, and licensed pets running freely in a public park with their owners watching, and the pack of hungry strays they'd encountered in the same park, or near one of those abandoned buildings or empty lots that became fixtures of the New York landscape in the 1970s. Their fears were seldom justified since the vast majority of bites occurred, as they do today, outside of parks. Joggers, however, were occasionally chased and bitten in parks by dogs, licensed or not, who mistook them for predators or, worse, for prey. The classic image of Dustin Hoffman in the opening scene of *Marathon Man*, being pursued by a German shepherd while he's trying to jog in Central Park, was meant as a reference to the treatment of the Jews during World War II. But the scene was also an accurate reflection of what running pedestrians feared might happen to them in New York parks. "Unleashed Danger" read one of many headlines addressing the problem. "The unleashed dog," wrote a federal judge, "either in its owner's presence or left unattended to its own devices, is as great a hazard as a stray dog, and with less excuse."[21]

It was difficult to deny that unleashed dogs were causing problems for some New Yorkers. And not all of them were muggers. But why "with less excuse" than the dogs that ran wild because they had no owners? On the contrary, many dog owners believed, what was truly inexcusable was the fact that their government was allowing stray dogs to roam the city. Not only did strays make pedestrians and bicyclists nervous, they attacked other dogs, and eventually died under the wheels of automobiles. Why were no efforts being made to control New York's canine population? And why was there no one to look out for the welfare of homeless animals? However rightly dog owners could be criticized for sacrificing public safety for their own, or for allowing their dogs to take the exercise they so desperately needed to the detriment of jogging (which wasn't even that fashionable yet), the more pressing urban problem resulted from the fact that a large percentage of New York dogs didn't have owners at all. "Mangy, starving dog packs are on the increase in many parts of New York City," wrote another federal judge. "These pitiful animals menace pedestrians and endanger motorists night and day. Visitors to our city regard these filth-ridden dogs with horror and ask what we are doing to control them."[22] By the 1970s an estimated 100,000 stray dogs roamed the streets and parks of Brooklyn alone. Lacking the necessary structures to help guide them through a treacherous human world, many of these animals returned to a semi-feral state and traveled in packs. Even if these "wild" dogs tended to shy away from humans and to mind their own business—the Department of Health's studies indicated that having dogs on leashes could, in fact, increase the likelihood of bites occurring—the fear unleashed at the mere sight of free-ranging beasts was enough to inspire a panic. Catching them, however, could be dangerous. Police of the Central Park Precinct often accompanied the ASPCA on "animal safaris" and packs were found to number as many as 20 dogs. Onlookers like Cleveland Amory were alarmed. "The day is coming," Amory told the *Daily News*, "when there will be so many stray dogs that they'll create a disease problem. And people are going to say, 'Let's get rid of all of them.' That's happened elsewhere. It could happen here."[23] The nearby Yonkers Animal Shelter reported that the number of dogs abandoned in that area had doubled from a few years before. New York City had between 600,000 and 1,000,000 dogs by 1976, about twice the number from a decade earlier. Between 150,000 and 400,000 of these dogs were thought to be unlicensed, and many of them homeless. The ambiguity in estimates is but one of many examples of what happens when a city undergoes a near-complete breakdown of its government. "Nobody was counting *anything* in those days,"[24] recalls Stephen Zawistowski of the ASPCA. This number-guessing also reflects the very primitive state of New York's policies toward animals. By all accounts, New York had more dogs than any other city in the nation. And yet it had very few agreed-upon standards for the care and control of these animals. While people were squabbling over what to do with the poop, the dogs themselves were often ignored. Granted, other cities had also tried, unsuccessfully, to enforce canine waste laws, and with as little success. But contrary to the belief of some New Yorkers, animal care and control involved more than just waste disposal. Did the City have a viable plan for its stray population, which grew exponentially each year?

A popular solution to the stray problem was to place the blame entirely on dog owners. As in the unshakable assumption that canine waste was an *individual* responsibility, or a matter of "community participation," many people believed that dog owners themselves should be held responsible for the many strays running wild in the streets and parks because *they* were the ones, after all, who had brought these menacing animals to the city in the first place. These thoughtless pet-fanciers, they believed, should clean up the "mess" by paying higher taxes or increased license fees. But was this judgment fair or even realistic? How could dog owners be responsible for the stray problem if they were, in fact, still dog owners? And why shouldn't the broader task of animal welfare and control be the duty of municipal government?

Whenever people couldn't pass the blame for poor animal control onto dog owners, they shifted it to the ASPCA, the private organization the City leaned on to handle many of its dog-related problems. But the ASPCA was in very much the same predicament as the City of New York by the 1970s. This single most important humane organization in the city, and the first of its kind in the nation, had been balancing on the brink of bankruptcy for several years and carried a huge deficit. How did the ASPCA find itself in such a predicament? The ASPCA did not survive entirely on government funding, not even during the fat years of prosperity and fiscal health. The ASPCA was funded largely by donations and by the animal licensing fees it was allowed to collect. Municipal government decided ultimately on any increases in the license fee but was slow to approve these. Even if the ASPCA had received the additional funding it was promised on so many occasions, there was still the question of how the money would be best spent. The Environmental Protection Agency under Jerome Kretchmer suggested raising the license fee in 1971 in the hope of discouraging people from having dogs in the first place. The EPA's stated reason for limiting the number of dogs was not to make New York more humane, but to get the feces off the sidewalks! And when citizens wrote to the local papers to suggest an increase in the fee, the typical suggestion was to use the additional funds to hire more street cleaners. This same concern for pristine pavement dominated the dog debate for years to come, the popular assumption being that, since the City didn't have the resources to pick up after dogs—and dog owners refused to do the job themselves—then it should be up to license-holders to absorb the cost of hiring additional workers. Cleaning up the poop, not improving the treatment of stray animals, was, in the opinion of many New Yorkers, to be the use of any increase in the dog license fee.

At first glance, the solution seems obvious: If only dog owners had been willing to pick up the poop, then maybe they wouldn't have been asked to pick up the tab for street cleaning. Any increased funding to the ASPCA would have been used to help the stray situation rather than for sanitation. But wasn't it just a bit absurd to believe that a poop scoop law would be a panacea for all of New York's dog problems? Some believed, instead, that attacking the problem at its root was the only solution. Why, they asked, not prevent stray dogs from being born in the first place?

Today's belief that preventing animals from being born can in itself be a humane act was not always popular in the seventies. Even some dog owners objected to the practice. Forced sterilization, they felt, was for concentration camps. Some believed that it was cruel to alter dogs surgically, as some continue to believe today. All creatures great and small, they thought, were "born free," as in the expression of the sixties, and had a basic right to survive and to reproduce as nature had intended. This was, after all, the age of free love. In fact, the belief in freedom for animals, a direct result of the growing respect for the non-human environment, led people to feel that dogs should not be leashed, caged, or even kept in dog runs. Control of reproduction and mandatory laws set by government to prevent the miracle of birth were viewed with suspicion as attempts by Big Brother or "the system" to limit personal freedom, if only the freedom of dogs to reproduce uncontrollably. And once again, the fear of a possible ban on dogs came into play. Though many dog owners believed the only way to make New York humane was to create free spay/neuter clinics, others were quite nervous over the question of spaying and neutering because they viewed these particular solutions to the dog problem as yet another attempt to get rid of dogs altogether.

The libertine attitude toward dog breeding in the 1970s might seem obscene by today's standards. So different were conceptions of what, exactly, made a person a responsible dog owner, that a story reported by the *Soho Weekly News* will surely shock and appall. "Cathouse for Dogs in Village?" asked the headline. "To this place dog lovers could bring their faithful Fido and he would be provided with a female dog in a state of artificially induced heat with whom he would be free to fornicate, for the sum of $50 (Bankamericard, Amex, and Purina in bulk not accepted). Included in the $50 fee would be pictures snapped by the Cathouse's resident photog of your number one pooch working out with Fifi, Bobo, or whichever brassy bitch he is confronted with. These photographs would then become the property of the dog's owner to do with as he wished. And if you were weird enough to take your dog there in the first place you must have enough imagination to recoup your $50 . . . limited editions of dogfuck sequences, squalid animal porno stills, or even, as one dog lover suggested, Christmas cards for your special friends. . . . The mildest of mutts can be transformed into a kill crazy canine once he gets a whiff of that pheromonal odor."[25]

It should be recalled that one of the most serious "epidemics" in New York of the 1970s was human venereal disease. Pup porn aside, even the ASPCA was against spaying and neutering for many years. How could this have been? Some critics have ventured the opinion that, since stray animals were the bread-and-butter of the ASPCA, it was very much in its interest to have as many of them as possible to round up on the streets of New York. Otherwise, the little funding it had might dry up altogether. The ASPCA has often been accused of exaggerating the number of strays the city actually had. And the reason for opposing spaying and neutering seems bizarre by today's standards. It was believed that rendering dogs incapable of reproducing would somehow "subsidize"[26] dog owners to go on breaking New York's leash law. In this strange turn of logic, dog owners, who might otherwise keep their pets on leashes to prevent them from mating randomly in parks, were thought to be less likely to limit their dogs' movement if they were sexually altered. Sterilizing and spaying dogs, it was believed for many years, would result in more dogs running away from their owners, increasing the likelihood that these dogs would end up on the street and perhaps be killed by automobiles. According to this theory, spaying and neutering were not in the dogs' best interests. The net result of population control—even with automobile fatalities figured into the equation—was predicted to be *more* stray dogs in New York City than there already were.

Not until 1973 did New York's ASPCA begin requiring dogs (and cats) to be spayed or neutered before adoption. And even then, the owners had to cover the costs of these operations. It's easy to see how the dog population grew out of control. Prior to that time, animals were adopted out sexually intact, which ultimately increased the number of strays in New York and made the ASPCA's job more difficult in the long term. What about subsidizing the costs? The President of New York's Veterinary Medical Association was against publicly funded population control. State- or city-subsidized spay/neuter clinics, he warned in 1972, would be the first step toward "socialized medicine for dogs and cats." This opinion was shared by many New Yorkers who were decidedly against shifting any of the burden for dog-related problems to government agencies. The weight, it was widely believed, should be carried by license-purchasing dog owners. "Keep the ASPCA," wrote one citizen, "or some private agency, tell us the true cost of dog care and make dog owners pay full costs; don't bury those costs in a general city budget."[27]

Dog owners were hesitant to view the ASPCA as a panacea for all of the city's dog problems. On the contrary, the ASPCA's popularity was rapidly declining. The troubled organization was unliked partly because of a state law that still required it to hand over a certain percentage of live animals each year for laboratory testing. This law had been in effect for over 20 years and contributed in no small way to the public's distrust of state-regulated shelters. Although New York City's ASPCA began defying the law in the early 1970s, the mere possibility that animals might be requisitioned by laboratories led many New Yorkers to abandon their unwanted pets on the street rather than bring them to the ASPCA. Whether it was more humane to let dogs take their chances on the street, to have them spayed or neutered, to have them euthanized, or to expose them to possible experimentation was still very much an open issue for New York dog owners. When the state finally repealed the laboratory testing law in 1979, this was done with the view to encourage dog owners to bring their animals to city shelters rather than set them loose on the streets or in parks, as so many people were still doing. "Bill Would Curb Tests on Animals," the *Times* announced, unable to resist making a clever reference to that *other* canine issue that had been fixating the city for so many years.[†]

The ASPCA's bold defiance of the animal testing requirement was not enough for it to regain the popularity lost in recent years. On the contrary, this single largest collector of stray animals in the city came under increasing scrutiny from pet owners and animal rights groups alike. The ASPCA euthanized approximately 400 animals each week in decompression chambers, a mass extermination that was less than humane in the opinion of critics. Due to recent austerity measures, shelters would close around the metropolitan area. Would an increase in the dog license fee alone have solved the ASPCA's many problems? While successive directors pleaded with New York leaders to press for desperately needed funding, a rapid turnover of directors and board members, even a lawsuit filed by board members for alleged financial mismanagement and neglect, did little to help procure additional funding or regain the public's trust. Stories circulating about poor conditions in shelters only accelerated the ASPCA's decline in popularity, and limited resources and allegations of animal cruelty made it difficult to perform the most basic tasks. "People won't take their animals to the ASPCA," said the head of United Action for Animals. "They would rather put them on the street."[28] So villainous had the city's dog catcher become that ASPCA

[†]This tendency to view all dog-related issues in terms of sanitation, and to equate dogs with their waste products, was widespread and would have residual effects for some time. When Albany passed a poop scoop law in 1977, New York State Attorney General Louis J. Lefkowitz wrote Governor Carey to say that, although the law was "laudable," a more effective method for handling canine waste would be in controlling the stray population by offering a lower licensing fee for altered pets. Today New York City's license fee is $3 higher for unaltered animals, though dog owners might not imagine this has anything to do with keeping the sidewalks clean. Lefkowitz's "fee-differential" idea, he believed, would "*curb* [italics mine] the proliferation of dogs . . . not spayed or neutered." Such a "self-enforcing law," he explained, would also take pressure off the overburdened criminal courts. But most important, the sliding fee was supposed to solve the stray problem and the poop problem in a single stroke. "This would reduce both forms of litter."

workers were often stoned by onlookers as they tried to "rescue" animals. They began requesting police escorts to accompany them on their rounds for protection against self-appointed pet vigilantes. Meanwhile, waiting for a license fee increase was like waiting for Godot. Governor Wilson did finally approve an increase in the dog license fee for New York City in 1974. But two dollars per dog would not be enough to save the ASPCA. That same year, the Governor vetoed a bill to authorize municipalities to operate low-cost spay/neuter clinics.

The pro-dog lobby's suspicion that certain parties wanted to ban dogs from New York doesn't seem so paranoid in light of the very strange priorities of the day. Concerned that Fido might be thrown out with the feces, dog owners reacted harshly against any attempt whatsoever to control their behavior, or that of their dogs. Like other cities, New York was still unable to decide on what were the basic responsibilities of dog owners toward the rest of society. But without a system in place for the responsible care and control of animals, there was little hope of convincing them that they had duties toward anyone at all. What people really needed was a show of faith and a willingness on the part of their leaders to take animal issues seriously.

"Stray dogs, dog litter on streets, the conditions under which animals are marketed and pet care in general"[29] were *all* major concerns according to City Councilman Carter Burden, a long-time defender of dogs and their owners. Burden had been the first Council member to remark that "a lot of other animals" contributed to the city's litter problem while many New Yorkers sought to blame dogs alone for the shameful state of sidewalks and parks. Burden was still decidedly against a poop scoop law. Instead, he believed, the important animal issue was the treatment—or lack of treatment—of New York's stray population. "I've reluctantly come to the realization that the ASPCA is doing a woefully inadequate job," Burden announced in 1974 when he began campaigning for a new City agency to handle animal affairs. Many pro-doggers agreed: An epidemic of dog bites, the deplorable activities of puppy mills, the tens of thousands of stray dogs and cats, and the mass extermination of these animals made for a shameful situation that demanded more than the ASPCA *or* a poop scoop law. "All of these factors contribute to a problem which can no longer be handled piecemeal by private organizations and fragmented city agencies," Burden insisted. "It is a problem which cries out for a complete commitment and strategy on the part of city government."[30]

The editors of the *Times* agreed that the dog situation in New York had gotten out of hand. A few days after a child had been fatally mauled by a pack of dogs in the Bronx, they wrote: "This spreading canine terror is only one of many dangerous and disagreeable consequences for New Yorkers of the failure of municipal authorities to deal with what has become a major problem for urban areas throughout the country—the proliferation of pets. There are about a million animal pets of all kinds in New York, yet the city today has no comprehensive system of laws to control—and protect—them. Nor does it have any single agency responsible for seeing that existing statutes, such as leash and curb laws, are strictly enforced."[31] The original thought behind forming a Bureau of Animal Affairs, as stated by a group called Citizens for Animals when it first gathered the required 50,000 signatures on a petition in 1973, was not to enforce the curb or leash laws, but rather to handle the one problem which, in their opinion, stood out before all others: the stray problem. Citizens for Animals called for low-cost spay/neuter clinics that would prevent many of the city's stray dogs (and cats) from being born in the first place. The group also supported having clear standards for the humane treatment of animals. Eventually, as stated in the five bills submitted by Carter Burden a year later, the purpose of a Bureau of Animal Affairs was extended to include a new law that was supposed to require landlords to allow pets, and even the creation of "dog runs" in all new housing developments so that dog owners would no longer need to run their dogs off-leash in public parks. Whether people liked it or not, dogs had arrived in New York and they were here to stay. The time had come to accommodate them with a greater vision and a long-term plan. "Unless the city takes over the enormous task of animal welfare and control, as other cities have done," Burden warned, "what is now a series of unpleasant circumstances is going to become a plague."[32]

Thanks to a media that had been primed by the claims of Fran Lee and others, the "plague" that most concerned so many New Yorkers was still the so-called poop epidemic. Responses from those opposed to Burden's plan for a Bureau of Animal Affairs came mainly from people who didn't see a complex urban problem but rather, like turds on the sidewalks, blatant reminders of a few inconsiderate individuals who had no qualms about imposing their filthy animals on the rest of society. They continued blaming dog owners for the canine waste problem and to view the stray problem as the fault of the many pet fanatics who had brought these unwanted animals to the city in the first place. Added to the disdain for dogs and their owners was a basic distrust of Big Government, which was, in fact, shared by some dog owners in the wake of the Lindsay years. After all, the city had sustained a vast bureaucracy at an enormous cost for nearly a decade, and the results had been disastrous. Carter Burden's proposal to group all animal-related issues under a single government office bore an unwelcome resemblance to Lindsay's "superagencies," which had failed so miserably to solve the city's problems. Why should animal control have been any different? Even the ASPCA, as desperate as it was for help, was against the idea of forming a new government agency to share in its thankless task. General Director Encil Rains argued that a "municipal Bureau of Animal Affairs would only create a bureaucratic monolith."[33] This opinion was shared by the anti-dog lobby. "The city is $1.5 billion in the hole," wrote one critic to the *Times*, "its transportation system is bankrupt, yet a combination of soft sentimentality and vote-grabbing is going to saddle the city with more costs for caring for dogs . . . Up the license fees, substantially. Fine them for the mess."[34] Most New Yorkers understood "the mess" to mean the poop on the sidewalks. And a license fee increase, if not a poop scoop law, was seen as a panacea for all of New York's dog-related problems. (Next to this letter demanding a license fee increase to help pick up the poop was another letter about a proposal to limit where, exactly, on city streets taxicabs should be allowed to pick up fares.)

City Council approved portions of Burden's plan and a Bureau of Animal Affairs was created as a division of the Department of Health in 1974. But this was probably not the best time to be expanding the role of municipal government. A year before Burden's plan was even approved, Health Commissioner Lowell Bellin had warned that his agency didn't have the resources to sustain a new division devoted to animals. He was partly right. A year after the Bureau of Animal Affairs was formed, the fiscal crisis arrived and the state-run Municipal Assistance Corporation began deciding how money would be spent. The ASPCA continued its downward spiral despite Burden's warning of a coming plague. And the new Bureau of Animal Affairs would be under the same fiscal constraints as the City of New York. Though the Bureau would play an important part in controlling dangerous dogs, in educating New Yorkers about dog-related issues, even in handing over $1.7 million to the ASPCA, it would have little to do directly with the stray problem in New York City, which had been one of its purposes when Citizens for Animals first gathered the list of signatures for City Council's consideration. The Bureau would be charged with other important tasks such as monitoring guard dog schools and gathering and disseminating statistics on dog bites and terrestrial rabies. The latter had not been seen in New York for nearly 20 years but it was the Department of Health's responsibility to be on watch for signs of epidemics. The recent pet population explosion had not, despite widespread fears, brought rabies back to the city any more than it had increased the threat of *Toxocara canis*. But the incidence of dog bites was, on the contrary, reaching alarming proportions, and educating citizens about this problem was a major goal.

The one "epidemic" that threatened to overshadow the poop problem during these years was the incidence of dog bites. The increased presence of watch dogs was a contributing factor. The number of bites reported annually in New York City had more than doubled in a decade to reach approximately 38,300 by 1974. The real number was believed to be at least twice that number, since many cases went unreported. Most of these bites were suffered by children. The Bureau responded to a vital need for any information that might help prevent attacks and calm fears about a pressing new urban problem that affected many people directly. If the Department of Health didn't have the resources to attack the problem at its very roots—and until the virtues of birth control were disseminated by government or approved by the Catholic Church—then at least the Bureau could advise people on how to minimize the risk of being bitten by dogs. The educational campaign was launched in the summer of 1975. Posters were displayed in subway cars instructing citizens on how to avoid potentially aggressive dogs while at street level. Summer was the worst time, not only for feces that filled the air with their presence, but for dog bites as well because more dogs and humans were outside in the warmer months. Bites, however, were becoming less seasonal. One medical doctor from Mount Sinai Hospital conducting a study of bites warned that the heated controversy over excrement that had dominated the dog debate almost entirely in recent years was obscuring the more serious and immediate problem of bites. "We have been worrying about the wrong end of the dog,"[35] he said, trying to divert the public's attention away from poop and onto bites. Bureau Director Alan Beck agreed. "Guard dogs are an increasing hazard in the city," Beck said. "Of course, the problem of dog feces is a major health one in New York," he added about the subject that kept rearing its ugly head. "It's unhealthy, it stinks, nobody wants to walk through it. But I think the greater problem today is dog bites."[36]

"The Worst Doggy Do Is Biting,"[37] agreed the *Daily News*. As a result of the Bureau's campaign, dog bites soon began to distract from the poop problem, as they should have. This very real and alarming epidemic of attacks in New York City came about as a direct result of the fact that dogs had grown, not only in number, but also in size and temperament over the previous decade. The increase was a direct measure of a growing malaise. Studies in cynophobia had shown that fear levels in humans corresponded to the size of dogs. Once again, the Bureau provided the numbers: The average weight of a New York dog increased from 25 to 33 pounds between the mid-sixties and the mid-seventies. New Yorkers were no longer satisfied with the fluffy lapdogs that looked like wigs or small rodents. The miniature poodle (the dog whose owner was accosted by Jack Lemmon in *Prisoner of Second Avenue*) had been a breed of choice among New Yorkers since the early sixties and was still quite popular. But these dogs were outweighed by a distinct trend toward larger models like Rottweilers, Weimaraners, Komodors, and German shepherds (the dogs that terrorized Jack Lemmon, "piddled" on his car, then went on to chase Dustin Hoffman in Central Park). Populations of certain breeds had increased as much as 35 times since the 1950s. Many of these larger dogs were bred specifically for their aggressive tendencies and were purchased as guard dogs. These big, strong, tightly wound animals, while they made their owners feel safer, were having the opposite effect upon others. "The bigger the dog, the bigger the mess," said the owner of three Great Danes on the Upper West Side, noting that when people saw a large dog they usually thought of one thing: more poop. But larger-breed dogs caused other concerns as well. "Pit bulls" were still known as Staffordshire bull terriers and had only a minor presence in American cities. The guard dog of choice in the 1970s was the German shepherd. New York's newspapers and Yellow Pages were filled with ads for training schools, breeders, and rental companies offering these and other breeds for protection. A typical guard dog advertisement showed a German shepherd lunging at the camera with teeth bared viciously—the same type of image used in psychotherapy to get a rise from cynophobists! This emphasis on encouraging dogs to attack was a far cry from today's focus on bringing out the kinder, gentler qualities in canines. Some breeders even crossed German shepherds with timber wolves to make them potentially more aggressive. The many descendents of these dogs so fashionable in the seventies can be found to this day in city shelters with the vague yet familiar label of "Shepherd Mix" affixed to their cages. The random interbreeding allowed by New York's lax control over its dog population has, ironically, selected against the unnatural aggression that was once encouraged by irresponsible breeders.

Controlling these dogs was a matter of the utmost urgency. Before the Bureau of Animal Affairs was created, New York had no rules governing the growing number of guard dog breeders and training schools. As a result, many of the canine graduates had been poorly trained. They were often dangerous, even to their owners who were not properly equipped to handle them. "Meeting an untrained dog is a desocializing experience,"[38] said Beck. Almost weekly, news stories told of fatal attacks by dogs, very often German shepherds or Rottweilers. The usual victims were children or infants left alone with these dogs. Roger Caras, the environmentalist and television commentator on wildlife (and eventually head of the ASPCA), expressed alarm over the new trend that was leading to these tragedies. German shepherds and other large guard dogs, he said, were being bred specifically for aggressive tendencies. Not only were most people unprepared to control these animals, providing them with the wide open spaces they required for exercise was very difficult in a place like New York City. When not properly exercised, these dogs became increasingly irritable and were much more likely to attack. There seemed to be no way for dog people to win. Being a responsible and humane owner to a big, powerful dog meant breaking the city's leash law and endangering people, or at least frightening the cynophobists.

Caras offered a solution: dog runs. Although this controversial idea had been part of Carter Burden's original plan, it wouldn't make it past City Council until 1997. In the meantime, Caras refused to let go of the idea. He suggested accommodating New York's growing dog population by requiring landlords to open "rooftop dog runs," fenced-in areas where dogs of all shapes and sizes could run freely without causing problems—except perhaps for the top-floor tenants who would have to live with the pitter-patter of paws. At least one New York landlord, rather than try to evict dog-owning tenants, actually took Caras' advice and opened rooftop dog runs on top of two of his apartment buildings. "Relative to the city dog problem," Jack Gasnick explained in a letter to the *Times*, "I have very nicely solved this question in the two buildings I own in the east Fifties. Realizing that my tenants possess these animals mainly because of safe-keeping reasons and also as pets for the lonely elderly, I have fenced off a good portion of my rooftops where the dogs can walk or ramble on leash or off leash, safe from automobiles, teasing children, and policemen. There is a sandbox and drinking water available and I hope someday to install some wooden prop fire hydrants. My halls are clean and best of all, my tenants are happy, especially those without pets."[39] Unfortunately, it would take many years of struggling before the rest of New York would accept the dog run idea. Even if these canine playgrounds were to be placed high in the sky, they were bound to stir some sanitary concerns. Caras suggested using hoses for cleaning the lofty sanctuaries. He recommended harmless enzyme cleaners used by farmers and zookeepers for breaking down fecal matter. But at no altitude did Caras, or most other animal advocates, consider a poop scoop law a viable option. The only solution to the city's poop problem, Caras insisted, was in limiting *where* dogs were allowed to go: outdoors, they should be "curbed" or kept in roof-top dog runs; indoors, they should be paper-trained. Caras thought the idea for a poop scoop law was absurd and totally impractical. "I want to give you an all-American scenario," he said. "Do I bring it as a hostess gift? Nobody is doing anything but talking."[40]

Despite government's inability to work out some of the practical details of urban dog ownership, progress had been made. The Bureau of Animal Affairs was, in fact, able to require many of the city's guard dogs to be registered. It also assessed the ASPCA's operations and provided extra funding. Across the city, the Bureau expanded pet shop and grooming facility inspections. Some order was imposed on a chaotic situation. Declaring New York to be the first city in the nation "rabies-free" did help to clear the air by keeping those "Rabidophobe extremists" quiet for awhile. For obvious financial reasons, the Bureau wasn't able to do all that was hoped for when City Council voted it into existence. But an office devoted to Animal Affairs managed to help both human and non-human animals to some degree. It also served to deflect some of the political heat over dogs, a leading concern of voters, away from City Hall and City Council during these difficult transitional years.

Whether dogs were the true source of the mass hysteria that swept over the city in waves with each new tale of an aggressive dog attacking some innocent pedestrian—or whether New York's dog problem was a symptom of a broader breakdown of society—the Bureau, despite its best efforts to solve the many *other* dog-related problems, was a highly political office and had to take issues as they came. Popular prejudices being what they were, and despite attempts to refocus the public's attention onto bites, the poop problem still demanded attention.

Once again, the Bureau supplied the numbers. Alan Beck estimated that New York dogs were depositing an estimated 500,000 pounds of "dog leavings" on city surfaces each and every day of the year, which was a big mess by any standard. "Of course," Beck explained, "this is distributed over a fairly large surface area."[41] What was the Bureau's official stand on the matter? "No one can deny the fact that it stinks, it's dirty, and it's saying something about ourselves to pollute our environment,"[42] Beck said in another interview. "We wouldn't tolerate people defecating in the street," he added. "And dog feces are at least as dangerous as human feces."[43] But what did all this *mean*? Much to the disappointment of Fran Lee, who had spent years campaigning against exotic diseases, Beck concluded that the presence of dog feces on sidewalks and in parks did not constitute a public heath problem per se. Instead, he explained, feces were "very much a psychological and aesthetic problem, so in that way they are a health problem, too."[44]

There it was, intelligently put but bound to cause an uproar. After years of bitter fighting and a long list of elaborate programs and experiments, dog poop in New York City had become a mental health problem, or at the very least, a matter of personal taste that was causing some serious social problems. "Fran Lee was pissed," recalls Beck, "but we remained friends. It made sense. *Visceral larva migrans* was serious but relatively rare while stepping into dog waste was a major annoyance."[45] Beck was right but the cynophobists were beside themselves, as were others who had grown tired of stepping into crap and learned to equate dogs with the very waste products they left—why not increase the license fee by one dollar per pound of dog, as one desperate letter to

the *Times* suggested? Alarmists were losing patience and official pro-
nouncements were not enough to calm their growing rage. Each day,
they seemed more willing to take matters into their own hands, if not
to help pick up the poop, then to raise their voices to say that they were
mad as hell and not going to take this mess anymore.

The war over dogs in New York City, the same ongoing and
passionate dispute leading to no practical solution of the canine waste
problem and dividing the population along lines that ran contrary to
protecting humans or their pets, reached a new extreme in March 1976
when two stray dogs were reported creating bedlam in Kew Gardens.
The *Times* reported:

> Two large German shepherd dogs that have been running loose for
> more than a year have created an atmosphere of terror and hostility
> in a quiet residential community of Queens by biting anywhere from
> 20 to 50 persons, mainly children, in recent weeks.[46]

The vast gulf in the estimate of the number of victims was typical of these chaotic times. The story continued:

> Parents of bitten children in the Kew Gardens Hills section have begun
> hunting the dogs with axes, baseball bats, snares, walkie-talkies, and
> even guns. Some angry fathers have tried to run down the dogs with
> automobiles. One man was seen at 3 in the morning, standing with a
> shotgun under a tree near where the dogs had been sighted. The police
> and the American Society for the Prevention of Cruelty to Animals
> have been unsuccessful in efforts to capture the dogs. Many parents
> will not allow their children out alone in the street. Some elderly per-
> sons no longer sit on porches; they carry sticks when walking through
> this area of private homes and garden apartments, in which dogs can
> lope for miles through a maze of backyards and driveways and appear
> suddenly on a street from behind a house.[47]

Something was awfully askew in New York City. Two dangerous dogs, it seemed, had managed to elude both the ASPCA and the
police. The bands of armed vigilantes provided a strange foreshadowing

to public responses to the Son of Sam a year later. Maybe Alan Beck was right: Had dogs become a source of mass hysteria? Residents of this normally peaceful family neighborhood in Queens were comparing the two German shepherds to the killer shark seen in a recent film called *Jaws*. Like the beach community portrayed in the movie, residents of Kew Gardens were in a state of panic over the presence of loose predators they believed were stalking their children. Queens Borough President Donald Manes said that neighbors were demanding these "four-footed sharks"[48] be hunted down and killed at once.

"There is, however," said the *Times* "one very important difference between the situation in Kew Gardens and in the movie about sharks. There are residents in the community who are on the side of the dogs.[49] A group of neighbors, each of them described simply as a "dog lover"[50]—were alarmed by the harsh approach to the stray dogs which were, it turned out, a male and a female protecting their pups. The dogs' defenders claimed that the mates were only doing what came naturally when they attacked humans wandering too close to their litter. For lack of a man-made order that might have protected their pups, or perhaps even prevented the parents from being born in the first place, the dogs were resorting to their own devices. They'd been moving their family to a new location after each encounter with a human, and their present location was unknown. Concerned that the mob of armed parents might discover and kill both the adult dogs and the pups, the dog lovers started their own patrol of the neighborhood. They, too, carried axes and bats—but they didn't plan to use them against the dogs.

The situation was clearly getting out of hand as people who had nothing against dogs were suddenly forced into conscription in the war being fought over them. A local rabbi, whose six-year-old daughter had been knocked down and bitten on the leg by one of the dogs, started his own one-man posse. For several days, Rabbi David M. Fuld was observed patrolling the neighborhood with an ax, a baseball bat, and a handmade noose. "The idea of killing a dog with an ax sounds gruesome," Rabbi Fuld confessed. "But my children were being attacked by these dogs. Because of these dogs, our community has become a sort of vigilante community."[51] Fuld made a point of saying he'd always taught his children not to be afraid of dogs. But these had to be stopped. "When I saw the blood on my daughter's leg, I became furious,"[52] he said. "Some people think dogs are more important than children. Thank God, I still don't hate animals."[53] Nonetheless, Rabbi Fuld felt compelled to take action and began hunting the two dogs. But before he could find them, his campaign ended abruptly. The caption to the photo of his young daughter in the *Times* explained: "She is seen through a hole in a window made by a rock thrown by a dog lover in retaliation for Rabbi Fuld's attempt to hunt down the dogs."[54] Fuld admitted he was powerless to make his own neighborhood safe for his family. "I cannot take a chance worrying about the dogs outside and about what happens to my home too,"[55] he concluded helplessly.

A week after the two German shepherds were reported creating bedlam in Queens, a letter appeared in the *Times* imploring dog owners to consider a social problem of the utmost urgency.

> As president of the Veterinary Medical Association of New York City, I would like to comment on the relationship of dog owners and the city in the hope of preventing hostility between those who own dogs and those who don't. It is imperative that dog owners act in a responsible manner toward the people in their community. For instance, New York City has a law stating that dogs must be kept on their leashes when outside. This is a positive idea since it prevents dog fights, mismatings, traffic accidents, dog bites, etc. There is no possible ill effect on dogs. Our city also requires dog owners to curb their pets. This keeps our sidewalks cleaner, keeps our parks and other planted areas free of dog litter, and makes the city an easier place to keep clean. In addition, many dog owners are starting to "pick up" after their pets. We applaud and encourage such actions.[56]

The unlikely events in Queens might have been viewed as the culmination of campaigns to instill fear in parents, combined with the City's inability to control the dog population. This was bound to be an explosive mix. But instead, the ASPCA was held to blame. In fact, if New York's Bureau of Animal Affairs served to deflect political heat from City Hall and City Council, then the ASPCA would serve for decades as a convenient scapegoat for all of New York's dog-related problems. Just what was the ASPCA being paid to do, anyway? The problem was, the ASPCA wasn't being paid enough. There were two German shepherds running loose in Queens because the ASPCA had been forced, for financial reasons, to close its shelter there, as it would soon be forced to close others around the city. The end result of the Kew Gardens incident was the introduction in the State Legislature of a bill that would actually *decrease*, not increase, funding to the ASPCA, which was to be penalized for not having a shelter in a borough where it collected license fees! Meanwhile, the ASPCA's fiscal state, and the stray problem, worsened.

The family of German shepherds was never apprehended in Kew Gardens. It was assumed that one of the militant dog lovers had taken them in. But later that year, the same neighborhood was once again drawing attention. This time, a police officer had been bitten by a large dog, an Irish setter, while attempting to serve the dog's owner with a summons for walking it and another dog, a female German shepherd, off-leash. As usual, the press sensationalized the incident, which began when the Irish setter, running off-leash, chased the officer as he rode by on a motorcycle. He had a serious bite on the leg and would be unable to work for several weeks. "When an animal comes after you," he told an already uneasy public, "it's an unbelievable feeling."[57] The owner of the dogs, too, had panicked, running away when the officer pulled out a gun to defend himself. It appeared that the dog's owner had no more control over himself than he did over his dog.

In response to the policeman's report, ten of the man's neighbors showed up to defend the dog owner's character—and the dog's— in Criminal Court. They all swore under oath that the animal standing accused of attacking a police officer had always been friendly toward *them*. A proud picture of this coalition of "character witnesses"[58] was shown in the *Times*. The end result was a further confusion of issues, and yet another melodrama portraying the dastardly enemies of canines on one side, and their faithful and unconditional "lovers" on the other.

Depending on how one looked at this scene, it could have been a politician's dream—or his own worst nightmare.[‡]

[‡]While residents of Kew Gardens hunted down stray dogs with rifles and axes, humorist Russell Baker tried to make light of the war over dogs. But Baker, like most New Yorkers, couldn't hide his strong feelings on the subject. The *New York Times* piece was called "Dog Day Evening,"[59] referring to the film *Dog Day Afternoon* starring Al Pacino, which, like so many films of that era, depicted New York City as a place where citizens resorted to their own devices and respect for law and order was at one of its all-time lows. Baker wrote:

> New York is a city of dogs. There are more than a million in all walks of life. Most of these walks go right past my house, which makes for a great deal of cursing on dark nights. Guests who come to dinner usually refuse invitations to come back. I am ill-disposed to dogs in cities, though I am careful not to say so, since dogs have numerical strength and owners obviously capable of great ruthlessness.

Baker goes on to tell the story of his son who decides to visit from the country. Unfortunately for Baker, his son insists on bringing his two very large mutts. Admittedly, Baker doesn't like dogs but is obliged to welcome the "two unkempt, loutish dogs named Spike and Irma" if he ever wants his son to visit. But he puts his foot down when it comes to sleeping arrangements, insisting the dogs be placed in the neighborhood kennel. "Irma was obviously delighted to be in New York," Baker remarks, "but Spike sniffed at the air with the uneasy disdain of a rube among the city slickers, one who knows he is out of his class and wants to show nothing but contempt for the whole decadent scene." Spike, it seems, is aggressive toward other dogs and so he can't be boarded at the local doggy hotel, an elegant Upper East Side establishment where guests are allowed to wander around off-leash in a highly appointed setting complete with a bar, a dining room, and plush Oriental rugs. Baker, however, has a solution:

> That night I tied them illegally to the grill fence in front of my house. Next morning the sidewalk was remarkably clean except for large batches of dog hair torn from neighborhood canines who made the mistake of pausing there for their usual nocturnal excretions. It warmed me to them so strongly that I might have kept them if it weren't against the law to keep a clean sidewalk.

Baker's opinion was shared by many New Yorkers. First of all: dogs belonged on leashes, even if this meant tying them up all night on the sidewalk. Then: dogs, especially large dogs, were both dangerous and dirty. In Baker's view, repressing one bad quality could only mean cultivating the other. There seemed to be no way for the poor creatures to win. The prospect of pristine pavement could only be realized by chaining an aggressive dog on the sidewalk and allowing it to replace the piles of crap with the clumps of fur that would inevitably be torn from passing pets. But the dogs had to do their business *somewhere*! After years of bickering and debating, humans still could not agree on exactly where that should be. The bad feelings that arose during these frustrating, deadlocked days would color the entire experience of having a dog in the city for years to come, lingering and festering and shaping New York City's future policies toward animals. As dogs were equated with their very waste products, the fear of them and the distaste for their droppings merged inextricably. Like that proverbial bear in the woods, they left deposits as a constant reminder of their presence nearby. The *Daily News* seemed to agree when it said that "The Worse Doggy Do Is Biting," and then showed a photograph of dogs on a New York sidewalk with the caption: "On the scent of another threat."[60] Feces, the source of that mental health problem afflicting New York on a mass scale, had become not only an unpleasant item to encounter, but the sign of some imminent danger.

CHAPTER 9

A NEW PRAGMATISM

> "People who bite people are possibly the deadliest species of biters."
>
> —NYC Health Commissioner Reinaldo A. Ferrer[1]

"My husband has much more important things to worry about,"[2] said Mary Beame, the mayor's wife, the morning she led a pack of angry New Yorkers through Carl Schurz Park in search of polluting pet owners. The story made the front page of the *New York Times*. "Mrs. Beame Joins Protest at Mansion Against Dog Litter,"[3] read the headline in March 1976. While her husband tended to the city's finances and faced problems far more pressing than dogs or their doo, Mary Beame turned her guns on the small things. Barely two weeks after a pair of German shepherds were reported terrorizing residents of Kew Gardens, she took an odd course of action. Rather than speak up against the more serious pet-related problems like the stray situation and the bite epidemic, or endorse long-term solutions like population control or the enforcement of humane standards for animal care, Mrs. Beame reached for the only issue that seemed within anyone's grasp during these troubled transitional years.

The unattractive state of public parks was at the top of her list. Part Lady Bird Johnson fretting over rose beds, part the incarnation of her husband's dream for "Envirmaids" to tidy up city surfaces, New York's First Lady pointed a finger dutifully at the ground and vowed to tackle the job her husband didn't have the time to do himself. "You can't sidestep the issue"[4] was the slogan that propelled her as a major proponent of the government-backed, institutionalized vigilantism that seemed the only way to get things done in New York City. She found many willing participants. As government approached a standstill, concerned citizens were more eager than ever to take matters into their own hands. "The streets are lost,"[5] Mrs. Beame conceded sadly before leading the group of about 100 members of the Carl Schurz Park Association, which was over 600 strong by this time, on its first official rampage. "Let's save the park!"[6] She encouraged "the muttering majority,"[7] in this case a group of disgruntled gardeners, to stop talking under their breath and rise up against a dog-owning minority who sabotaged their efforts to beautify the city. "Parks are for recreation, not defecation,"[8] read the placards they waved.

Hearing the mob approach from around trees and behind hedges, perplexed morning walkers were quick to leash their frolicking beasts and get out of the way. Catching these lawbreakers wasn't easy. "It's an obstacle course,"[9] Mrs. Beame cautioned her followers, meaning they should keep one eye open for leashless dogs and the other on their next step through a minefield of dog litter. As the rowdy bunch slowly and carefully edged its way across the patchy lawns, tying not to step into anything, fleeing pet owners, their own eyes half-shut because they hadn't had their morning coffee, dispersed to all four corners of the park. The ultimate goal was to push them out, then off surrounding curbs where their pets could do no more damage. Innocent bystanders in the park were also drawn into the campaign with handbills praising flora and showing a photograph of the alternative: two large dogs defecating in fearful symmetry. "STOP THIS!"[10] implored the caption.

Dog owners weren't the only focus of Mary Beame's campaign. She'd also lost patience with City Council for failing to confront them head-on. If her brand of community participation didn't do the job, she warned, and Council continued to dodge the poop scoop proposal, then

elected lawmakers would be passed over and humiliated as the cow-
ards that they were. She swore, as a last resort, to involve her husband
personally—and he'd be very angry at having been disturbed. The
mayor, she promised, would take his wife's advice and protect lawns
from the ravages of running canines, and all the other unpleasantness
they left behind. He would invoke the City's original Charter, which gave
him "personal power to sit in judgment on miscreants brought before
him."[11] The Chief Executive "shall be magistrate"[12]—in other words,
New York would have a kind of poop tribunal. "Ms. Beame meanwhile
had been collared for television comments,"[13] said the *Times*.

Old Abe Beame, it turned out, did have more important things
to worry about—like rescuing the City from bankruptcy. He never de-
livered on his wife's promise to hold people personally accountable for
their pets' evacuations. But Mary pressed on with her beautification
campaign for the duration of his term, hunting down any fauna that
threatened the flora, then trying to shame its caretakers into complying with a law that didn't yet exist. Her confrontational approach had
repercussions in neighborhoods throughout the city. Downtown, Greenwich Village dog owners were not only being chased out of children's
playgrounds, but were accosted simply for walking their pets on the
sidewalks. In other neighborhoods, like-minded citizens with an axe
to grind continued their scourge in the name of surface beauty, venting their frustrations over a world gone out of control—if only at the
expense of a few animal lovers whose dogs needed exercise. While
time and energy were spent trailing those dogs with rightful owners,
the stray situation only worsened and Carter Burden's visionary bill
for spay/neuter clinics was never passed. Unfazed, the militant flower
people carried on their mission in Carl Schurz Park, encouraging others
to follow their example. Where, they wondered, would New York find
a mayor who wasn't afraid of getting his hands dirty?

* * *

Many New Yorkers, in and out of parks, grew tired of fooling
around with City Council. During the course of Mary Beame's cam-

paign to curb dog owners, a host of alternatives and a wealth of patience had been exhausted. As various approaches were tried and failed, one Sanitation Commissioner became so furious that he threatened to lobby for a municipal tax on dog food. If this didn't discourage people from having pets in the first place, then maybe it would starve the poor animals to death and finally get those sidewalks clean. "He'd Tax Doggie Intake to Curb Output,"[14] read the *Daily News* headline. Commissioner Anthony Vaccarello never made good on his threat, though he was famous for calling New Yorkers "slobs." Meanwhile, pavements and parks remained as they were and frustration mounted. A day after the Cunard Princess was christened in New York Harbor in 1977, the *News* noted that the sheer tonnage of pet feces left on city surfaces each year outweighed the luxury liner by three times! Talk of a possible tax on dogs according to their size, or "poop potential,"[15] also led nowhere.

"Nearly four years ago," the *News* recalled bitterly, "legislation to require pooper scoopers was introduced in the City Council, only to be knocked down by vehement dog owners."[16] Here was Ed Koch's ticket to ride. Local lawmakers clearly couldn't be relied upon to get the job done. Once at the helm, Koch made one of his very first acts in office a jaunt to Albany where he bypassed local legislators and rallied, instead, for a statewide doggy cleanup. Only a state law, Koch believed, could control those anti-social misfits who were making life so unpleasant for everyone in New York City.

While campaigning for mayor, Koch had presented himself as a serious candidate, a man who would mend the errors of the past once and for all. He would introduce a new kind of pragmatism into politics that excited some New Yorkers and terrified others. Much would be accomplished under his reign. Though Koch would one day be accused of having sold out the city to real estate interests, he remained faithful to the spirit of his campaign. He kept focused on the lessons he had learned from what he called "the three c's"[17]—none of which stood for City Council. Instead, the first *c* referred to *clubhouse* and Abe Beame's corrupt old cronies of the city's Democratic Party he believed best represented the forces standing in the way of progress. The second *c*, for *charisma*, referred to that seductive but illusory quality in John Lindsay that had, in the opinion of Koch and others who had forgotten the many great things that man had done, led the city astray. Against a long tradition of fancy failures, Koch was packaged as the no-frills, no-nonsense candidate who had arrived to clean house (and the sidewalks). New York needed a man with *competence*, he said, that third and final *c* on the list, that would help him undo the damages of the previous two and set the city back on course.

Chutzpa might have been added as the fourth *c* on Koch's list. Shockingly original though it seemed, the decision to turn to Albany was in reality part of a broader trend to which he could lay no claim. Just as the city's spending habits were now being monitored by the state, the behavior of dog owners, too, was about to be regulated by outsiders. Once again, the mess in New York City had been handed to someone else on a silver platter, whether they wanted it or not. "It wasn't the dog law,"[18] Koch would recall years later as an aside to the Westside Highway project. Looking back, he would try to downplay the importance of the dog law, the success of which was one of his first mayoral coups. But he couldn't resist taking credit for boldly going where no local leader had gone before. "In August of 1978," Koch mentioned in a footnote, as though in passing, "the City of New York became subject to the new 'Canine Waste Law.' It was at that time that dog owners had to begin using pooper scoopers or be subject to a fine. I had gone to Albany during the 1978 legislative session to lobby for the bill."[19] Maybe Koch was tired of fooling around but he wasn't fooling anybody. Poop was one of the single greatest public concerns when he was first elected. New York, his support for the law suggested, could only be fixed from the ground up. He aimed low and found many supporters who shared his view.

"How come they do-do us like they do?" asked the *Daily News*. "New York City has many problems, so who would think one of the major ones comes complete with four paws, a wet nose, and a wagging tail? Simply stated, New York is going to the dogs, and a lot of people are concerned."[20] *New York* magazine also noted this tendency to view certain smaller problems through a magnifying glass. "To some officials and elected representatives, fouling the footpaths is an ecological crime, the eastern equivalent of using the Grand Canyon as a landfill site."[21] This was no minor irritant. Perhaps out of some feeling of embarrassment or a sense of the absurd, or daunted by feelings of impotence in the face of challenges larger than dogs or their leavings, Koch and much of the city had been agonizing for years over an issue that had always seemed so much larger than it should have been in the greater scheme of things. Struggling to put poop into its proper perspective, to keep their wits and maintain some semblance of style, many New Yorkers were barely able to hide their anger whenever they encountered this small item on the pavement. They seethed through their teeth each time they got a whiff of the curb, or showed up to meet friends at restaurants, only to find when seated that they'd dragged a pungent pile to dinner. Rolling over into some unexpected surprise during picnics in Central Park was no laughing matter. This was all too much for some people to take sitting down. Mary Beame had worked for years to embolden the gardening set. Koch would be the first New York mayor to go a step further and give voice to those gut reactions of fed-up pedestrians, the ones who'd been too shy or polite to talk about the problem at length, much less to join a poop posse. The wider "muttering majority" had finally found a leader who would confront dog owners head-on without reservation or apology.

As far as Koch was concerned, the situation was as plain as the nose on his face. Dog owners, he believed, were acting selfishly and had to be taught some manners. Their anti-social behavior was, it seemed, destroying the city. The poop scoop idea was presented as a matter of common sense and common decency. Though admitting this was difficult, passing such a law was, in fact, a crucial first step toward rebuilding New York—what good were the MAC and federal assistance if no one wanted to live there? Fixing the city from the ground up meant taking a trivial complaint seriously. Only by clearing the air would the ailing metropolis regain the faith and credit of the nation and the world. Koch's handling of this problem, however small it might have seemed in the greater scheme of things, would help to set the tone for his future in politics.

But Ed Koch hadn't been sworn in yet. While he waited in the wings, Senator Franz Leichter and Assemblyman Edward Lehner of Manhattan officially co-sponsored Health Law 1310. The two absconded quietly to the halls of Albany in 1977 with a hot topic tucked under their arms, an explosive prospect that had left local lawmakers shell-shocked. Here they hoped to settle the matter secretly and without interruption, to be free of all the rowdy demonstrators and last-minute oratories. They had tried, the year before, to pass a poop scoop law upstate but the idea had died in the Health Committees of both Houses. But a new mayor would soon be in office, one who didn't believe in coddling people. Sure, dog owners were going to be upset when they found out about this. But in time, Leichter, Lehner, and Koch believed, they'd see reason and agree to lend a helping hand in saving their city from certain doom. Such an easy solution to a complex problem that had dragged on for years might have seemed suspect. Was Koch forgetting the long and ugly war waged, for the better part of a decade, over what appeared on the surface to be a cut-and-dry issue? Hadn't the lessons of the past offered a clue as to what might be expected from that small but growing and increasingly vocal part of the population that would be most affected by this law?

Getting Albany to see things their way was not as easy as the pro-scoopers had predicted. Though the chaos of that mad day in City Council's Chamber five years earlier would have been hard to match, proponents of State Health Law 1310 ran into serious snags that were preventing the law's passage. They were not about to see this happen a fourth time. Two failures in City Council, and then a recent debacle in Albany—they weren't going to stand by and let the problem be buried and forgotten again just because it was controversial. "There is a sort of dog lobby up there," an embattled Leichter reported home with dismay. "They are permissive to dogs and cruel to people."[22] Leichter, a regular jogger in Riverside Park when he was in town, had his own personal reasons for taking on the cause. He said that New York had become "one big dog latrine."[23] But the owners of those animals that chased him daily and befouled the footpaths weren't the only contingent trying to block what would one day be called "the Koch-Leichter law." Along with the dog lovers was a united front of conservatives from across the state who, whether or not they even liked dogs, opposed the legislation that they viewed as yet another unwelcome interference from Big Government. The most surprising aspect of New York's poop scoop law is not that it took so long to be accepted, but that it was passed at all. Allied with the conservatives and the pro-doggers were rural representatives who were eager, regardless of party affiliation or feelings about animals, to poke fun at the overblown concerns of the city folk. Despite the prevalence of *Toxocara canis* in rural areas, they were decidedly un-alarmed. In their opinion, this was another example of those arrogant and pretentious Manhattanites trying to impose their inflated concerns on everyone else. It was bad enough that state and federal governments were being expected to bail them out financially. Now Albany was being asked to vote on a silly law that no one would be able to enforce? Rather than indulge those overstuffed New Yorkers and flatter their sense of self-importance, many rural representatives voted against the bill. Their unkind opinion of us wasn't entirely unfair. No one in the state cared as much as the city folk did about having a poop scoop law. In fact, hardly anyone cared at all.

The debate dragged on while Lehner and Leichter struggled against all odds to push the bill through, and representatives from that vast territory stretching northward as far as Canada wondered why on earth they were wasting so much time on this.

* * *

"There seems to be something about this bill and Mr. Lehner's hinted explanation of it that has upset the entire Chamber," said acting Speaker Jean Amatucci. "Could we have some order, please."[24]

This wouldn't be the last time Ms. Amatucci would have to intervene. Repeated calls for self-control punctuated both debates in the Assembly and Senate where the sponsors' grasp on the poop scoop bill was in constant danger of slipping. New Yorkers in favor of this law would have to work hard to make others share their enthusiasm for the cause of cleaner sidewalks in big cities.

"Mr. Lehner," said Amatucci a few moments later to the man trying to lead the way, "excuse me. I cannot hear you and I don't think anybody else can hear you. Members please take your seats. Will those people that are not members please leave the aisles and go to the back area."

Lehner was not a dog owner himself, a fact not in his favor. To prove the practicality of this strange new idea, he held, in clear view for anyone who cared to pay attention, an odd contraption the likes of which his fellow legislators had never seen or imagined. He praised the "pooper-scooper" just as manufacturers had tried to push similar items on City Council five years earlier.

"I have with me a simple device which I will demonstrate whereby dog owners, for a device that costs less that $10, can simply comply with the law."

From the onset, proponents of the bill tried to base their case on this odd contraption. It was assumed that a favorable vote, and the law's eventual success, would hinge upon the "pooper-scooper," which was really nothing more than a three-foot metal rod with a plastic bag attachment, and mechanical jaws that snapped the bag shut. Introducing a miracle cure in the Assembly Chamber, like a circus barker or a potions salesman pushing some promising tonic, was unusual behavior for a legislative hearing. In fact, when Senator Leichter tried to perform a similar demonstration for the Senate a month later, he was reminded of a prior ruling against the use of "proprietary products" and visual aides. The Senator's sideshow would be banned for being "a form of commercialization."[*]

---

[*]In years to come, Health Law 1310 would be known popularly not as "the dog shit law" or even "the canine waste law" but rather as the cuter "poop scoop law" to focus on the mechanism and distract from an unpleasant topic that made people feel uncomfortable.

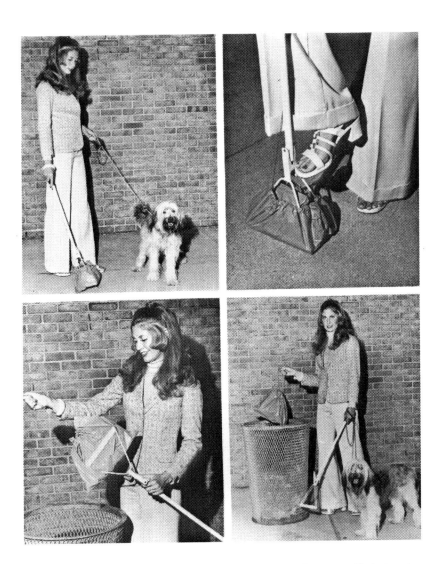

"It's in the bag with Dogmatic™." This poop-scooping device was demonstrated by its inventor, Robert Veech, before City Council in 1972, and then again by legislators in Albany in 1977. In the product literature, an attractive woman shows that scooping can be easy. "How many times have you wished you could clean up your dog's litter without embarrassment and awkward, conspicuous motions when you walk your dog?" asks the manufacturer. The device "exceeds all legal requirements for pickup and disposal," has a "lightweight compact design," and a "light reflective color for safety" when stepping off the curb.

Source: Used with permission of Robert Veech.

U.S. Patent Mar. 8, 1977

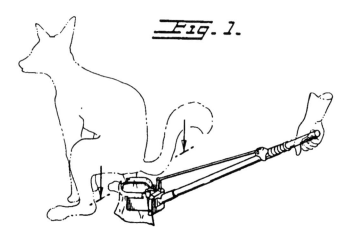

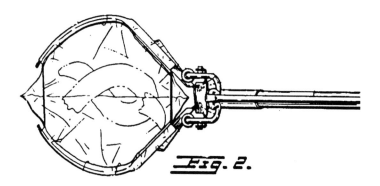

One of dozens of pooper-scoopers invented and patented over the years. This device was created by John R. Campbell and was listed as a "waste receiver for dogs." Similar devices were modeled after various litter collection tools and, in some cases, fruit pickers.

Source: Used with permission of John R. Campbell.

186

Assemblyman Lehner was allowed to proceed with his demonstration, inviting howls from the gallery.

"Any walkers without this device may be subject to criticism of their neighbors," Lehner continued explaining to the Assembly, which still refused to settle down.

"Madame Speaker," Thomas Frey of Rochester intervened, "would it be possible, my colleagues, to give attention to the speakers, please. We have to have some order in the Chamber."

"There is this one device that exists," said Lehner, taking up the cause once again with gestures to the alien object in his left hand. "There may be others."

Critics of the bill, and the pooper-scooper, couldn't resist jumping in.

"Will Mr. Lehner yield to Mr. Betros," asked the Assemblyman from Poughkeepsie who was leading the "nays" that day.

"Yes, sir."

"Did you say in your remarks this was a legislative recommendation?" asked Betros.

"Well, it more than recommends."

"Mandates?"

"Creates a violation . . . The people of this state will inevitably have to enforce this by mere pressure. The people walking dogs, without this device to have the feces removed, there will be pressure on those people with the result that there will be compliance . . . and I must say seriously, Mr. Betros, it is one of the things that annoys people more than anything else. Because of the crime problem, we end up having more and more dogs, because they use them for safety."

"Madam Speaker, will Mr. Lehner yield to another question?" asked Betros, trying to keep his high emotions within the rules of a formal hearing.

"Yes, sir," said Lehner with some reservation.

"I noticed that on lines 6 and 7 you talk about the '. . . removal of feces left by dogs on any sidewalk, gutter, street, or other public

Source: Alan M. Beck

area.' If I understand this correctly, if you were walking your dog down a street, and you were on the sidewalk—"

"I'm sorry, Mr. Betros," interrupted Amatucci again. "Will the members please sit. We will not continue with the debate until all members are sitting and the conferences are broken up around the room. Those people that wish to have a conference, please go out into the outer areas where they are permitted. It is impossible to hear in this room today. Mr. Lehner."

"I had this certified by my secretary who has a dog," posited the Manhattan Assemblyman in his defense. Betros wasn't satisfied.

"Now," continued Betros, "assume that you are walking your dog down a street and you are on the sidewalk walking your dog. If the dog chooses to go, you know, to make a deposit, so to speak, on the sidewalk, you are now in violation of the law. But if he chooses to go off the sidewalk and on the front lawn of somebody's house, you are no longer in violation of the law?"

"He probably committed a trespass, that is, on the property."

"That may be, but you don't violate the law that you are proposing. . . . Why did you limit your bill to just the public areas, why don't you—"

"The police cannot enforce—why did I?"

"Yes, sir."

"Because I don't know that the police," said Lehner, a New Yorker who had limited knowledge of front yards, "I am not sure, Mr. Betros, if they walk upon your lawn, the dogs, I don't know, and if you are not at home, if they can get a ticket. They don't know if Mr. Jones gave Mr. Betros the privilege of having his dog go up on the lawn for fertilization or other purposes, so I think it might create more of a degree of abuse, but you have to prove that the private land owner did not consent to that."

"Did you say a minute ago you thought some law would be violated?"

"I think a trespass. I know it is a civil law."

"You don't think any criminal law—I still have the floor."

"Will Mr. Betros yield to a question," interrupted Amatucci.

"No. One more question, then I will yield. I would like to know how do you differentiate—let's assume that you are walking your dog, and the fact is that it does happen on the sidewalk, and then later somebody calls the police, and the police come up. Does one have to visually observe the taking place of this particular deposit? Is there a way of differentiating a deposit from one dog as opposed to another? How do you anticipate enforcing all of this?"

"I would think, Mr. Betros, the police, for all practical purposes, would have difficulty enforcing this without a scientific device that I would not recommend them spending money on. I would think if I saw your dog doing something illegal, I can report that to the police and I would be the complainant."

"Can you tell me where we are going to preserve the evidence for the eventual trial if somebody pleads not guilty?"

". . . I think a *habeas corpus* will be needed in this particular situation."

Source: Alan M. Beck

"Can I ask you another question? Do you remember when you and I were kids, they used to call this number one and number two? What happens if it is number one, is that a violation of the law, or is it just number two?"

"Mr. Betros," Lehner answered, hinting he was losing patience with his provincial colleague who clearly didn't understand life in the Big City where people didn't even have lawns, where virtually all outdoor property was public, and where poop was more of a concern than pee, "that would be the number two bill on the agenda. This is my number one bill on dogs. This is probably my only bill on dogs. I will let you handle a number bill, one or two."

"Excuse me," said Amatucci, forcing Betros to back down. "We have a list. Mr. Pesce, you have the floor."

"Mr. Lehner, I am wondering when you became an expert on dog feces?"

"Walking around Washington Heights."

Pesce picked up where Betros had left off, insisting the proposed legislation had some serious flaws. But unlike Betros, he was not against having dog owners pick up. He would vote in favor, but he questioned the bill because those officials who would enforce this law, the Sanitation officers and the meter maids, weren't typically on duty during the early morning and evening hours when most of the evacuations took place. And in the unlikely event that dog owners were caught breaking the law, he said, bringing them to justice would "clog up the courts with debates, and if it's about whose dog is involved and whose feces this was . . ." The two men argued back and forth, with Lehner tiptoeing around the grey area of enforcement until Pesce was finally stopped in his tracks by Amatucci.

"The five minutes have expired, Mr. Pesce. If you want to sum up, it is permissible, but—"

"I am not familiar with this gadget of yours," continued Pesce, unphased by the request to wrap it up and intent on returning this debate to the nuts-and-bolts of compliance. "Will you demonstrate this?"

"I will show you," said Lehner, only too eager to comply. One would step on this."

Lehner held the device awkwardly, placing a foot on one end. Having neither dog nor doo, he used a wad of tissue paper to demonstrate. In the months to follow, he'd be performing this same mime act on the sidewalks of Manhattan to publicize the law. ("The Real Poop Sends Him for a Loop," said one paper. "See, He Was Paper-Trained.")

"Mr. Henderson, you have the floor," said Amatucci to the Assemblyman from Hornell.

"Mr. Lehner, now that you have scooped all of this, what do you do with it?"

"You put that in a trash can."

"You put that in a trash can?"

Lehner continued clumsily. He hadn't been properly trained for this and struggled shakily to collect the paper ball and then seal it inside the plastic bag. The ball and bag fell to the floor. He tried again.

"It comes apart, the bag comes apart simply—I am not mechanically inclined—it can be done simpler than that."

"How much experience have you had with this procedure?" pried Mr. Henderson.

"Excuse me, before you proceed." said Amatucci. "We cannot hear you. Please can we have some order in the Chamber."

"My secretary tried this and she advises me it works perfectly," Lehner tried to reassure the skeptics whose voices began to rise.

"Your bill does not apply to cats, does it?" asked Henderson.

"Nor does it apply to your District," Lehner answered sharply.

"That is what I am afraid of. I have had experience with dogs next door to where I live. For some reason or other they think my lawn is softer than the rest, and it does not work as easily as you are saying."

At least one person had apparently handled a pooper-scooper before and he was not impressed.

"It works easier—"

"Can you please use your mike," interrupted Amatucci.

"It works easier on cement than it does on the lawn," Lehner explained to another out-of towner ignorant of the urban landscape, "and the major offenses in the City of New York are on the sidewalk and streets. On the lawn I am advised it is more difficult because of the factors that you, as a dog owner, are aware of."

"What do you think is left on that cement once that is taken?"

"I am told it works pretty well. It is much less than if we did not have this law and device. Maybe it will not wash a dish, but it will do the job, and I am advised by science, which puts men on the moon, if we do take the leadership there will be better devices, such as vacuums and brush devices that are being considered, but this essentially does the job on cement."

The bill, and the pooper-scooper, were debated to a length that far surpassed that of the average hearing. A vote would not be taken until every possible angle had been considered. Amatucci intervened again and again, calling for order and getting some, if only until the next outbreak. As the debate dragged on, accusations of "grandstanding" were made, and several members requested that their "nays" be recorded without delay. Assemblyman Henderson asked whether dog food manufacturers might be enlisted to help "make your gadget there work better?" Lehner referred him, for reasons forgotten with the passage of time (except that he voted "nay" that day), to Louis DeSalvio of New York City who said nothing. Issues of evidence, witnesses, and intent were touched upon but never resolved. For example, leaving the scene of a crime, a member of the opposition pointed out, wasn't actually illegal so long as the dog owner could claim he'd forgotten his pooper-scooper and had every intention of running home to get it. This led George Murphy of Seaport to rise and state that he was opposed to the bill "due to a couple of technical objections." Once again, the automobile analogy would come into play. Leaving the mess on the pavement, Murphy said, was like having a "fender-bender" and then not reporting the event promptly enough. With the same sort of vaguely defined interval between an "accident" and the moment a citizen should register it with the authorities—"immediately"—Murphy said this bill "mandates that the dog owner remove the deposit, but it doesn't say *when*. . . . I don't think we ought to subject citizens to this kind of fine in such an ambiguous type situation. . . . You are calling upon some arbitrary function that he didn't intend to comply with this law, and I don't think we ought to subject our residents to that impact of the law, and therefore I withdraw my request and I vote in the negative."[†]

When Mr. Fink implored the Speaker to begin a roll call and get this matter settled with a vote so the Assembly could move on to

---

[†]The problem of how long a dog owner had to pick up would prove to be a nonissue in years to come. For example, one Sanitation officer reported to the *Daily News* in 1998 that a Coney Island woman, already some distance from where her dog had dropped a deposit, claimed she had every intention of picking up. It was just that her brother had been hit by a milk truck and she had to get to the morgue. She got a summons along the way.

other matters, Mr. DeSalvio hastily took the suggestion and spoke out of turn, only to be chastised for trying to perform a function for which the clerk alone had authorization. This debate was not over yet. David Greenberg of Brooklyn rose to request that he be "excused from voting" due to the controversial nature of this bill with which he did not wish to be associated. Then he changed his mind.

"As much as all legislators here, I find a lot of humor in the debate that we have just heard. But I also take the laws of our State very seriously, and in times like this when the public temperament is below par, they seem to be scrutinizing and evaluating the laws being passed in this Legislature now more than ever before. I feel that the people in the State are being taxed overwhelmingly now, and I think by passing a law such as this we are relieving the burden of the Sanitation Department and those who are responsible for cleaning our streets. I think we are putting that burden on the taxpayers. . . . For that reason I ask that my vote be recorded in the negative."

Attempts to kill the bill were barely offset by pleas to take the problem in New York City more seriously. Lehner claimed that a majority of residents in his Manhattan district were now in favor of having a poop scoop law—"90 percent" of his constituents had said as much on a questionnaire. If this number was accurate, and reflected the true feelings of the rest of the city, then it showed a distinct increase from the findings of that survey presented to City Council in 1972 when dog feces were shown to be a marginal concern that most New Yorkers didn't think government should waste any time discussing. The problem hadn't worsened all that much but people's perceptions of it had. Based on the new findings of a stronger commitment to the cause, appeals were made to the good nature of the residents of other cities who, though they didn't seem to care as much about their own dog problems, might at least sympathize with the horrendous predicament of New Yorkers. If only outsiders would try and put themselves into their shoes . . .

"We, in Long Island," said Armand D'Amato of Mineola, "for years have had the reputation for being called the bedroom community of New York City, and we certainly don't want to be called the bathroom, so I urge your support of this legislation."

The law, it was added, was for everyone's benefit, including the tourists from upstate who'd probably appreciate being able to get around town more easily. Some of the "nays" were, indeed, from members not opposed to having a statewide law but who thought that it should apply to all cities, not just New York.

The toughest hurdle was a constitutional one that would require some fancy footwork. Bypassing New York's City Council meant breaking the law of "home rule," which stated that municipal legislatures had the right to determine certain laws locally. If State Health Law 1310 were to be passed without Council's ratification, then it would have to apply to more than one city in New York State. All cities with populations over 400,000, it was decided, would be affected. Apart from New York, only Buffalo fit that description. This remote northern outpost that neither needed nor wanted a poop scoop law was dragged into New York's fecal fixation.

To more than a few legislators attending that day, the population rule was yet another random condition to an unsound law, a cheap trick designed to serve the needs of a few self-important New Yorkers who didn't agree with the decisions of their own local officials. Buffalo's City Council, it had to be admitted, hadn't even been given a chance to consider a poop scoop law and was being bypassed altogether. Many Assembly members resented being asked to impose decrees from afar and to fix problems that didn't concern them personally. Others voted against the bill out of genuine respect for City Councils and their right to decide on certain local matters. New York City's legislators, Mr. Pesce pointed out, had turned down the idea (in fact, Council had never even brought a bill to a vote) because "in receiving public debate it was found to be ineffective." Lehner, who still had his contraption in hand, seemed to think "it" referred to the pooper-scooper and not to the law itself and responded: "They have tried this realistically, Mr. Pesce. There are devices that are available that can be sold, and this is really a simple device, cheap, and it works . . ."

Here was an opportunity to do some City Council bashing, to let off some of the steam collected from nearly a decade of frustration over local leaders' continued refusal to take a stand on canine waste. The same window would be used in the Senate debate a month later with repeated references to "Jerome Fleischman" and "The Fleischman Pooper-Scooper Bill" that New York's City Council had avoided when Jerome *Kretchmer*, not Fleischman, made a first attempt. But anti-Council comments were not well taken. Why, asked State legislators, were they being asked to interfere in this local matter?

"Are you here on this floor," asked David Martin of Canton, appalled by the brazen move, "telling us that the City Council in the City of New York is incompetent to deal with the problem of dog waste on its streets?

"I might have put a period after the word 'incompetent,'" Lehner answered, explaining that, although Council did have "a lot of serious business and a lot of street name changes to work on," perhaps they might have turned their attention to the streets themselves. "They haven't dealt with this issue, and unfortunately, Mr. Martin, I think, unfortunately, they defaulted, and it is up to us, who deal with the issues of public health, to deal with it, and I must say at certain times I have thought in terms of abolishing the City Council."

"I am sorry, Mr. Lehner," said Martin, "but I am going to have to vote against the bill until you can show me where the City Council took up the question and failed, or due to incompetence, or whatever, did not deal with it. Because I think this is a decision that should be made locally, and it is a matter of principle with me, sir, I would like to help you out but I can't."

"I don't wish to denigrate the importance of this bill," Mr. Fink interjected, "but I would like to point out that there are nine more speakers on the list, and I am wondering if I could read off what some of the various groups around the State have said, and perhaps we could end debate on the bill. The Conference of Mayors supports it because 'the dog owners should live up to their responsibilities.' And New York City opposes it because traffic people would be overburdened. The Humane Society says 'The largest polluters in rivers are disposed diapers,' and they will come back on this bill. And the Police Conference of the State of New York has no objection."

But the debate was still not finished, and applause broke out whenever someone suggested that others be given a chance to speak. Over this long and drawn-out affair, the ultimate justification for the law—the claim that it would solve a "public health" problem—came only in passing. The dangers posed to children were mentioned but no evidence was presented. Scientific innuendos gave way to harder pleas for common decency from fellow officials who were implored to think of the welfare of their neighbors on the Hudson, or at least to consider the safety of their children, even if they didn't like New Yorkers all that much.

"Mr. Betros," said Peter Mirto of Brooklyn to his backwater peer who persisted in refusing to yield in a matter of human dignity, "in the City of Poughkeepsie that you represent, do the people walk there with their heads high or with their heads lowered?"

"We have always walked with our heads high," Betros answered defiantly.

"Well, Mr. Betros, let me inform you in the City of New York we cannot walk with our heads high. We must walk with our heads low to look from one place to another. That is why there is merit in this bill, Mr. Betros. Do you hear me, Mr. Betros?"

"From a prosecutorial standpoint, do you believe this is going to be a good and enforceable bill?" Betros went on, underestimating the power of peer pressure in New York City, as well as this New Yorker's persistence.

"Mr. Betros, this is not a crime, this is a summons, and you don't need the evidence. A summons can be handled by a Sanitation policeman or police officer in the city. It is not a crime that he has to arrest someone for. We want to walk in New York City with our head held high, Mr. Betros, so please vote for the bill."

"I think," added Mark Siegel of Manhattan, "Mr. Lehner's legislation is intelligent, creative, and should be adopted by this House because it certainly is something that is on the minds of the constituents in my district, and on some of their feet, too."

Ronald Tills of Hamburg disagreed, and at the very last minute, just before the vote was taken, slipped in one final objection.

"I am very concerned about your discrimination between dogs. And why have you forgotten the cats, the horses, the mules, and the animals being walked in the streets in the City of Buffalo and the City of New York? For that reason, Madame Speaker, I would like to be recorded in the negative."

The bill was passed by the Assembly. But Betros, and over a third of the legislators attending that day, had given firm "nays" to Lehner's pooper-scooper—and to his law.

*   *   *

One month later, the Senate debate took a less formal tone than the Assembly hearing. Polite attempts to remain true to form were a thin veil for the animosity that was almost palpable in the Senate Chamber.

"Once the kibitzers around me are quiet," opened Franz Leichter of Manhattan, the major proponent of the bill, "I want to address myself to Senator Johnson's request for an explanation."[25]

New York City, Leichter explained calmly but not with detachment, had became "one large open toilet for canine waste. You can walk around parts of the city, residential parts of the city, and the stench can be just overpowering, and you have got to zigzag your way on the sidewalk, on the streets, to avoid the dog droppings . . . you take a real risk if your kids go into a sandbox, they will come out of it smeared with dog feces. Now, in some respects, it may seem funny, and I know there have been a lot of jokes about his bill, but it is really important."

Senator Leichter went on listing the reasons for why this was a good law. New Yorkers, he said, cared more about the poop problem than they did about crime. Dogs could be trained not to go on the sidewalk. The elderly, contrary to popular opinion, would have no trouble complying with this law. Everything he said was more or less true, except for the part about the people of Buffalo wanting a poop scoop law.

"Now," he concluded, "this bill—now, if there is no negative vote, I promise to keep quiet right away."

Leichter then proceeded to demonstrate the pooper-scooper device as Lehner had done a month before but for one specific reason: to allay the fears expressed about the inability of elderly people to comply with this law. Leichter had had more time than Lehner to practice with the device and his grasp was confident. Bending over, he planned to prove, would not be necessary with a pooper-scooper.

"Senator, I have it right here," he said, trying to reassure William Conklin of Brooklyn. "Do the rules of the House permit a demonstration? Without a dog."

"Senator Pavadan, for what purpose do you rise?" asked acting President Jay Rolison.

Frank Pavadan of Queens, the Majority Leader who was unable to keep himself seated, explained that he wanted Leichter to yield for a question.

"Senator Leichter, have you finished your presentation?" Rolison asked, though Leichter had barely begun and was only just considering the ball of paper he'd dropped on the Senate floor.

The demonstration would have to wait because Pavadan had more statements than questions. First of all, he pointed out that prior rulings, based on objections raised in similar cases, had forbidden the "use of aides of this sort in the Chamber," adding, "I think we know what the thing does anyhow."

"Mr. President," Leichter implored, his heart set on having a chance to make a demonstration.

"Senator Leichter," Rolison answered.

"Mr. President," Leichter repeated.

"Senator Leichter," said Rolison once again.

Pavadan was not about to give Leichter the slack he needed to show that the elderly could comply with his law. Leichter tried to ignore the gadfly and began giving the Senate President reasons for making an exception in this case.

"Are you asking me a question?" Pavadan interrupted sarcastically, angry at having Leichter go over his head.

"I am trying to find out whether I may display this, and I want to see if you have any objection."

Then why hadn't he asked? Pavadan had already made his feelings about pooper-scooper demos crystal clear, and knowing that Leichter's question was not a question at all, he said that prior rulings should be respected and "consistency in this regard" be maintained. He was unmoved by a plea "for understanding on your part," even though Leichter saw no harm in "this innocuous little mechanism." Leichter would be forbidden from operating it because, Pavadan said, this was "a form of commercialization, and I do not think it has a place in this House."

"Then, Senator Leichter," said Rolison, "in view of the fact— Senator Leichter, that you may not use that—whatever it is . . . I do not want to use the common vernacular, which I am sure it will be referred to later on by others. The Chair regrets that ruling, Senator, but Senator Pavadan has persisted."

"I understand," said Leichter. "I will try to explain to you how it would work."

Leichter set about demonstrating the device, still in hand, verbally without actually operating it.

"You just very simply take this pooper-scooper, as it is called. You open it up by pressing the lever. You then put it over the dog dropping. You activate it by touching sort of a little lever there, and without even having to bend over or anything else, it automatically clamps shut on the dog's feces, picks it up. It is in a bag. You take the bag and you put it in the garbage can, and you have no further problem with it. You have not had to bend down. You have not had to touch it. It is all very clean and sanitary, and you have removed the offending dog feces from the street so a child is not going to fall in it, an old person is not going to step in it. Now, let me just mention, I think a factor—"

"Mr. President," interrupted Pavadan, seeing through Leichter's ruse. Will Senator Leichter yield now?"

Many reasons were given for why this was not a good law. Enforcement problems were mentioned, and questions were raised about recent violations issued by City law officers for an act already illegal, failure to "curb" a dog. How could the City be expected to enforce a new law when existing ones were being ignored? All of this led to a nasty exchange.

"My inquiry indicates that there have been none," said Pavadan, referring to the violations of the "curb" law recorded in the previous year.

"Excuse me?" asked Leichter.

"My inquiry indicates that there have been none."

"I would doubt that very much."

"Well, I asked you a question. I said my inquiry. My inquiry may not be correct nor the response to it, but in any event, I am sure we would both agree, knowing how City agencies of all sorts operate, that if it is not none, it is very few."

The "home rule" issue was also raised, and "Jerome Fleischman's" failed attempt to rally City Council. This led Leichter to say that "if we waited for the Council to act in this area or any other area, that we would be waiting until doomsday . . . and you know that the City Council is a do-nothing body." Once again, the "technical deficiencies" of the bill were brought up. Pavadan criticized the "reasonable time" stipulation for being too vague, predicting that law enforcement would take advantage of this and abuse its authority by not allowing dog owners however much time they needed to pick up. "I think we have enough harassment in the City of New York without adding that to it." And then how in the world would evidence be presented in court?

"Senator," Leichter answered, "if that is the only objection you can think of to this bill—"

"I have many."

"This must be an even better bill than I think because, Senator, with all due respect to you—"

"Point of order!" intervened Mr. Lewis of Brooklyn.

"Point of order!" seconded Mr. Galiber of the Bronx.

"The multiple points of order are well taken," said Mr. Rolison, "Now, Senator Pavadan and Senator Leichter, please. You know the rules of the House, and we are not going to have a dialogue or colloquy back and forth. Let's observe the rules of the House."

The two men volleyed to and fro despite several warnings and an objection on the grounds that it was "ridiculous that we are spending our time when two gentlemen are arguing this matter." Pavadan still had ammunition and planned to use it. He said that the City Sanitation Commissioner himself, Anthony Vacarello, had written the Senate to say that he did not have enough manpower to enforce this law and to ask that the dog problem not be dumped on Sanitation. Finally, Leichter responded to Pavadan's concern over abuse and harassment by saying that if a citizen were given some super-human time constraint for picking up, then of course the violation would be thrown out of court—which led to another deadlock.

"Senator, let me rephrase—" started Pavadan

"Let me finish," said Leichter.

"I am sorry. I thought you had."

"I submit to you, Senator, that there are enough sanitation policemen, there are enough meter maids, there are enough policemen—"

"There are enough policemen?"

"There are enough policemen."

"That is very interesting—"

John Caemmerer jumped in where Pavadan left off, hurling punches with new vigor as though this were a tag-team event.

"Then you are acting as the conscience of the City Council?" he asked.

"Senator, *touché*," conceded Leichter.

In time, Israel Ruiz of the Bronx rose to Leichter's defense, explaining in calm if not always rational terms the effects that thoughtless dog owners were having on New York City. Equating the poop problem with the urban crisis, he said:

"I think that we in the inner city must ask of people that they have to become more disciplined, more responsible, because if they don't, within the next ten or twenty years none of us will be able to live in the cities because the cities will be completely destroyed, and they will be so bad off that none of us would want to live there, so I think Senator Leichter's bill, if it is not enforceable, will at least drive the point to the dog owners that they have the responsibility to the rest of us in the City of New York."

Martin Knorr agreed, arguing not that officers would be over-burdened, but that it was a good idea to divert resources to enforcing this law because tax dollars were being wasted the way things were. "It takes away from the meter maids some of the time so that they would not unnecessarily be going around tagging parked cars, which never hurt anybody." Dogs, the Senator suggested, were clearly more of a nuisance than automobiles.

John Marchi disagreed, saying: "I represent probably the only upstate county in the City of New York, and I take serious exception to this bill. If the sponsor would amend his legislation to confine it to counties [not cities] of more than 400,000 I would gratefully vote for the bill, but under these circumstances, Mr. President, I must rush to the defense of our canine population in Staten Island."

"It is not as innocuous as Senator Auer said," added Richard Schermerhorn, referring either to the bill or to the device, "but it bothers me. First of all, we are forcing the sale of a new product . . . and, secondly, I don't think that we should set a price on it. . . . I think there should be a fine there but the fact that we are selling a product on this floor is unac-ceptable to me, and that is the reason I am voting against this bill."

As in the case of Kretchmer's—*not* Fleischman's—"commercial venture to sell pooper-scoopers," the contraption designed to pass a law and then to make it palatable to society at large actually did more harm than good that day. Bad feelings about this tool accounted for an extremely close vote, nearly sabotaging the bill.

* * *

Health Law 1310 was finally passed, though by a surprisingly narrow margin, winning by only two-thirds in the State Assembly and closely split with 31 "ayes" and 24 "nays" in the Senate. Though many upstaters failed to see the importance of this law, representatives of Manhattan were for the most part in favor. Those New Yorkers against it tended to come from the outer boroughs, mainly from Brooklyn. Four senators abstained from voting on the controversial bill and were excused. Three of these would have had to answer to voters in New York City. The fourth, James D. Griffin of Buffalo, also abstained. Alas, dog owners in both cities would be required to pick up, though they weren't required by any law to carry pooper-scoopers.

Assemblyman Lehner celebrated prematurely. "Notwithstanding the reference to the 'clumsy' user of this instrument referred to in the attached newspaper article," he wrote in a note to Governor Carey that was attached to a pooper-scooper he'd sent as a gift, "the device is quite simple to operate and I would appreciate the opportunity for a bill signing ceremony."[26] But other representatives were refusing to back down and pressured the Governor, whose support for the bill was far from certain, to veto the measure.

"Carey Won't Sidestep Bill on Curbing Dogs,"[27] the *Times* sighed with relief on June 27, a week after the bill's approval in the Senate. "Walking Tall," rejoiced another headline for a newsflash announcing gleefully that "the State Legislature has moved in where City Hall has long feared to tread." After nearly a decade of civil war, the anti-poop movement had finally won! The possibilities seemed endless. "This law could change the streets of New York. People might even start to walk with their heads up. Good for posture."[28] Most important, Governor Carey, though he was a dog owner himself, had decided after some reflection to take the side of the pro-scoopers. "I'm going to try and sign that bill without putting my foot into it,"[29] he said on that historic day. "I don't think Olmstead and Vaux, when they created Prospect and Central Park, meant they were for dogs. People have to pick and choose their way around the clumps. Some of those dogs are so big they ought to put saddles on."[30] Aware of the implications of siding with this controversial decision, Carey knew he had to show that being in favor of picking up didn't mean being a dog hater, despite the assumption still held by most animal rights groups and much of the press that this new piece of legislation came, as *New York* magazine said, as "a prime indicator of the strength of the anti-dog movement."[31] Trying to depolarize the issue, Carey made sure that New Yorkers knew he loved dogs and that his devotion to them was beyond question. He pledged to avoid a $100 fine himself by doing his civic duty whenever in town, promising that he, personally, would "take full responsibility"[32] for whatever came out of his 11-year-old Labrador retriever.

Back in New York City, people weren't exactly dancing in the streets over the good news. But many New Yorkers were immensely relieved that if ever they wanted to in the future, they'd no longer have to watch their steps. Did they, in fact, have cause for celebration? Was this long, drawn-out, treacherous affair really over? The controversial law had only narrowly entered the canon, and for the wrong reason. Why, in the end, did the State legislature finally decide that New York and Buffalo needed a poop scoop law? During the course of the debates in Albany, proponents probably learned early on that they could not fall back on the argument that aesthetic concerns were extremely important to New Yorkers, that the delicate natures of urbanites had been offended, or that dog poop was the source of a mental health problem afflicting city folk on a mass scale—the farmers would have had a field day if they'd been so honest. Instead, Leichter, Lehner, and their supporters had exploited concerns over extremely marginal "health" hazards, matter-of-factly but much more effectively than anyone had been able to do before City Council.‡ In a stroke of pure politics, and with a very slim

---

‡"As yet," said the *Times* in 1978, "no doctor anywhere has been able to document that VLM, or other zoonoses, such as leptospirosis which affects the kidneys and liver, account for truly perilous health problems." Dr. John Marr, Director of the Bureau of Infectious Diseases of the NYC Health Department agreed, pointing out that "the health issues are not the hard issues. What it boils down to is an esthetic issue."[33] The Counsel to New York State Health Commissioner Robert P. Whalen, however, took a more political stand. "The public health significance of uncontrolled feces," he wrote

file of scientific evidence, Fran Lee's campaign against *Toxocara canis* had finally paid off. But had dogs been given a fair trial? The obvious absence of outsiders who might have gainsaid the various disease theories had surely played a role in helping the bill get past Albany. Despite all the disorder in both debates, the list of invitees had been suspiciously short.[§] But some people are never happy. Even though Ms. Lee had

---

to Governor Carey in June 1977, "particularly in densely populated areas, is obvious. Such uncontrolled deposition involves the transmission to humans, primarily children, of the diseases hepatic capillariasis, larva migrans, and salmonellosis. Dog feces also facilitate the breeding of flies and present a physical hazard to humans who may slip and injure themselves." But New York's City Hall, currently occupied by Abe Beame, kept curiously silent about all this. "Please be advised," wrote the City's Legislative Representative Richard L. Rubin to Governor Carey, "that the Mayor has no recommendation with respect to said legislation."[34]

[§]The Board of Directors of the Pet Food Institute, representing a long list of big players the likes of Ralston Purina and Quaker Oats, wrote Governor Carey to question the legitimacy of Health Law 1310. "We are concerned," wrote Executive Director Duane Ekedahl, "that this bill may have been adopted without adequate debate and consideration of alternative suggestions which would be more effective in reducing the problems created by dog owners who do not properly control or clean up after their pets. When Assembly Bill 2391 was introduced in the legislature and referred to the Committee on Health, we requested an opportunity to testify in hearings when the bill was considered. However, no hearings were held, either in the Assembly or the Senate, and as a result we had no opportunity to present views on the bill. We doubt that other groups, such as dog owners, shelters, or humane societies were aware that the bill was pending or had an opportunity to present their views. . . . We would suggest that the bill would be far more enforceable, and therefore of greater benefit to the citizens of New York and Buffalo, if it focused on the problems of dog waste in the most offensive areas. . . . A number of organizations concerned with pets, including the two national humane societies, the American Veterinary Medical Association, and our own group have been active for a number of years in attempting to reduce the nuisance problems caused by uncontrolled or abandoned pets. The emphasis has been what we perceive as the most pressing problems—failure to keep pets on leash or to prevent excessive breeding. . . . By attempting to require dog owners to remove all wastes, we fear that Assembly Bill 2391 would antagonize dog owners, fail to achieve its purpose, and miss the opportunity to improve the condition of parks, beaches, and sidewalks—an important objective which is achievable. We would suggest, for this reason, that the bill be returned to the legislature for careful consideration and for hearings to which these alternatives could be explored."[35]

won, she was very angry over how long the decision had taken. The bill wasn't going to be signed until August 4. "Shocked," she wrote to the Governor via Western Union, "that all the medical material I sent you on dangers of diseases from dog feces to children prevented you from signing dog bill immediately. . . . You've allowed another hot summer to pass while children playing in the filthy sandboxes are exposed to blindness, death. . . . Dr. Cahill is aware that polio and epilepsy are carried in dog worm eggs."[36] Fran Lee, "New York's foremost fighter against dog dirt," may not have succeeded in forcing dogs to go "in the owner's bathroom," as she'd have preferred. But making it illegal, for whatever outlandish reasons, for people not to pick up in public places came as a major victory.

"The pooper law is Leichter's folly,"[37] said Sheldon Farber, a Republican Senator from Queens who'd voted against the law, suggesting to the *Westsider* that its support at home came mainly from a few wacky Manhattanites. It was, in fact, true that the "nays" tended to come only from the outer boroughs. "I am as concerned with the city's problem with canine waste as anyone, but to pass laws that will not be enforced is to create contempt for the law. I'd like to know how Senator Leichter justifies his claim that this law will be enforced when the leash your dog and curb your dog laws are not."[38]

Farber was right. Passing of the law was no guarantee of its success. In fact, the basic question of enforcement had always been what kept leaders from taking the poop scoop idea seriously. And no one had answered that question yet. "The situation presents a sticky problem," wrote Mario Cuomo, then Secretary of State, to the Governor's Counsel, "particularly when expert testimony may be required that a particular piece of evidence emanated from a particular aperture."[39] When word got out about the coup in Albany, it was predicted that the law would "have no more effect on the habits of dog owners than the law of relativity."[40] Ed Koch thought differently. All that Leichter, Lehner, and supporters had to do was push the bill through—once Koch was in power, the Office of the Mayor would see to enforcement. But was City Hall up to the challenge? A few men in Albany had gone out on a limb by endorsing a possibly unsound law that might have no practical application. Already lawmakers seemed nervous about what they'd done, and perhaps afraid of what all the controversy might do to their careers. It didn't take a political genius to see that the price for the law had been dumped on the State. Would dog owners be rioting in the streets, as one of their leaders had vowed? Making this law work would be a top priority for both Leichter and Lehner, not only for the greater cause of cleaner sidewalks and parks at home, but because failure of the law to take hold, after those ugly debates upstate, would have allowed their critics in both Chambers to say "I told you so."

The oddest part of this whole process was the decision on timing. Before Health Law 1310 even took effect, dog owners were given a full year to get used to the idea because, as the *Times* noted, they would need "time to ponder the matter."[41] It was assumed that a safe period of psychological adjustment was necessary to help the target group recover from its initial shock, overcome an emotional block, conquer a social phobia—and see the many good reasons for a law that many dog owners still believed was unfairly aimed at them. A year would also give the pooper-scooper manufacturers time to respond to the overwhelming demand expected for their products. "Since the law will not become effective until one year from the date it is approved by the Governor," wrote Assemblyman Lehner, "I am confident that there will be a wide variety of devices then available."[42] Government, too, would need time, if only to gauge the reactions of dog owners and plan accordingly.

Local responses to the state's decision ranged from mild and apathetic to severe and catatonic. One woman on West 66th Street with a bulldog named "Archie" told the *Westsider*: "I haven't started scooping yet, but when I do I'm just going to use a piece of cardboard and a baggie. Then I'm going to make it easy by telling myself I'm doing kneebends."[43] Others felt no need to pretend, deciding instead to face the task head-on without flinching. The owner of a Samoyan named "Morgan" was actually relieved to finally have a law that made it socially acceptable to scoop. "I'm going to pick up," she said. "I used to do it, but stopped because people looked at me like I was crazy."[44] But the general attitude toward this revolutionary measure was mixed, to say the least. In Greenwich Village, steps were already being taken to prepare an alternate solution in case the law—and pooper-scoopers—failed. The *Westsider* cheered "that wonder of modern technology—The Doggie Flush at 207 West 10th Street. Dogs can do nature's bidding in a 45-inch bowl that is set into the sidewalk. The owner flushes by stepping on a conveniently located valve handle. Nearby, on a window ledge above the toilet, are suppositories and biscuits that the owner can offer as a reward."[45] One can only guess at what happened to this charming addition that appeared briefly in historic Greenwich Village. As the months passed and the day of reckoning approached, dog owners wasted no time in finding other creative ways around the law. Unable to imagine the possibility of actually picking up feces, one of them decided, instead, to un-housebreak his dog. He converted his walk-in closet into a ceramic shower with a drain connected to the toilet in the next room—just as Fran Lee had wanted all along. Others took Jerome Kretchmer's advice too late and began paper-training their pets. One East Sider lined an entire room of his apartment with Astroturf as if to try and trick his golden retriever into believing it was Central Park. A dog trainer started offering special "sewer-breaking"[46] classes in the hope of reviving an old idea. And then there was the option of paying someone else, a professional dog walker, to do the dirty deed. So humiliating and revolting was the thought of complying, especially in public, that people were open to ideas.

To put their minds at rest and make the thought more palatable, a vast array of opportunists swarmed around the new law like flies around shit. The moment Health Law 1310 was passed, patent-holders, manufacturers, wholesalers, and retailers were all seeing dollar signs and they spent the next year preparing for hefty profits. "We expect to have a windfall from this law,"[47] said the owner of Fauna Foods on East 72nd Street, who planned to sell pooper-scoopers. Dog walking services, too, saw a future for the law and planned to increase their rates by as much as 40 percent due to the extra work involved in picking up after the dogs in their care. Those owners who could no longer afford their services, or who simply preferred to walk their pets themselves, would be overwhelmed by the wide selection of newly patented poop-scooping devices that came to their rescue. Dozens of bizarre, new-fangled contraptions and gizmos promised to make the experience less vile and the act more respectable. At the lower end, there was a simple pail with an extra–long-handled shovel to prevent back strain (included were a pair of barbecue tongs). More elaborate inventions included a machine that looked like an elongated bicycle pump. The operator was instructed to pull the handle and suck the offending matter scientifically into a plastic bag. For the bigger dogs, there was the "Super Dooper Pooper Scooper." Consisting of a set of gigantic crisscross metal jaws at the end of a lengthy handle—designed to keep the user at a safe distance from the poop—this would help with the gargantuan task of picking up after Great Danes. For those having extremely violent reactions to the thought of handling the feces, there were products on the cutting edge of scooping technology. One of these might have been invented by Dr. Seuss—a sleek fiberglass parabola for use on street corners and in basements, which discharged a self-cleaning flush at the touch of a foot pedal. Not only did these and so many more quirky contraptions offer ways around the problem, a pooper-scooper was viewed as a kind of *deus ex machina* arrived from the sky to rescue dog owners from their terrible fate. Wild speculation over these lifesavers, the vast majority of which would vanish not long after they had materialized, made an important assumption: perceptions had to be changed, it was widely believed, before a task so gruesome and onerous as handling dog feces would ever become a part of daily life. The devices were supposed to distract from the grizzly task at hand. In the process, pooper-scoopers were given more attention than the poop itself. In the way that some people fetishized feces, others were giving undue attention to the machines designed to get rid of it. After all, legislators had considered these machines crucial both to passing the law and to making it work.

The technological boom, however, was very short-lived and the pooper-scooper bubble soon burst. Eventually the more affluent or style-conscious pet owners would solve their problems with simple but expensive designer plastic bags that came with and without wrist attachments. These attractive items had names like the "Poshy Quick Curb Bag" and were often done up in bright colors to distract from the obvious. In a town where being seen with the right shopping bag can be crucial to one's social survival, these helped to glamorize an inelegant act and to make the users feel more confident about lowering themselves in public. Meanwhile, average dog owners on the street decided they didn't need custom-made bags or any of the dazzling inventions flooding the market. They settled for old grocery bags, newspapers, magazines, even cardboard shirt inserts from the drycleaners. But not in the beginning. The possibility of picking up with whatever happened to be lying around the house assumed a nonchalance toward scooping, a desensitized attitude that would not set in for some time yet.

Pooper-scoopers, whether they were complicated or home-made, sexy or Spartan, expensive or free-of-charge, wouldn't solve every problem attached to the new law. Assuming the matter could be successfully bagged, another concern that manufacturers addressed was the still unanswered question of what, exactly, to do with the unwholesome mess once it was in hand. Koch had warned dog owners that they would not, under any circumstances, be allowed to burden the Department of Sanitation by filling public waste receptacles with feces. They cringed at the thought of being forced to carry home a smelly parcel in the backseat of a cab, or to endure the disgusted looks of their neighbors as they boarded crowded elevators in high-rise apartment buildings with something offensive. One company tried to exploit this fear with a proactive solution called "Minus." This supposedly harmless substance could be added to a dog's food and would miraculously deodorize its stool. Another company began manufacturing a "low residue" dog food, starting a trend that would last to the present day. This questionable advance guaranteed hard and round deposits that would be more convenient to collect. "A gastrointestinal work saver," praised *New York* magazine, "it makes the end product of digestion small, compact, and eminently graspable."[48] Nutrition and sanitary convenience, it seemed, were equally important. What did it matter if dog food was made of chicken beaks and claws, pig tails and snouts, cow hoofs and ears—sometimes even other dogs—so as long as everything came out alright?

What about those dog owners who were physically unable to pick up, even if they didn't mind the idea all that much? While his colleagues quibbled over the nitty-gritty details of the law, Senator Leichter saw these as unnecessary red tape and dismissed his critics as "absurd nitpickers."[49] Nonetheless, certain exceptions had to be made. The blind, naturally, would not be expected to pick up after their Seeing Eye dogs. And what about the elderly and the paraplegic? Senator Farber of Queens lambasted Leichter for his lack of foresight. "In his own myopia," he told the *Westsider*, "Senator Leichter fails to see that the handicapped and the aged will have just as much difficulty complying with the law as the blind"[50]—to which Leichter was quick to respond: "There are devices that enable one to pick up canine waste without bending over."[51] The vast majority of dog owners, Leichter insisted, would have no exemption. Unless they were blind, they would need to comply, no matter how awkward the task and whether they liked it or not. If they resisted, offenders would risk being caught leaving the scene of their crime and then face heavy fines and perhaps prison sentences. Mayor Koch was, in fact, already amassing a standing army to enforce the law. Police officers, Sanitation enforcement officers, and meter maids were said to be joining forces and gearing up for confrontations with renegade pet fanciers. Also enlisted were the already overburdened staffs of the Departments of Parks and Recreation, Health, Housing, and Air Resources. All officers were authorized to issue summonses and were warned to expect the very worst from dog owners.

* * *

While leaders were working out the tiniest details of the law and summoning legions to enforce it, they lost sight of the bigger picture. So thrilled were they over this bold new step for mankind, and so focused on the task before them, that they failed to ask themselves an important question: What would life be like in a post-poop world? Maybe it would be a little cleaner. But besides the hostility this campaign was bound to stir up in an already tense population, the most serious pet-related concern had been forgotten: What effect, if any, might the law have on the city's stray dog problem?

The number of strays roaming New York, either alone or in packs, was currently estimated at approximately 400,000 (about the human population of Buffalo), though it was difficult to determine exactly. Unlike the presence of feces on sidewalks, this was a legitimate health problem, and it hadn't been solved. If the poop scoop law would have little effect on the city's health or environment, then what effect might it have on the dogs? ASPCA officials had warned all along that it could not support a canine waste law because this would, in their opinion, lead to the "wholesale abandonment" of dogs across the metropolitan area. Rather than perform such a demeaning task as handling feces, the owners were said to be ready to set their animals free and let the City—or rather, the overburdened ASPCA—take full responsibility. As a result of the poop scoop law, said the ASPCA, the streets might become filthier than ever. Senator Leichter was flabbergasted. "Are you going to tell me," he asked the *Westsider*, "that instead of cleaning up after Fido people will just throw him out? I don't believe that."[52] Nonetheless, the ASPCA cautioned leaders that New York's devotion to its four-legged friends would only go so far. "There is no doubt that many people will just get rid of their dogs," said one ASPCA spokesperson. "And we are concerned." Why hadn't lawmakers foreseen this scenario? "If we don't win our fight with the City for funds," she warned, "we won't be able to handle the existing number of strays. This added burden will be a real problem. As far as I know the ASPCA has not been consulted regarding the Pooper Law. And as the increase of strays will be our problem I think we should have been."[53] For many years, the ASPCA had, indeed, been denied the money it needed to handle the city's stray problem in an efficient and humane way. And now it seemed that a new law was about to make its job more difficult than ever. What was government thinking? By the time that the mandate went into effect, the ASPCA was about $1 million in debt. Each year into the law, it would lose roughly another $250,000. By the mid-eighties, the ASPCA would be forced to shut three of its five shelters. The remaining two facilities, overcrowded and run by skeleton crews, would be balancing on the brink of bankruptcy.

On several occasions in years to come, the ASPCA would tire of pleading for extra funds and would plan to stage a strike instead, as it had already threatened to do if the situation didn't improve. In fact, while the poop scoop bill was still being debated in Albany, Director Duncan Wright had announced that the ASPCA was quitting. The first humane organization in America would resign, he said, and stop rounding up stray animals, a thankless task it had been performing since 1894. Citing a critical lack of funding and misplaced priorities, Wright said: "If the only program the city can think of is to pick up animals and exterminate them then they'd better find another boy. If all they want is a slaughterhouse then to hell with them."[54]

CHAPTER 10

No More Mr. Niceguy: The Final Confrontation

"I don't care if it's good luck to step in it. I don't want to."

—Ed Koch[1]

July arrived and the air was electric with predictions of how different life would be in just another month. But optimism over the poop
scoop law's enlightening effects was tempered by critics who found
reasons for doubting its usefulness. Dog-walking moods only darkened
as that long-awaited day drew nearer. Koch showed no signs of backing
down, despite the many symptoms of resistance over the previous year.
The hard-nosed mayor continued to view the law's justification as self-
evident and its enforcement as a can-do, though he did make gestures to
the dog-owning community to soften the blow and avoid appearing as a
cold-hearted scoundrel. "I love dogs," he said a few days before the law
was scheduled to go into effect. "I even had one once. But I've stepped
into their stuff enough times to know what a problem it is to people in
this city."[2] Many New Yorkers were, indeed, very upset about the mess
and the inconvenience. But was it fair, or even realistic, to expect a
simple law to be a peaceful settlement of what had proven over the years

to be a terribly complex and divisive issue? Across the city, a mixture of glee over victory and dismay at defeat added to an atmosphere thick with ambivalence over how, exactly, this decree would be received in a town with so many radically different points of view on everything under the sun.

Hinting at this complexity, an episode of *Saturday Night Live*[3] featured a sketch that was as hilarious to some as it was disturbing to others. "Mr. Bill Visits New York City" showed the famous little boy made of playdough walking down a city sidewalk with his faithful clay companion, Spot. As the tiny yellow dog prepares to squat and do his business, Mr. Bill reflects: "I'm sure glad you don't do it on the rug anymore." But before Spot can make a mess on the pavement, Mr. Bill's nemesis, the local bully called Sluggo, appears to tell him that dogs are no longer allowed to soil the walkways. "Go where, huh?" asks a perplexed Mr. Bill as Sluggo points to a sign that reads: "Leash, Gutter, and Clean Up After Your Dog, Please." Mr. Bill has no choice. It's either get his dog off the curb or end up on the sidewalk with a black eye. He watches helplessly while his best friend is placed in the gutter by two giant intervening hands.

Then the laugh track goes wild. "Oh no-o-o-o!" cries Mr. Bill as a car drives by and flattens Spot into a little yellow pancake. "New law says you have to clean up after your dog," say the forces of law and order as their giant hands intervene again, this time with a pooper-scooper to scrape the offensive animal matter off the street.

Was this law really so unfair and heavy-handed? Might it actually be harmful to pets? Whatever one's point of view, waiting to find out was causing quite a stir. In the middle of the commotion, had anyone stopped to ask poor Buffalo how it felt about all this? Unlike those high-strung New Yorkers who were making all the hoopla over poop, upstaters weren't in the least bit jubilant or alarmed. In fact, Buffalo didn't give a shit. Having been dragged into the conflict, a tale of two cities that didn't concern his own in the least, Mayor James D. Griffin expressed no interest whatsoever in the cleanup mandate soon to be imposed from afar. Buffalo's SPCA confirmed this utter lack of concern.

Source: Alan M. Beck

As August 1 drew nearer, Mayor Griffin was asked by New York City's Department of Health what measures he had taken to ensure compliance. "If you don't know, don't give me a call,"[4] he answered.

New York City dog owners couldn't afford to be blasé like their apathetic neighbors to the north. This new law was aimed at them and they knew it. As the dreaded day edged uncomfortably close, many of them started losing sleep. They imagined their enemies lining the sidewalks to push them off. Hordes of dog haters across the city, they feared, would finally be in a position to take their revenge. Eventually, they thought, their dogs might be taken away, as Cleveland Amory had predicted. Every neighbor they'd ever told to piss off for complaining about their pets; every neurotic parent worked up over Fran Lee's predictions of doom; every self-appointed nut who'd screamed them off the lawns, out of the playgrounds, and into the gutter—they'd all be ready and waiting in legions, breathing down their necks and trying to humiliate them in public. On the sidewalks, anyone with a leash would become a suspect. In the parks, any dog without one would be condemned without a trial. One false move and they'd be reported to one of the 6,470 enforcement officers standing by in a state of orange alert. Little did anyone know that, within the first year, the number of poop police would increase to a mind-boggling 22,000.

Bracing themselves for a storm of retribution, many dog owners opted, if not to collect their pets' excretions, to limit their movement altogether on August 1 when the law went into effect. There were no riots, despite Max Schnapp's threat of a mass uprising. On the contrary, an eerie stillness descended upon the city that morning. Sidewalks and parks were conspicuously shy of dogs. Many of the owners seemed to be avoiding public places. At Park Terrace on 218th Street, they were bringing their pets to the rooftop rather than deal with their enemies on the sidewalks and be forced to dig the mess from the gutter. But not everyone in the city had rooftop access. Dog owners in other neighborhoods cowered in dark apartments, knowing that their pooches would have to go out at some point. Some bit the bullet and did as they were told. They bent over, under the glaring eyes of their neighbors, picked up, and tried to get on with their lives. Others popped out briefly, trembling and paranoid, let their pooches relieve themselves, then speedily dragged them back indoors without cleaning up. On the Upper West Side, walkers were observed running nervously along Riverside Drive as they clutched homemade cardboard scoopers (the stores had sold out of all the patented devices the night before). They were said to be using them only when police officers were watching. Others hiked great distances to try out the only two doggy comfort stations in town. One facility was on West 10th Street. The other was on West 43rd in front of Manhattan Plaza, the home to a number of famous actors, actresses, and playwrights that was drawing more attention than usual that morning. On nearby 39th Street, a man described as having hair as red as his two Irish setters was hurrying to make an appearance but one of his dogs apparently didn't quite make it. He tried, briefly, to collect the mess from the sidewalk but gave up and was last seen traveling east. Later that day, "Toto" from the Broadway musical *The Wiz* was successfully escorted to the experimental "dog toilet" on 43rd where he was made to rest his paws in wet concrete to dedicate the doggy latrine. But when he sniffed at the hole in the sidewalk, he decided that he wasn't interested. Nor were any of the other dogs that made the pilgrimage that day.

After a full year of reflection, many dog owners still took scooping as a hard pill to swallow. Across the city, they left their pets' mess on the ground because they saw no other option. In Brooklyn Heights, the stronghold of the Dog Owners Guild that had fought so fiercely against the law's passage, people were choosing to keep their animals indoors for most of the day. Occasionally someone was seen dashing down the front steps of a brownstone, rushing a dog to the curb, then running back upstairs and bolting the door before neighbors could raise any objections to their doing business as usual. One Bay Ridge resident was seen picking up but not without protest. He couldn't afford a pooper-scooper and used a political campaign poster with a picture of Governor Carey! In Queens, people tended to be less upset on the whole about poop. Obeying the law in that borough seemed to be a matter of personal choice. Those who complied did so without drama. Those who refrained didn't bother looking over their shoulders. In the Bronx, a woman reluctantly decided to pick up rather than pay a $25 to $100 fine. But she said she planned to dump the mess in a public wastebasket no matter what Koch had said. "They don't have enough people to pick up after we pick up," noted the member of the Bronx County Kennel Club. "I don't blame people if they put it in a trash can. Then what?"[5] In other neighborhoods, dog owners were reported walking their pets in cemeteries just to avoid being forced into picking up. "There aren't going to be too many people around a cemetery to follow you and say 'Clean up after your dog,'"[6] said one Community Board member. No place was sacred.

The vast majority of confrontations, however, were staged on the isle of Manhattan, where one member of the resistance movement called the law "the stupidest thing in the history of the city."[7] This man was not about to lower himself to the gutter. "If I see the cops around," he said, "I'll just pull back on the leash until they go away and then let Ralph continue to do what he's been doing for six years."[8] Another Manhattanite said she would most definitely *not* be cleaning up after her German shepherd, her standard poodle, or her large mixed-breed dog. Unable to embrace the logistics of such a daunting operation, she said: "I can't. If I had to do that I'd need a forklift."[9] In Greenwich Village, where dog owners were particularly belligerent, one woman was threatened with citizen's arrest for not scooping by a foul-mouthed man in a passing van. She returned a few of those guttural *bons mots* for which New Yorkers are famous when they're riled. Then, on a higher note, she told the press she planned "to read Thoreau to my cocker spaniel and teach her civil disobedience."[10]

Rebellion across Manhattan was widespread and couldn't be traced to any particular group or special type of dog owner. Although many people were, in fact, complying with the law, many others seemed to share an aversion to handling feces and a feeling that the measure was unfair. This attitude was encountered in a variety of neighborhoods and defied all the socioeconomic indicators. Even the more conservative New Yorkers, it seemed, didn't want to cooperate with what they saw as an unreasonable request and they were willing to be called menaces

Source: Alan M. Beck

to society, or even go to jail if necessary. "Elegant Dirt," read a *Times*[11] headline for a story reporting that "the greening of Park Avenue will require special help: the islands are covered with a bumper crop of litter and canine waste."[12] The poop scoop law was making even effete Upper East Siders into anti-socialites. Rather than face curbside harassment, they were taking their chances against the traffic and heading for those islands in the middle of Park Avenue, once sanctuaries to tulips, grass, and the occasional sculpted hedge. "The proper and privileged people of Park Avenue, rather than pick up after their pets on the streets, have turned the islands into a dog run."[13] Each day they grew bolder in their disdain for a petty-minded law. "It can't be blamed on lower-class culture shock," said the *Times*. "The shock is the view from upstairs windows."[14]

Politicians were out in scores on that first day to try, against all odds, to nip any insurgency in the bud. On hand to monitor the law's effect, or perhaps to make sure that it had some, was Sanitation Commissioner Anthony Vaccarello, the man who only recently had called New Yorkers "slobs." He was keeping watch on Central Park West when a woman emerged from the park with her toy Dalmatian and a summons she'd just received from a friendly ranger. When Vaccarello asked her if she planned to start obeying the law, she answered: "Sure, and I'll use this to scoop it up."[15] Dealing with dog owners wasn't going to be easy. Standing by to help fend off the sarcasm were Senator Leichter and Assemblyman Lehner, also stationed at the western border of the park. Both wore Bide-A-Wee t-shirts—from the only humane organization to back the law officially—and gave out handbills detailing what, exactly, dog owners had to do. According to witnesses, an elderly man approached the two statesmen and shouted "I always cleaned up!"[16] The senior citizen felt the law was insulting and paternalistic. Why, he asked, weren't leaders out protecting him from all the muggers running off-leash in the park? Senator Leichter, who didn't believe the old man had any intention of picking up, was said to have suggested he trade in his cane for one of those newfangled pooper-scoopers, to which the man replied, limping away with his faithful companion: "I carry this cane to protect myself from the criminals you do nothing about."[17]

Contrary to Senator Leichter's suspicions, many dog owners were, in fact, complying with the poop scoop law on that groundbreaking inaugural day. Though counting them was impossible, "most," according to some accounts, were already doing as they were told. In time, others would take their example, though not without a struggle and a profound change of mind. Within a few months, the *Times* reported "Gadget Boom Seems Over,"[18] a sign that people were learning to perform the onerous task casually and no longer feeling they needed all the fancy gear—or had some of them given up on the idea altogether? Many dog owners, too embarrassed today to admit how many years they spent resisting the law, hadn't the slightest intention of giving in. They made up a significant portion of the pet-owning population who still believed the law was unfair. For a time, their stand continued to draw strong support from animal rights leaders and humane organizations, and by many dogless New Yorkers who sympathized with their plight and agreed that the measure was a smokescreen for political ambitions and anti-dog agendas. Who was government trying to kid? Even if every single dog owner in town could be made to pick up one day, that wasn't going to cure all of the city's ills. On the contrary, the new law was causing some disturbing social problems in these early months, and might actually work against New York's recovery. In many neighborhoods, having the law was creating more tension than *not* having it. After years of thinly veiled hostility on the sidewalks, a new kind of directness had been unleashed. As soon as government gave the go-ahead, people were practically at each others' throats. Dog owners were trailed everywhere they went, and left alone only if their dogs defecated. They were expected to prove to onlookers that they had planned to pick up all along. If they refused to pick up or to back down, an argument ensued and the screaming could be heard from blocks away. Often these rows became physical, with harsh words leading to clenched fists and an escalation of violence. One year into the law's enforcement, the sidewalk situation had grown so unpleasant that one prominent dog owner decided he'd had enough of the city's anti-poop vigilantes and was taking his put-upon pooch to live where people were more animal friendly. "Sandy," the dog who co-starred in the Broadway musical *Little Orphan Annie*, was moving to the suburbs of Glen Rock, New Jersey, in protest of the law. The pup who'd warmed the hearts of millions, who'd had personal meetings with Nixon and Kissinger, was leaving New York because of the unwholesome atmosphere created when this whole sordid affair began. "When they started enforcing the litter law," said the dog's owner and trainer Bill Berloni, "I had to think about the effects of bad publicity if Sandy were to be given a summons for littering. It's not that I disagreed with the intent of the new law, it's just that I didn't want to put up with it, and for some reason, Sandy hates the sight of a pooper-scooper—it upsets him."[19]

Who could have predicted that New Yorkers would go so far in their defiance of the poop scoop law? And who could have known that unofficial cops would break so many other laws just to enforce this one? People were angry on both sides of the curb. Some dog owners were willing to go to whatever extremes they felt were necessary to protect their right to keep animals, and to live in dignity while doing so. Meanwhile, their pursuers did whatever they could to shame or threaten them into compliance. Was the prospect of pristine pavement really worth all the trouble this was causing? The tension on the streets was palpable. A measure that was intended to avert what was being called a "civil war" over dogs seemed to be having the opposite effect. The staunchest supporters of the new law believed that all the ugliness and unneighborly acts were unavoidable parts of the process. "Meaner Streets, Cleaner Streets,"[20] reasoned the *Times* in 1984, referring to a Scorsese film in which mafia thugs, by applying ruthless pressure, were always able to get what they wanted. The questionable means, it was widely believed, would be justified by the end result. Average New Yorkers were, indeed, helping to bring about change by making the streets and parks a little cleaner, and some of them were having a lot of fun doing it. For the more seasoned vigilantes, getting after those self-centered dog owners became a full-time sport. Was this what Koch was aiming for?

"Peer pressure" was a nice way of saying government-backed vigilantism. By pushing private citizens to take a leading role in enforcing the law, Koch had managed to tap into the endless rage of New Yorkers who had passed through the ordeal of the 1970s. He had breathed new life into "community participation," that buzzword from the Lindsay era. He had also created a monster. Unlike the more positive acts of civil resistance in recent years of peaceful demonstration and open discussion, Koch's campaign was fueled by mean-spiritedness and a do-it-or-move-to-Russia mentality. Actively encouraging civil unrest and often brutal opposition, turning neighbor against neighbor, fanning the flame of bad feelings between dog lovers and their critics, diverting the rage that New Yorkers felt after two decades of nerve-wracking urban decay, forcing people off the curb and perhaps out of the city—this strategy didn't seem like a good formula for restoring health and sanity to a town that had just stepped back from the brink of disaster. Then there was the effect that an ongoing civil war might have on public safety, a scenario that should have made the thought of having dirty walkways seem a petty concern. Not only could the controversial law fail to solve the poop problem, as similar laws had failed in other major cities, there was evidence that the plan was backfiring and causing an explosion of the stray dog population. If pet-related problems were really as important as some people were making them out to be, this could put off New York's recovery for years to come, scaring away investors and businesses, and making the trend toward "white flight" irreversible. New York could end up like Detroit.

Who would take the blame if this promising new law didn't solve all of New York's problems?

* * *

The poop scoop law had another effect that one of its leading critics had predicted all along. The ASPCA reported that, in the first three weeks since the law had been in effect, the number of dogs abandoned had doubled. This figure, like most estimates made in these chaotic times, should be taken with a large grain of salt. But the numbers shouldn't be written off. Overall abandonment was said to have increased by 25 percent in the first few months of the law, a suspiciously round figure but one that commands attention. The total number of dogs admitted to some shelters was said to have tripled. It seemed that those pet owners who weren't arguing on the sidewalks or begrudgingly picking up from the gutter were letting their animals, even the expensive pedigrees, loose to take their chances on the streets against the cars, trucks, and buses, as well as the ASPCA, which vowed to at least try and pick them up but not their droppings. How could this have been? Was scooping really such a big deal, after all?

At the risk of raising the specter of a feud that nearly tore New York apart, one might at least consider the other side. It was probably true that anyone who preferred to throw out a best friend rather than dispose of its waste products never should have had a dog in the first place. But if it's permissible to play devil's advocate for a moment, then it's possible to believe that the ASPCA was just doing its job by opposing the poop scoop law. In the view of animal rights advocates, *anything* that encouraged people to get rid of their otherwise well-treated pets was unacceptable. After all, weren't dogs better off living in safe homes where they were fed and walked than starving on the streets where they roamed until meeting some violent death? The ASPCA, unlike those dog owners who refused to keep their pets because picking up bothered them too much, apparently didn't have the heart to give up on the city's animals and didn't resign as promised. This was a dirty job but someone had to do it. Since the law had been in effect, their job had become dirtier than ever and repercussions were felt throughout the entire metropolitan area. Those fair-weather animal lovers who didn't dump their pets on the streets of New York City or on the doorstep of the ASPCA were schlepping theirs all the way to fields in Westchester County where they thought the poor things might stand a better chance of surviving. The Central Westchester Humane Society reported that it was filled beyond capacity.

Had the ASPCA been right all along to oppose the poop scoop law? However difficult it is to believe that someone would throw away a dog rather than pick up after it, many of the owners who showed up at the shelters admitted that they simply weren't up to the task. Others claimed "we're moving," "we're allergic," "the apartment's too small," or "we got new carpeting." The ASPCA knew better. "We know it's because they didn't want to pick up after the dog,"[21] said a spokesperson. While shelters in and around New York struggled under the added burden, other cities looked on with horror at the scenes of betrayal. But not everyone blamed the dog owners for these acts of cruelty. Some faulted the poop scoop law, instead, for forcing people to give up their beloved companions.

"He was old and the small, black dog had been his for 14 years," read a heartbreaking story in the *Washington Post*. "It was hard, painful for him to stoop over in the street to clean up after the dog, he said, and living on a fixed income he couldn't afford the fines under the new law. So, his dog would have to go. Tears streaming down his face, the man signed the destruction slip with a shaking hand and quickly shuffled out, leaving the dog with the woman at the American Society for the Prevention of Cruelty to Animals. 'He'd had that dog for 14 years and you could tell it was well-taken care of,'"[22] said an ASPCA worker.

The rise in abandonment after the poop scoop law went into effect, however large or small, was a good reason for both sadness and shame. The ASPCA and other shelters under the added strain often had no choice but to exterminate the vast majority of the dogs they received. But while the gruesomeness of these developments cannot be measured in mere numbers, the suffering of these animals might have been reduced, and their final moments made less brutal and traumatic, if only there'd been more money. The ASPCA had been in serious financial trouble for years before the canine waste law arrived. Successive directors had begged for additional funding and, with rare exceptions, their pleas were denied. Another increase in the dog license fee might have helped to dig the ASPCA out of debt, and to ensure that animals under its care were treated more humanely. But the increase was slow in coming. Just before the poop scoop law went into effect, Governor Carey had signed another decree to revise the existing licensing laws and increase fees in order to better fund the shelters. Not since 1973 had the city's fee been increased, even though many dog owners said they'd be happy to pay more if it meant improving the shelter system and reducing the animal population in some humane and thoughtful way. Finally Albany had approved an increase, which might have been good news for local dogs except for one problem: New York City had its own licensing procedures. As in the case of imposing a canine waste law, it would have been up to local leaders to increase the fee. But unlike that daring initiative taken to resolve the fecal dilemma, no progress was made because no one wanted to go to Albany and break the law of home rule. As a result, many cities in the state *except* New York benefited from this humane measure.

Koch continued throughout the eighties to keep a critical eye on the ASPCA's performance. Mismanagement and improprieties were, indeed, exposed. The ASPCA was having problems. But wasn't this a bit like blaming the poor for being poor? Was it possible, by some wild stretch of the imagination, that the City's dogcatcher was being used as a scapegoat? After all, the Koch administration was trying to rebuild New York and had other problems on its plate. An animal cruelty scandal might have worked against these efforts. Koch did finally approve an additional $1.7 million for the ASPCA. But this apparently wasn't enough to make up for the years of bad press the shelters had received while government was spared the embarrassment. Allegations of mismanagement weren't unfamiliar to the old and battered organization. But in the process, alternative sourcing efforts were all but crippled by a scandalous reputation that made independent fundraising extremely difficult. The ball was in City Hall's court. Any help would have to come from the government. One official dealing with the ASPCA is said to have intimated that, no matter how much help the City did or didn't provide, written into the ASPCA's original charter was a duty to round up stray dogs no matter what—which simply was not true. On the contrary, the stray animal population had always been, technically, the City's own responsibility. As in the reliance upon "peer pressure" to keep the streets clean, this was a classic case of transferring the responsibilities of government onto others. The fiscal crisis was a good excuse—but only for as long as it lasted. According to Stephen Zawistowski of the ASPCA, the failing humane organization that the City leaned upon to fix its pet problems would be forced to operate on a budget that, as late as the 1990s, would still allocate just 30 percent of what other major cities devoted per capita to stray animals.[23] This situation would go unchanged, and long after New York had become prosperous again. The local licensing fee would not be increased at all until 1997. By that time, however, the ASPCA had already resigned, and for good. Government was benefiting from the extra revenue.

One possible effect of having given all the attention to the poop scoop law was a bit less negative, though not entirely positive. Oddly enough, the stray problem in New York City, despite the ASPCA's deteriorating state and its inability to handle the job, was said to have improved in the years after Health Law 1310 went into effect. Like any estimate of the city's animal population, the ASPCA's latest claim was vague, difficult to substantiate, and thus very much open to wishful thinking. But following the brief increase in the rate of abandonment that was also said to have occurred in the months following August 1, 1978, the situation had supposedly stabilized to a small degree. If this was true, then it made perfect sense. Most dog owners who had cared enough about scooping to throw out their pets were promptly eliminated from the game. By 1982, the steady decline in the city's animal population that shelters were claiming based on intake was a mixed blessing that would have come largely in response to the poop scoop law. After picking up became a legal duty rather than a courtesy, people were probably thinking twice about buying or rescuing dogs. The heated controversy surrounding them, and the harsh treatment their owners would have to endure each time they took them out for their walks—whether or not they planned on picking up—became important considerations when making the decision to have a furry friend. More than ever before, keeping a dog in the city meant making a solid commitment. At least until the law became a more normal part of daily life and sidewalk relations calmed down, that doggy in the window was priced a little high. The poop scoop law did not, as its critics had warned all along that it might, lead to an outright ban on dogs. But it might have, indirectly, impacted the pet population and made the stray problem a hint more manageable in these early years, though no less shameful than it had been before cleaning up was viewed as a central part of responsible animal care.

* * *

Whatever facts or fictions were behind the official estimates, the nation's first humane organization continued its downward spiral while Koch kept getting tougher on poop. In this way, government remained faithful to a long tradition of favoring human "health" issues over humane concerns. In response, a contingent of dog owners and their leaders decided that fighting for better treatment of animals meant fighting *against* the poop scoop law.

Much of the rebellion came, like the passage of the law itself, in the more civilized setting of the courts. Max Schnapp, the leader of POPA who had threatened a mass uprising of dog owners if a poop scoop law were ever passed, was among the first to challenge the law on the grounds that it was "unconstitutional."[24] Schnapp claimed the law "denies due process; violates municipal home rule; is unreasonable, arbitrary and capricious; and creates hardship and injustice for dog owners."[25] He said that "dogs' feces is no more harmful than chipmunks',"[26] declaring: "Dog dirt on the streets is good but the law is bad."[27] He also expressed a deep concern over the new wave of "vigilanteeism."[28] But his objections fell upon deaf ears. In *Schnapp vs. Lefkowitz*, the opposition argued: "With an estimated 600,000 dogs in the City of New York making their daily contributions, it is doubtful whether anyone these days could 'trip the light fantastic' on the sidewalks of New York, or in the streets or gutters, either." A Supreme Court judge agreed, ruling that the law would be not only helpful to humans, but beneficial to their pets. The law, he told the *Times*, "reduces the hazards the dog must confront in its diurnal and nocturnal peregrinations about the city."[29]

Other reasons were found for challenging the law's legality. One case was filed by a group of Orthodox Jews who claimed the law violated their religious freedom because they were forbidden from scooping on the Sabbath. A judge ruled that anyone capable of walking on a holy day could also bend over and pick up. "The sacred cow may wander without let or hindrance and leave its dung on the streets of India," read the decision. "Whatever the claims of religion, in the name of individuality and of liberty, the dogs may not do so on the streets of New York and Buffalo." Sanitation, it seemed, was the more sacred duty. "Since cleanliness is next to godliness, it is doubtful whether an all-seeing deity would approve the desecration of public places in the name of orthodoxy."[30] Another case involved a loophole in the law. A judge ruled that there would be no legal distinction between a dog's "owner" and "walker." Both would have to scoop. Still other questions surfaced about the practical details. What, exactly, did it mean to "remove" feces from the sidewalk, street, gutter, or grass? How far were dog owners being expected to travel once armed with the putrid parcel? And was it fair to forbid them from unloading it into the nearest public waste receptacle?

While these questions were tackled in the courts, individual dog owners faced the wall of retribution on the street. Against them stood not only the overly zealous vigilantes, but the legions of hired hands that Koch had engaged to defend public places. Perhaps to lighten the load of law enforcement, Koch soon changed his mind about disposal and told dog owners they'd have the privilege of using the trash cans that their tax dollars were paying for, provided their deposits were sealed securely in plastic bags. In order to minimize friction and hostilities, he instructed his army to issue only warnings in the first few months, not summonses. Not all dog owners appreciated the gesture. Many continued to dodge the law unless reminded, and even then some still refused. As time passed, law enforcement's job became more, not less, frustrating. There were no two ways about it. Dealing with uncooperative pet owners was going to be extremely unpleasant, not to mention bad for community relations. Who would be willing to take on such a dastardly task? Early on, meter maids, among the most highly paid and uppity of law enforcement officials, turned down a job they felt was beneath them. On the contrary, the NYPD did take part in the campaign, though only for the first two months, at which point cops stepped back and tried to blend in with the crowd. Pat Livingston complained to the *Times* in 1978 that "a lot of police officers don't consider it a problem for them to handle, despite instructions from the Mayor."[31] But public relations were still a bit shaky since an officer named Serpico had gone to the papers with tales of widespread police corruption. The Department didn't need any more bad press. Besides, officers on the beat had earned a reputation for looking the other way at dog problems, and maintaining these good community relations seemed to be the priority.

With no one left to take the job, Sanitation enforcement officers, whom nobody liked anyway, got stuck with most of the burden of making people respect Health Law 1310 in years to come. Known for their rough manner and intrusive methods—they spend much of their time sifting through public wastebaskets for names and addresses of local residents who dump their household trash into them—even these shady characters were learning to treat dog owners with kid gloves. Norman Steisel, the new Sanitation Commissioner, saw the error of his predecessor who had called New Yorkers "slobs" and announced his department's change of plan. "One reason the public response was slipping," he said, "is that the Sanitation Department was not working well—we've got to do our jobs before we start calling dog owners slobs."[32] To help him do his job, Koch transferred 80 of the 140 Sanitation officers to full-time dog-watching assignments, but was harshly criticized for making this move at a time when the Department didn't even have the resources to empty wastebaskets regularly. "What explanation is there for this bizarre order of priorities?" someone asked in a letter to the *Times*.[33] The total number of Sanitation workers had, in fact, dropped from 10,800 to 8,700 between 1975 and 1979. After a few months of issuing milquetoast warnings, officers were instructed to shift gears and go straight to the ticketing. "In February," Koch said in a press release, "I decided that people had had enough time to familiarize themselves with the law, so I ordered that warnings be discontinued and that summonses be issued to all violators."[34] But for taking this no-more-Mr.-Niceguy approach, and for taking part in a plan to humiliate law-breaking dog owners by publishing their names, addresses, and photographs in the papers, enforcers came off as bullies. "It takes two cops to arrest one dog?"[35] asked a perplexed dog owner who was shown in the *Times* with his 12-year-old Lab, flanked on both sides by grinning Sanitation police. "But I haven't left the park yet!"[36] Peter Richter of East 96th Street protested over a mere technicality. "I don't have to pick up until I leave the park,"[37] he pointed out, though he got his summons just the same.

Confrontations with dog owners were not as smooth and easy as government wanted to portray them in the media. The fact was that, apart from a handful of staged ticketings, precious few summonses were actually handed out, even after Koch had taken his harsher stand. By February 1979, 7,316 warnings had been made but only 363 summonses had been issued citywide. The bulk of the tickets were given in Manhattan, with only three in all of Brooklyn, one in Queens, one on Staten Island, and none in the Bronx. The number of summonses issued would increase greatly from that point forward, though considering how many lawbreakers the city had this number was practically meaningless. Apart from counting the few trophy dog owners caught in a conspicuously central park, enforcers were, in the vast majority of cases, unable to spot anyone leaving the scene of a crime. "As soon as one person gets a ticket in an area," complained one officer, "it seems as if word spreads quickly. Dog-walkers have some sort of grapevine."[38] Sanitation police were also having trouble confronting the minuscule number of lawbreakers they could even catch. "They'll tell the agent, bug off, quit following me. They'll grab hold of their dog and walk away, screaming harassment."[39] Once suspects were caught, detaining and ticketing them represented yet another hurdle. In no time at all, dog owners got wise to the legal details of enforcement. Only members of the NYPD, they learned, were authorized to detain citizens and demand identification before releasing them. Sanitation officers, saddled with the bulk of enforcement of this law, had no such authority. They would have to content themselves with requesting I.D. and then writing tickets, whether or not documents had been produced. If they were lucky and suspects agreed to cooperate at all, they might very likely be given fake names and addresses, and a few insults. This was a miserable job that no one but a few thick-skinned zealots cared to have—which only helped to exacerbate the situation and to sour community relations. "I'm the bad guy,"[40] said one of the more dedicated enforcers whose superiors understood what he was up against. "We warn our people now not to push to the point where they'll get assaulted,"[41] said a commander. A few years into the law, Sanitation officers were resigning by the dozens, citing the tendency of dog owners to be "verbally and physically abusive."[42] The Department struggled to keep them on board, even offering them the rare opportunity of entering the Civil Service and enjoying the many benefits attached. But this wasn't compensation enough. Eventually, staff dropped by nearly 50 percent, with fewer officers than were needed to cover the early morning shift, which everyone knew was poop rush hour.

Not all successes or failures were so easily quantified. In the course of government's uphill climb, less showy tactics were suggested by New Yorkers who wrote discouraged letters to the *Times*. Secret surveillance vans to cruise the curbsides, cameras hidden in trees, undercover poop patrols planted to make dog owners feel paranoid, police dogs trained to infiltrate the enemy camp—the list went on. Despite the revelation that enforcing this law by legal means was, just as critics had predicted all along that it would be, next to impossible, Koch persisted in making it seem that he was not backing down. Discreet measures would never be strong enough to get his point across. Success had to be made conspicuous if anyone was going to believe the law was working. And only by making rebellious dog owners think that their numbers were dwindling could government win this war. Highly publicized ticketing sprees weren't the only strategy. Softer but more blatant approaches were explored. Among these, a public show of support from other powers-that-be was helpful. New York's City Club lent prestige to the struggle when it gave its seal of approval to City Hall in 1980. The annual award for urban design went to the animal waste law. This was the first time that the honor had been bestowed upon a piece of legislation. Then there were the gala anniversaries celebrated by the mayor and his commissioners in parks throughout the city. Free pooper-scoopers, leashes, bowls, balls, and biscuits were handed out as peace offerings—and gentle reminders to dog owners that they were still being watched. At first, these events were celebrated annually, then sporadically according to the number of complaints coming in.

Along similar positive lines, the Bureau of Animal Affairs took a new position under Koch. Rather than try to divert public attention from canine waste, considered a minor issue a few years earlier, Director Alan Beck began making friendly radio and television appearances in support of the law. Beck led a broad educational campaign stressing ownership responsibility, and these efforts would be crucial to the law's eventual acceptance. In the process, the Bureau gave a kinder face to the administration. But even this more sensible approach met with much resistance. Beck could have been assaulted when attending meetings of dog owners and trying to convince them that being pro-scoop didn't mean being anti-dog. Despite the confusion, he managed to win over many converts, proving that positive examples and open discussion could be at least as effective as force and humiliation. "The idea was to put in place a culture and then work on the other problems,"[43] Beck recalls of the Bureau's long-term goal. The plan made perfect sense. Dogs were extremely controversial. If only the leashed and the leashless could find some middle ground on which to live in peace, then the dogs themselves might find a safe and permanent home in a city where many residents, even some dog lovers, wondered if they belonged. If dog owners would accept the poop scoop law, then their dogs would, theoretically, be treated more humanely in the long run. But how was the Bureau finally able to devote its limited resources to canine waste? The situation had changed since the mid-seventies. The Bureau no longer had reason to be concerned about a dog bite epidemic and could focus, instead, on the hot potato that leaders, until recently, had been dodging. Consistent with the new mood on the street, the Department of Health, which oversaw the Bureau of Animal Affairs, announced in 1981 that dog bites were down by 16.7 percent while human bites were up 24 percent. Health Commissioner Reinaldo Ferrer said that bites from other people could be far more harmful than the canine kind.

"Can an immediate, specific reward for good behavior succeed where an unconvincing threat of punishment has failed?" asked the *Times* on one of the law's gala anniversaries. "Sociologists should take note. So should strollers who appreciate clean parks and sidewalks."[44] Attempts at using carrots instead of sticks came at a time when dog trainers, too, were turning to more positive reinforcement methods and proactive enticements. Punishment was losing its appeal, at least in some circles. "Choke" collars were being tossed aside to make way for clickers and liver treats. "No" was becoming a dirty word. The same philosophy had much to do with turning an embarrassing public act into a show of respect and a cause for pride. Rather than degrade and further alienate dog owners—which the sidewalk vigilantes seemed to enjoy so much that keeping the pavements clean was almost a secondary concern—the goal was to befriend and then praise the target population. Gradually, scooping was entering the mainstream. Support for government's more gentle methods came from many places. Actress Gretchen Weiler made television appearances with her Doberman to discuss the many benefits of the law. A *Times* story entitled "Curbing Dogs With Kindness"[45] announced that a group called "We Care About New York" had arranged for Girl Scouts to wander the parks with free Alpo dog treats and books of detachable "Good Citizen" certificates. Even the most hardened New Yorkers were finding it difficult to scream at sweet little girls who followed them around with rewards they got only if they picked up. Overall, it seemed that sugar was going a lot farther than vitriol. Pat Livingston, the founding member of the Carl Schurz Park Association—and whose calming influence kept some members from waving sabers while Mary Beame encouraged them to sharpen their claws—formed a new group called The Coalition for Dog Control. Livingston's latest peaceful approach would be instrumental in making the law a success in years to come. The Coalition, rather than chase dog owners down in the parks, tried to lure them in of their own free will. A man was hired to dress up as "Scoop the Scooping Dog" to hand out literature and be seen picking up after himself (what, exactly, he was picking up remains unclear). Also enlisted was jazz bassist Jay Leonhardt, who was commissioned to compose an inoffensive jingle about "scooping the poop" that was played by radio stations. In many creative ways, Dr. Livingston tried to reach out to dog owners rather than alienate them. As in Beck's approach, the idea of ownership responsibility was the key to her success. She tapped into the very feelings that dogs evoked in their human guardians by appealing to the "parent" in everyone. But her quiet victories were sometimes laced with bitterness over the long and ugly struggle that had dragged on for so many years. However much she smiled, Livingston couldn't always hide her resentment at those arrogant ones who had insulted her, thrown things, and threatened her life, and who were now expecting to be thanked for following the law. "Dog owners feel righteous when they pick up droppings in a park," she said, "but it was already illegal to let a dog defecate, urinate, or go unleashed in a park."[46] According to Livingston, many dog owners thought they were doing someone a favor by doing their parental duty.

Sugar would only go so far to sweeten those sour memories of the recent past. Ancient feuds wouldn't die easily, and the temptation to scold and denigrate was always around the next corner.* This was war. Staying to his course and consistent with his more confrontational approach, Mayor Koch announced that he was installing a special "computer system"[47] to track repeat offenders, an impressive thing in the early eighties, though a bit excessive. Meanwhile, press releases provided the latest numbers on summonses issued, hotspots were discussed, and government provided its own analysis on what this all meant. By the end of the law's first year, the Office of the Mayor was able to boast that 1,616 people were in possession of summonses for failing to clean up after their dogs. "There were those who were initially skeptical about the City's ability to enforce this law," said Koch. "I think that these figures indicate that the City can enforce the Canine Waste Law. In addition to our enforcement officers, the public has been most helpful in applying peer pressure upon those who have failed to pick up after their pets."[48]

Unfortunately for Koch's jubilee, only 35 percent of the dog owners receiving notices of violations had willingly paid their fines. The remaining 65 percent of the cases had been either scheduled for

*Koch's personal style for getting things done came with a broader trend and represented a clean break from the past. The new hard-nosed approach to urban problems, or simply to matters on which not everyone agreed, stood in stark contrast to the touchy-feeliness of the 1960s when more faith was placed in human nature and laws were often viewed with suspicion. New York had passed through the ordeal of the 1970s. Many liberals had been mugged, and people with the noblest causes to defend had abused the public's trust. By the end of the decade, the city was in a state of near-disaster and people's nerves were frayed. Talk of a harsher paternalism was in the air, and by the 1980s many New Yorkers were taking a less indulgent approach toward their neighbors. Others, however, tried to resist being drawn into the new cynicism. In 1986, City Council received a proposal for a law to ban smoking from restaurants and other public places—inspired by the poop scoop law and its reliance upon peer pressure. Among the opponents was former mayor John Lindsay. His "Courtesy Committee," along with the tobacco companies that funded it, still believed New Yorkers could be trusted to consider each other's health and comfort without being forced into good manners at gunpoint.

hearings or dismissed, or the accused had been found in default of the law. Tracking down ticket-dodging deadbeats, forcing them to pay up, dragging them into court and perhaps to jail—all of this was going to add to the costs the City was already incurring from added law enforcement. Unwilling to back down, Koch noted further "slackening of compliance"[49] in 1980 and announced that the lowest fines for failure to scoop or keep a dog on a leash were doubling from $25 to $50. By 1981, the Office of the Mayor's annual poop press release could proudly announce that the number of summonses was rising abundantly each year. Since August 1, 1978, nearly 5,000 New Yorkers had been slapped with one. By 1985, Sanitation Commissioner Norman Steisel and Parks Commissioner Henry Stern were tooting triumphantly that more than 18,000 New Yorkers had been caught and added to the list. As always, these numbers were interpreted to mean that the law was working better as time passed.

The numbers didn't lie, at least not 100 percent. The condition of pavements and parks had, indeed, noticeably improved since the law went into effect. All that gainsayers had to do was to go outdoors and find that they could stroll more carelessly than they had perhaps since the 1950s. Edgy New Yorkers could once again relax while promenading, no longer needing to look down every step of the way. They, and their necks, were getting less sore. "I can recall when it was difficult to walk down a Manhattan street without having to wince at the unmistakable reality that you had stepped into IT," said Commissioner Steisel in a press release, wincing at the thought. "Today, however, we can once again enjoy the spectacular lofty sights of our magnificent skyline without having to constantly be on the alert for IT—the annoying sloshy danger that used to lurk below."[50] Parks Commissioner Henry Stern agreed ebulliently. "The 'pooper scooper' law is one of the best things that ever happened to New York City's parks,"[51] he beamed. The situation was still far from perfect, though something, whether or not it was the law, was clearly working.

Maybe there was some cause for rejoicing. But to use the number of summonses issued as official proof of success was to distract from reality. In fact, interpreting the rising number of infractions to mean that fewer people were breaking the law was absurd. These figures suggested, if nothing else, quite the contrary. It was a bit like saying that the latest ticketing drive for speeding motorists proved that streets were getting safer.[†] And for every dog owner caught, there were thousands more who weren't, and who knew that they never would be. One need only peruse the headlines to see the madness behind this method. "Success of Dog-Filth Ban Is Called 'Spotty,'" read an early assessment in 1978, perhaps prematurely. "Dog-Cleanup Law Praised After a Year," reported the follow-up story. "Don't dump on poop scoop efforts" pleaded another a few months later when public praise appeared to be drying up. "2 Lawmakers Fault Dog Cleanup Effort" read a headline in 1980, referring to Senator Leichter and Assemblyman Lehner, who went against official wisdom by saying they were disappointed over the City's inability to collect as much as a third of the fines imposed, even though 25,000 city employees were now, at least in theory, authorized to write summonses. "Dog Clean-Up Laws Need More Teeth," complained another article in 1980 when the total number of summonses was higher than the year before, even though this was the case every year—and did this mean that the streets were getting dirtier or cleaner? Just when there seemed to be no end in sight, "Summonses for Not Cleaning Up After Dogs Increase Sharply" claimed yet another victory for government in 1983 when, due to a city-wide crackdown, the number had doubled from the previous year. Still no champagne. "Steps Forward and Back" suggested the need for some critical distance when it was found that summonses from one fiscal year totaled 1,155, a distinct drop from the 2,326 issued in the previous year. "Poop scoop still draws growls" confirmed that the war was still on, and that monitoring the law's effect was a tricky business.

[†]Jerome Kretchmer had tried to pull a similar fast one in 1972 when he claimed that new anti-pollution standards were being better respected because the number of violations had doubled.

"A Matter of Communication—or a Lack of It,"[52] asked the *Times* in 1986 when, due to an argument among government leaders, the eighth birthday of Health Law 1310 passed without the usual celebration. The annual party was skipped because local and state leaders couldn't agree on whether or not the law had been successful, or whom should be praised or blamed if it had or hadn't. Over the years, state leaders responsible for pushing through the legislation in the first place had been critical of local enforcement efforts. Their reputations, too, were on the line. Did Albany have to do *everything* itself? wondered the senators. Were City officials incapable of using this great gift bestowed upon them? The law's failure would make everyone involved look ridiculous and this was serious business. Leaders at both levels shared a keen interest in joining forces to make this thing work—or did they?

Senator Leichter's jabs were much resented back home. But given his personal interest in cleaning up Riverside Park, one can assume that his motives weren't all strategic. Yet when he tried to hijack the anniversary of the poop scoop law, his devotion to the cause was called into question. Before the festive event scheduled to take place in Carl Schurz Park on August 1, Parks Commissioner Henry Stern, who'd arranged for the celebration himself, and Sanitation Commissioner Brendan Sexton had planned to co-issue yet another victorious press release announcing the law's steady march forward despite the few bad apples who still plagued the city and made their jobs so difficult. Leichter beat them to the punch. His own office sent out a press release stating, in no uncertain terms, that he would be on hand to "criticize the City's enforcement activities."[53] Stern, a fierce protector of the public green known for ferociously guarding his turf, and jealous of anyone who threatened his personal relationship to the mayor, was kicking up the sod. This was to be *his* press conference, after all, and Leichter had been invited as a mere courtesy. "Even in matters of dog litter there are some proprieties,"[54] Stern explained to the papers when he announced that both he and Sexton would be boycotting their own news event. The senator's faux pas had apparently weakened the Koch-Leichter alliance. "I don't know why they pulled out now," said Leichter in Carl Schurz

Park where he stood completely alone before the media on August 1, "except that somebody's feathers have been ruffled and those feathers belong to the Mayor."[55] Stern, perhaps assuming Leichter was referring to those courtiers Koch had placed around himself to cushion any falls, responded: "That's totally preposterous. The Mayor didn't even know about it. We were afraid to tell him."[56]

Despite what anyone upstate might have said, confronting dog owners was a primary occupation of some local leaders, and no one in Albany was going to get away with criticizing their record on enforcing the poop scoop law. City government was getting too hooked on claiming annual advances, and would never quite wean itself off the habit of counting summonses. But like that vast and unfathomable gap between the number of enforcement officers and the countless dog owners they were expected to oversee, any numbers that politicians could concoct were negligible compared to the untold masses of offenders that were targeted. From the very beginning, the poop police were hopelessly outnumbered. In all truth and fairness to the way in which things actually happened, it was not government or its hired hands who were enforcing the poop scoop law. Instead, the lone vigilantes and individual block associations did the vast majority of the work by chasing down and intimidating dog owners. Like the ASPCA, which still assumed the City's own responsibility to handle stray animals, and dog owners, now viewed as non-salaried Sanitation workers, average New Yorkers were suddenly cops. City Hall wasn't entirely passive. Showing official support for vigilante efforts was seen as proof that leaders were still serving the public and helping to make New York a nicer place in which to live, even when it already was. Each year, larger numbers were published to embolden the vigilantes and to help them frighten the dog owners into compliance. How far could this strategy possibly go? Supporting, if not enforcing, the poop scoop law became a sign of good government in years to come, a measure of performance, and a vested interest that was closely guarded. Long after non-scooping dog owners had truly become the exceptions to the rule, leaders would go on spewing forth the latest figures and adding them to a grand tally that was supposed to mean something. Anniversaries would be celebrated and subtle threats, as unconvincing as the numbers, would be made. No other subject managed to stir up a crowd so easily or to distract the public's attention away from other matters.

Behind all the padded estimates and puffed perceptions was a simple fact: New York's poop problem had been dramatically reduced in a very short time, even though the situation would never be to everyone's liking. The smell had dissipated but the bitterness lingered on, as did the hostility that was kicked up with each new encounter. The vigilantes, like government, had acquired a taste for battle. They would continue chasing down dog owners long after most of these had gotten the message and started doing as they were told. This was the social price that was paid for having encouraged such bad behavior in citizens. The pursuers of pristine pavement were not unlike those believers in the myth of "zero pollution" who had helped to drive New York into bankruptcy. Having the sidewalks *almost* feces-free was never enough to quiet the most militant anti-poopers or to calm their rage. Nostrils flared at the slightest hint of a rude aroma, and all that it took to keep some people perpetually off-balance over poop was for them to look down—once in a lifetime—and find they'd stepped into it. All that it took for *that* to happen, apart from a split-second of bad luck, were a few straggling mutts with irresponsible owners, perhaps just one or two lone aberrations per city block. These same dogs did their business, as dogs tend to do, in precisely the same spot, day after day, year after year, which always made the problem seem larger than it was. One diligent observer reported a cluster of eight separate piles on East 51st Street, "quite evidently a series by the same big dog."[57] The woman was particularly incensed because these mounds had been dumped right in front of the Seventeenth Precinct Police Station! The sheer mass of the mess, she thought, ought to have attracted attention to the culprits. But counting individual turds could be misleading.

In similar putrid pockets across town, the cumulative effect was as astounding as it was inflationary. One journalist noted with over-abundant disgust a stretch of pavement on one block that was "clearly a favorite for derelict dog walkers."[58] During the course of her "admittedly unscientific census"[59] on the Upper East Side, she had "counted an average of two dog piles per cement square, but lost tally and appetite when the total passed 35 piles."[60] However large and daunting, these numbers represented a minority of dog owners still resisting the law. If anyone hoped to catch the stray offenders—people who gave new meaning to the word—he or she would have to wake up pretty early in the morning. Short of calling in the National Guard or declaring martial law, the City would never have enough recruits to arrest more than a handful of the small number of civil resisters.

Did the poop scoop law really solve all of New York's canine waste problems? The law gave citizens the will to make sure that most of the poop got off the ground, but something foul was left over. The difficulty in catching every single offender continued to frustrate the vigilantes in years to come. Poop had become their raison d'être, and like pit bulls, some people just couldn't let go. Impotent before a problem they could do nothing about, they grew angrier and more aggressive each year. Again, the very success of the poop scoop law was having the opposite effect of what was intended. This wasn't bringing perfect peace to New York. On the contrary, having fewer lawbreakers meant that even fewer of them could be caught—which drove some people crazy. The vigilantes started blaming anyone with a leash, continuing the tradition of following dog owners for several blocks, then "thanking" them sarcastically for picking up (even though they wouldn't have it any other way). Despite the obvious improvement made to the city since the poop scoop law had been in effect, crackpots and neurotics went on blaming many for the crimes of a few. The mere mention of that offensive animal matter would be enough to resurrect the specter of civil war this law was supposed to have averted—which always presented leaders with new opportunities for getting tough on dog owners. The saddest part about this dynamic is that the unbroken attention to canine waste would also serve to distract from other, more humane animal issues in years to come.

If, indeed, it were possible to gauge the success of efforts on both sides of the struggle, perhaps a more accurate measure would be the raw tonnage of canine waste left on city surfaces, an unflattering figure but one that heralds a dramatic change. In 1972, New York's very rough estimate of 600,000 to 1,000,000 dogs (half of which were said to be strays) were relieving themselves two or three times daily. By 1975, Alan Beck estimated, again very roughly, that these dogs were depositing between 300,000 and 500,000 pounds of feces daily on pavements and lawns. In 1977, Sanitation Commissioner Anthony Vaccarello felt confident in calling New Yorkers "slobs" because of the annual total of 54,750 tons (or so he claimed—but who could say?) of offal that his department flatly refused to collect. In 1978, on the eve of the law that would make collection the duty of individual dog owners, John Marr, Director of the Bureau of Preventative Diseases of the NYC Health Department, said they would soon have to account for an estimated 20,000 tons of feces their animals were churning out each year (they could leave the 600,000 to 1,000,000 gallons of urine right where it was). By 1984, six years into the law, Alan Beck concluded that about 60 percent of dog owners were probably cooperating, which meant that of the estimated 22,800 tons of poo currently produced annually, an estimated three-fifths was being collected (and deposited into one of the city's overflowing wastebaskets where it might sit for days before finding a home, or end up back on the pavement once again, this time in a plastic bag, when the whole mess toppled over). This, it seemed, was the best that could be expected in a free and democratic society.

"It looks OK to me," said one sunbather in Carl Schurz Park. "But I still watch out when I walk barefoot."[61]

CHAPTER 11

SUMMARY: WHY IT HAPPENED HERE FIRST

> "The transformation of waste is perhaps the oldest pre-occupation of man."
>
> —Patti Smith[1]

The 1980s had an uplifting effect on New York. The dark decade was officially over and the city on its way toward recovery. Graffiti had been wiped clean from many neighborhoods. Fountains and subway stations were restored to their past splendor. Garbage was collected more frequently. By 1984, a victory could be claimed in the struggle against canine waste. More important, the unruly pet culture, believed to be a major obstacle to the city's renaissance, was fairly stable. Most dogs were finally "street-broken,"[2] according to the *Times*. Not only was the poop scoop law proving successful, at least 25 municipal governments, many having said that it could never be done, swallowed their pride and called to ask for advice on this crucial ingredient to urban renewal. What was New York's secret? "When something happens in New York—and it works—it becomes world news," wrote Alan Beck at the time. "For instance, I was called by a reporter from a Chicago newspaper who

asked how he could encourage his city officials to consider such legislation for Chicago; in fact, the amended version of the New York law
is modeled in part after a law that already exists in Chicago."[3] How
had New York leaders managed to enforce their dog law when similar
attempts had failed in other places? "For a while, I kept a list of cities
that contacted us for information," said a Sanitation spokesperson, "but
it got too long."[4] Chicago, Boston, Philadelphia, Toronto, Montreal,
London, Paris, Brussels . . . the turnabout was dramatic and suddenly
the whole world wanted to know: How did those pushy, arrogant New
Yorkers, who don't like being told what to do, manage to convince each
other that picking up after a dog was a good thing to do?

"What happens in New York gets either copied or criticized,"
says Beck of our thankless task of setting precedents. "First we're criticized, then we're copied."[5]

Despite all this eagerness to be let in on a secret, any practical
advice for outsiders must have been limited because the situation in
New York was, as it so often is, unique. The intensity of the problem,
whether real or perceived, demanded a special solution. Local leaders
had no surefire formula for success, and once again, New York would
be a tough act to follow. In fact, lawmakers had just barely been able
to pass their envied piece of legislation, and its justification, like its
enforcement, was still shrouded in mystery. Saying the poop scoop law
worked simply because New York was a world leader, however true
that was, would have been a bit off-putting. Claiming that New Yorkers
were natural-born trendsetters would barely have scratched the surface.
Giving anyone the real scoop on the poop, explaining why this particular
solution was chosen to handle it, and detailing the methods by which
people were made to take the law seriously could hardly have been of
much use to other governments. Nonetheless, the prospect of making
dog owners pick up suddenly seemed a possibility. For the simple reason
that New Yorkers were doing it, our private obsession became a personal
standard for our imitators who watched us and waited for their cues.

Health Law 1310, and its relative success, weren't born out of
thin air. Though the strange and awkward act of scooping a dog's leavings

eventually became so ordinary that it was no longer deemed worthy of discussion, this particular solution came in response to a specific set of circumstances. So basic an assumption about civic duty, as we've seen, was far from self-evident in the beginning. Asking New York dog owners to comply with this shocking new imperative, to commit an act they believed to be humiliating, dangerous to their health, and downright unfair was asking a lot. Changing their minds took years of gentle persuasion, subliminal hints, hard-nosed tactics, and fistfights until the new behavior took hold in a meaningful way. And even then, many New Yorkers would never be exactly satisfied with their performance. But before the daily habits of one of the city's most persecuted and understandably defensive groups of people could be changed at all, the subject matter itself—dog crap—had to be taken seriously. How was this issue transformed from a minor irritant into a major public health concern? How did scant evidence lead to legislation? How was government able to use a law to fuel a vigilante enforcement campaign? The answers to these questions are only as muddled as the subject matter itself. What, exactly, made dog doo a topic worth talking about? How did it become a problem in the first place?

New Yorkers shouldn't expect congratulations for geography. The physical layout of their city, an important factor for which they can claim no credit, had much to do with the birth of their famed law. Poop became a problem because New York is a sidewalk culture. Health Law 1310 came about because there were so many compelling reasons why it should have, though the first of these was as flat-footed as it was pedestrian. The local terrain not only drew attention to an inconvenience, it reshaped canine waste from a trivial concern into one of the most controversial issues of its time. Public walkways are vital in New York. Anyone who's lived in the city knows how much raw emotion is invested in the pavement. That thin strip between the curb (and the dangers that lie beyond) and the front door (a New Yorker's only source of privacy) is, for the most part, the out-of-doors, and the only way for people to get to where they're going. Overcrowding is a daily fact of life, and our discomfort is increased by the fact that we have so little space at home. New Yorkers are crammed into tiny apartments and

"O.K., I'm on my way home."

few of us are lucky enough to have backyards. Apart from our thinly stretched, hard-to-reach parks—those man-made expanses of fake hills, artificial lakes, and tortured greenery often mistaken for Paradise by nature-starved New Yorkers—the natives don't have many open settings in which to move about freely, to stretch, or to breathe clean air. The overall scarcity of space is a constant source of friction because people tend to lay their own separate claims to what little there is. On the sidewalk, bumping into a stranger accidentally can lead to an argument and perhaps assault charges. New Yorkers may not like being told what to do. But telling other people what to do is an effective way to cope with stress in a densely packed, fast-paced city where letting off steam is part of surviving. When it comes to using more civilized methods to decide the proper uses of our shared accommodations—discussing whether park land should be given over to playgrounds or dog runs, whether walking space should be taken up by outstretched leashes or three-headed baby carriages, whether motorized vehicles for the handicapped should weave through crowds at full speed, if bicyclists should have lanes of their own or hotdog vendors should be allowed to encamp on busy street corners—everyone's an expert and striking a balance is a never-ending struggle that sometimes seems more complicated than reaching an international consensus on global warming. Often the best strategy is to try and stay out of everyone's way.

Avoiding the issues, however, doesn't solve the problems. A dramatic rise in the city's dog population made one of these unavoidable. Humans were already overcrowded into limited space, and the subject matter, long-tolerated but never liked, soon took on a new importance—which only begs the real questions: Were dog feces worth getting so upset over? And if they were, then what could anyone possibly do about the annoying mess?

If it weren't for New York's fiscal crisis of the 1970s, the embarrassing topic might never have come up at all. Our groundbreaking poop scoop law very likely would not have been necessary because there wouldn't have been so many dogs in the first place. People would not have needed them for protection. Fewer deposits would have been a petty concern and government, if anyone, would have been held responsible. Even if we'd been a more prosperous city that just happened to have too many dogs, street cleaners, not unsalaried taxpayers, would have been expected to clean up their mess, and would still be scooping today as they do, however inefficiently, in cities like Paris. If New York had not been forced by severe circumstances into taking this drastic and eccentric course of action, then this particular solution to its dog problem—an option advocated by what many sane and respectable people for years considered to be a minority of extremists, opportunists, and downright nuts—would have been buried and forgotten by New Yorkers and by the rest of the world.[*]

---

[*]"In some cities," concluded a study made by Glickman and Shofer in 1987, "recently enacted poop scoop laws that require owners to pick up after their pets may be of some value, but a more permanent solution is to lower the prevalence of *T. canis* infection in pet dogs, especially puppies."[6]

Unfortunately for dog owners, by the 1970s New York was on the brink of bankruptcy and New Yorkers were on the verge of nervous breakdowns. The city was coming apart at the seams with tensions higher than their normal highs. Everything seemed larger than life and the smallest concerns were exaggerated under the relentless pressure of having to survive in an increasingly harsh urban environment. Many of the perceived dangers were quite real and life-threatening. Average citizens were importing massive numbers of dogs for protection because crime and police cutbacks left them no other choice but to fend for themselves. They discovered in the process that they also craved the warmth and companionship these animals provided in a cold and alienating city. In so many ways, dogs helped to carry New York through the urban crisis. They solved at least as many problems as they created. So why was this single by-product allowed to overshadow the many good things that these animals were bringing to the edgy, unhappy lives of stressed-out New Yorkers?

Anti-poop and often anti-dog sentiment first gained momentum when a loose coalition of special interest groups—mainly nervous parents fretting over marginal health risks—sought to convince government that the city had a serious public health problem that not only had a practical solution, they claimed, but demanded one as soon as possible. Magnifying the supposed risks at a microscopic level, and exaggerating statistics, they helped to create a sense of urgency, though scientific evidence would never back their claim that the presence of dog feces on city surfaces posed a significant danger to anyone. Blowing the threat of serious childhood illness out of proportion, one organization was able to spread panic among parents and to command government's attention. In a single blunt stroke, Children Before Dogs managed to put pet owners on the defensive by feeding their fear that any criticism of their animals was a veiled first step toward banishing them from the city. In time, the new fecal fixation would spread like a virus through the general population, much of which had neither children nor dogs because it was widely believed at the time that New York wasn't a healthy place for either. Average New Yorkers from all walks of life, as though they didn't have enough problems already, were suddenly awoken to yet another life-threatening obstacle in their paths as they forged their ways to work each morning, or tried to dash home after dinner without being mugged. Just when they were learning to accept the sidewalk mess as a minor irritant and another fact of life in a decaying city, to dodge this problem as they were veering away from so many other possible reasons to be frightened or annoyed during an urban crisis, New Yorkers were placed in an artificially heightened state of alert.

Their fear became official in 1971, just at the tail end of the Lindsay era when leaders were starting to run for cover. "The first thing that has to be done," said an EPA spokesman, "is to sensitize people to the fact that there is a problem that has to be addressed."[7] When *de*sensitization might have been the more prudent path, dog owners, a growing number of their peers began to believe, had a responsibility to account for their pets' waste products. Otherwise, said the EPA, they would be pressured into abandoning them. But threats were meaningless and getting that poop off the pavement, or the dogs out of town, would never be easy as anyone had imagined. Disagreements over the precise nature of the problem, and who had the right solution, assured that the subject matter would remain fresh and recyclable for years to come. Poop would need to be repackaged and recirculated several times before it was finally taken seriously by a majority of New Yorkers. The first official step taken by the EPA, however, that crown jewel of the Lindsay administration and beacon for a new-and-improved metropolis, brought a dog's leavings out into the open air where they could be examined in natural light. Dogs, claimed the EPA's rising star, Jerome Kretchmer, were harming "the environment." A reorganized bureaucracy took what might have been viewed as a traditional matter of sanitation and placed it under the heading of a global cause that commanded universal respect. New York City's pavements and its parks were approached as a natural ecosystem that required protection. Dogs were often compared to automobiles, the number one source of air pollution in cities, and number two was likened to fuel exhaust. For years to come, dogs would be viewed as dangerous, four-wheeled nuisances that belonged at the other side of the curb—if, indeed, they belonged in the city at all.

Concerned parents were disappointed with the EPA's official stand. They preferred to stress the more mundane aspects of dog dangers, and decided to take a more traditional, though no less tenuous, stand. They took the threat-to-shit-eating-toddler angle, which was about as half-baked as the car analogy. The mere presence of pet feces on city surfaces, they claimed, even if dog owners promised to collect as much of it as they could, was a critical public health issue. Nervous parents were also firmly against the solution being proposed. Dog owners would never comply with the EPA's law, they predicted, suspecting that government was using the poop scoop idea as a diversion from the real problems that it couldn't or wouldn't solve, and then trying to bury this one, leaving the subject matter to sit in the open air forever. Dogs, the anti-dog, pro-child people insisted for quite some time, should be taught to go in their owners' bathrooms, not in public places.

For reasons that should be obvious, alternatives needed exploration. New York's fecal concerns would be rethought and rephrased several times again before minds were put at rest. Seen in retrospect, dog dirt was as much the focus of a consistent governmental plan carried out with clearly stated goals across various administrations as it was a momentary response to other concerns as they surfaced. Changing perceptions of what, exactly, the dog problem was, and then how it should be remedied, were enough to prevent it—whatever "it" was—from being fixed for nearly two decades. This esthetic issue with sanitation undertones was draped in many different garbs before these troubled times came to a close. Once the matter had been cast as the subject of an environmental crusade, attempts were made to refashion it into a more traditional public health problem, though this idea encountered resistance. In the intervening years of urban decay and civil disarray, canine waste morphed into a matter of mental health and mass hysteria. In all the confusion, it was seen as one of the more noxious aspects of the urban crisis, and was often considered the cause. Not only was a poop scoop law viewed as the solution to all of the city's animal problems, it was believed to be New York's salvation.

One consistent thread runs through the lengthy dog debate. From the time it opened in the 1970s, keeping animals from befouling city surfaces was presented as an integral part of rescuing New York City from impending doom. Dogs and their littering owners were blamed for pollution and disease. They were thought to be indirectly responsible for crime, poor public schools, subway fare increases, and the mass exodus of taxpayers and corporations. In the end, it was economic necessity and the opportunity that leaders saw to restore New York to its former glory that framed canine waste as a legitimate threat to health, both public and fiscal. During the restoration years, the matter was transformed once and for all. Picking up after a pet came to be viewed as a matter of common sense. More importantly, compliance with Health Law 1310 was a demonstration of the renewed respect for law and order and a rekindled faith in leadership, ideals that had suffered greatly in recent decades when Americans learned to question all authority and rioting came to be viewed as a legitimate form of political expression. The times they had a-changed, and the poop scoop law was one of the early symptoms. Being a considerate pet owner, according to these new terms, meant being a responsible citizen who respected both his neighbors and public property. Sidewalk compliance levels, like the square footage of virgin lawn or the number of healthy trees, became measures of good government. Health Law 1310 was made sacrosanct and inviolable. It became perhaps the city's most revered monument to decency.

Exaggeration was key to making this law the cornerstone that it is today. A law inspired by a much older one forbidding the deposit of any "animal matter" that people might find "offensive" was inherently subjective, despite all the attempts to find objective reasons for its justification. The law was bound to encounter resistance. Looking back, local legislators were criticized for their unwillingness to take on the vague and slippery question of what, if anything, was to be done about canine waste. But should they be congratulated for having resisted going along with tenuous arguments for as long as they did? Was it a basic respect for truth or a healthy aversion to unnecessary controversy that compelled them to say "NO" to the idea? We forget that government had problems of its own. City Council devoted most of its time during the 1970s to financial matters. When the state finally intervened on the dog question, local legislators could not be blamed for being anti-dog. But neither could anyone be thanked for having addressed the city's more pressing concerns, human or humane, because so much fuss was still being made over this single by-product.

What, then, is the subject matter that's worthy of an entire book? Environmental issue or piece of propaganda? Public health epidemic or pet peeve? A question of civic duty or personal choice? In the end, Health Law 1310 became imperative because so many people believed that it was. Even New York City's Department of Health resisted focusing on the poop scoop idea until it had no alternative. In later years, studies would back the disease theory to some extent. An overabundance of uncollected dog leavings would, indeed, be tied to higher levels of *E. coli, salmonella*, and *Toxocara canis* in soils and waterways around the world. Large quantities of nitrogen and phosphorous, too, would threaten the environment. Advanced detection methods would show that canine waste was having harmful effects on plant and aquatic life in some places. However, the real impact on humans living in concrete cities and surrounding areas is exceptional. In fact, between 1977 and 1979, only one resident New Yorker was found to have contracted *visceral larva migrans*, at a time when New York was the unchallenged poop capital of the world.[8]

The subject matter? Dog feces in New York of the 1970s were primarily a *social* problem, one that snowballed over the course of one of the city's most trying ordeals and became, for various reasons, the single most controversial issue of its time. More attention was devoted to this hygienic concern than would have been thought reasonable under more normal circumstances. Unlike previous governments, the Koch administration took on any extremely controversial approach and was committed to following it through to the bitter end. While other cities tried and gave up on introducing or enforcing unpopular laws, a combination of fears made it possible to have one that worked in New York. The not-unfounded fear of prejudice against pets, and the profound distrust of government that was a sign of these times, kept the law from being passed for nearly a decade. On the other hand, the fear of predators, microbes, and assorted pollutants—and the possibility of losing the world's esteem and with it our cutting edge—conspired to make leaders take a firmer stand against dog owners. Once a course had been set, and a pragmatic and politically expedient solution agreed upon, then the problem would be solved by society itself and a wink from government. Removing this thorny issue from the city's sidewalks, integrating the keepers of unruly beasts back into good society, and bringing pets safely into the 1980s where they might be treated more kindly than in recent decades were part of the larger task of restoring a healthy balance. Allowing the blight to remain most definitely would not have been in the dogs' best interests, or anyone else's. As Alan Beck said many times, the poop scoop law was for the benefit of everyone. Though pets were in no way to blame for the urban crisis, they may have exacerbated it. Failure to clear the sidewalks and parks would have prevented corporations from moving back and their employees from believing that the city was once again a nice place in which to raise a family. Without a city-wide cleanup, people might have chosen to go elsewhere in search of fast-track career paths. "New Yorkers walk, talk, and think faster than other people," Ed Koch was known to say. The thinking part was debatable, the talking part beyond interpretation—and now that sidewalks had been cleared, New Yorkers could resume a fast pace and get on with their busy lives.

That wink from government would be instrumental in enforcing the kind of law that is basically unenforceable by legal means. "Peer pressure" is a dangerous force to unleash on the streets of New York. But when it's encouraged the results can be astonishing. Here lies the secret to the law's success and the reason why efforts would probably have to take different courses in other societies.

New York vigilantes are a breed unto themselves and the ability to stir up a crowd is a powerful skill that should be used responsibly, as it was by some leaders. The public education campaign led by Alan Beck, for example, was aimed at making friends, not enemies, and proved to be an effective way of changing behavior. The ultimate goal, after all, was to create a stable pet culture and to safeguard dogs, not to feed animosity and maintain divisions that would have allowed a bad situation to worsen. Notwithstanding Koch's tough rhetoric, which was probably expected of a mayor, government in the 1970s and early 1980s was in no position to be making demands. Instead, Beck's friendly television appearances, and the articles he wrote on why scooping was to everyone's benefit, played a major role in helping people to trust government once again. These efforts served as a model plan for cities throughout the world where, even if poop scoop laws were taken seriously by some leaders, they weren't always welcomed by dog owners. Beck also appeared, without a bodyguard, at those dicey neighborhood meetings at a time when many New Yorkers still believed the law was part of a broader plan to take their pets away. They had been told as much, not only by the dog haters, but by some of the most respected animal rights advocates of the time. It took skill, patience, and sensitivity to clear up, once and for all, a profound misunderstanding that had been further sensationalized by so many irresponsible journalists for more than a decade.

But while positive, educational tactics played a role in ensuring compliance, for every helpful hint, streetwise dog owners knew from experience, there was an imminent threat of dog removal. Irate neighbors could, at the very least, make their lives miserable. They could also try to make them give up their dogs or drive them from the city. The radical behavior of New Yorkers had become all the more pronounced after the crucible of the 1970s. The vigilante campaign worked so well because it had so many willing participants. Recreating the conditions that produced this mentality and then summoning the same social forces would be difficult in other cities. If dogs were to be made worth fighting over, then populations would have to reach the same levels of discontentment. They would have to become mad as hell about their hometowns but still refuse to move away. Public outrage would need to be nurtured, perhaps by taxing citizens more than anyone else in the nation and giving them virtually nothing in return. Living space would have to be redesigned to maximize congestion and pollution, and garbage would need to be left rotting in the streets. The world's highest violent crime rates would have to be achieved and an urban crisis extended long enough to harvest the sort of compulsive, relentless, hard-edged personality that came out of New York in the 1970s. If cities lost their middle classes in the process, then all was lost. In short, mayors would have to import angry New Yorkers to enforce their own poop scoop laws with the same kind of enthusiasm if they really wanted to do this the New York way.

* * *

What about New York's future? The city was ripe for change but maintaining this momentum would be the real test. Simply setting a precedent was a bit like making a splash on Broadway, only there was no guarantee that they'd be doing the same show across the country. Keeping the ball rolling would require years of hard work. Dog owners would need constant reminders and new generations would have to be educated. Gala anniversaries of Health Law 1310 would be celebrated with serious solemnity in parks throughout the city. Mayors would join forces with their Parks and Sanitation commissioners to hand out free leashes, chewy toys, and dog treats, and to remind dog owners they were still being watched. But the cutesy brand of persuasion that sometimes works in other societies was difficult to foist on New York dog owners. Always a convenient target for the city's rage, they had no illusions. Long after the urban crisis, they kept up their guards because they knew, probably better than anyone else in town, the lay of the land. Behind all the formalities of New York social life, underneath all that urbane exchange, artsy sophistication, and knowledge of good restaurants, was a kind of rarefied brutality always waiting to be unleashed. The target population picked up with forced smiles and eventually learned to de-sensitize itself to performing the task without embarrassment or resentment. Parks Commissioner Henry Stern said approvingly on the law's twentieth anniversary that cleaning up had become "a respectable and honorable act."[9]

Government and vigilantes can't take all the credit, only claim that by pressuring dog owners they helped to make New York a more attractive place. Demographic change was another important reason for the law's long engagement. The dramatic population turnover that began in the 1980s, a mass landing of new New Yorkers with values and expectations quite different from the old ones, helped to bring back to the city an outward calm unknown since the 1950s. Picking up after a dog still took some getting used to. The custom hadn't yet caught on back home. But recent arrivals were ahead of the game because they had no reason to feel humiliated when performing this dirty deed. Unlike the long-term residents, they hadn't fought in the local war over dogs. They and their pets had been spared all the misunderstanding, the ancient vendettas, and the bad blood from more spirited times. No one wanted to take their dogs away from them, at least not as far as they could tell. The slate, like much of the sidewalk, had been wiped clean. Standards for socially acceptable behavior had changed. Civil resistance was no longer fashionable. By the 1990s, picking up was part of becoming a New Yorker.

Whatever happened to those old-school dog people, the scrappy activists who had rallied with Cleveland Amory against the poop scoop law? Eventually, they gave into society's pressure, though not always out of a sense of civic duty. Many simply realized that they were fighting a losing battle. They grew tired of having their neighbors constantly yelling at them or chasing them down the block with fists clenched. The civil war had worn them out, and the chance that doing as they were told might one day make the city a safer place for their pets came as an added incentive. A few tough resisters lingered on from a bygone era, as did others who were just plain lazy, angering their peers and making the difficult task of raising a dog in the city more trying than it needed to be. Slowly but surely, these lawbreakers grew old and died off, as did their assailants who had made whining about pets into a lifetime vocation. To the present day, a few anti-doggers, permanently damaged by the 1970s, continue scouring the pavement like mad ghosts blaming other people for all of their problems. What unsuspecting New York dog owner hasn't been brushed on the sidewalk by some mumbling old curmudgeon demanding they get that damned animal out of the way? "Ban the dogs!" one decrepit vigilante wrote to the *Times* in the 1990s as a flashback to another era. But the constant complainers were wise to watch themselves. "You might walk up to the wrong person," Rudolph Giuliani cautioned while trying to stir up a fresh crop of fecal fighters, "and, who knows, you might get a punch in the nose."[10]

* * *

One last and unrecognized factor in the success of Health Law 1310 in later years came unexpectedly and almost by chance—and as a reminder that, although New Yorkers are trendsetters, they can certainly take their time about it. This final ingredient, like the poop scoop law itself, almost didn't happen at all.

Present-day dog owners are unaware of the long and grueling battle that was fought by their predecessors to secure this most basic provision for their pets. The public dog run—after New York's poop scoop law, the most visible advance taken home by tourists from across the globe—encountered fiery resistance from community groups, property owners, and government leaders who, for nearly 40 years, flatly denied dog owners' requests for meager parcels of land. Not only were dogs forbidden from running off-leash on lawns, they were also denied spaces of their own. Amtrak barred pets from trains in the mid-seventies, and taking dogs to the country for recreation was no longer an option for owners who didn't have cars. Dog runs would prove to be vital, not only to guard dogs needing the long periods of exercise that made them more manageable, but to dogs of all kinds. Still, it wasn't until 1997 that City Council made public dog runs legal in parks throughout the city. Until that time, canine playgrounds were treated as informal concessions to be taken away at a moment's notice, as necessary evils tolerated only because they spared the lawns, as oddities appearing in neighborhoods that no one really cared about, as private clubs with four-year waiting lists, or as unholy cesspools that should be avoided. Once City Council made them official, Parks Commissioner Henry Stern was quick to take credit for having single-handedly opened "over twenty dog runs in the city"—conveniently forgetting that he'd kicked and clawed every inch of the way.

What did dog runs have to do with the success of Health Law 1310? How did they make the sidewalks and parks cleaner once they were finally allowed? When urban dogs were given the formal right to the exercise and socialization they'd needed all along in order to lead happy and healthy lives, most of their unsavory side effects were localized. Dogs, it turned out, tended to save their business, both poop and pee, for these tiny, overcrowded, urine-soaked ghettos that they "marked" several times daily. The city's canine waste problem was dumped into the laps of dog-owning communities who had little choice but to patrol themselves for compliance with Health Law 1310. The only alternative was to learn to live with the mess while they sat sipping their morning coffee and reading their papers—not an inviting prospect.

The ultimate solution to New York's canine waste problem, like the problem itself, had been right under everyone's noses all along. In a single stroke, dog runs helped to remedy both the grass shortage and the poop surplus. When government finally gave in, a valuable lesson was learned: If controversial pet problems, both leash- and litter-related, couldn't be solved to everyone's liking, then at least they could be contained like feces in plastic bags. In years to come, the poop scoop precedent would be more fruitful than anyone could have possibly imagined. Based on this simple idea, virtually all aspects of animal care and control could be viewed in simple terms of sanitation, and as the responsibilities of dog owners themselves. Signs posted at the entries to dog runs across the city suggested nothing else. "If you're not responsible enough to clean up after your dog," they read, "then you don't deserve to own one." This sounded like a non sequitur to some people—surely caring for a dog involved more than obeying the poop scoop law?

Dog runs solved at least as many problems as they created. Why on earth would anyone have ever resisted them? What harm could possibly have been done by giving pups their own safe havens? Liability was a likely reason for government's resistance. If dogs were unleashed, it was assumed, then people and their pets might be bitten, even though studies showed that a chained dog was much more prone to attack than a free one. Limited space was another concern. Some New Yorkers were greedy about theirs and were not about to hand over parcels of public land, however miniscule, permanently to those filthy, marauding beasts that had, in their opinions, plagued the city. Nor did they have any interest in appeasing that group of anti-social renegades who, in their minds, had nearly destroyed New York. Law enforcement officers, too, had reason to oppose the idea. If running dogs were rounded up and kept locked in place, then whatever would those burly PEP officers on golf carts, who spent so much of their time bullying dog owners, do until their pensions came due? A combination of vested interests, misplaced priorities, bitter resentment after years of ugly encounters—and an almost primal fear of unchained animals—conspired to prevent these little sanctuaries from becoming part of the landscape. Even some dog owners were against the idea. They continued to see the world through the "don't fence me in" lens of the sixties and defended their dogs' free-ranging rights. Others predicted that dog runs would be unhealthy and dangerous places for pets and people alike. To legitimate sanitation concerns were added apocalyptic visions of blood baths. Too much freedom, many dog owners thought, would mean returning to "the law of the jungle." Critics imagined horrible scenes of loose predators, the large animals consuming the smaller ones in a single bite—as though a dog run would be a savage microcosm of the food chain in nature. Time would prove most of these prejudices to be unfounded, although the occasional dog fight and a handful of fatalities might have been prevented had government taken a more active role. But banning dog runs would have been like closing children's playgrounds because of the outside chance of a skinned knee. For the most part, the dogs got along much better in these places than their owners ever did. While neighbors fought over whose turn it was to take out the trash, Great Danes romped gently with Chihuahuas,

Jack Russells used the sheer force of their personalities to dominate Rhodesians, and lions laid with lambs.

Any problems would be our own. Once again, based on the victory of the poop scoop law, an analogy was drawn. Dog-owning communities themselves were saddled, in most cases, with the entire burden of constructing, maintaining, and patrolling these much-needed but much-aligned improvements. For nearly two decades, Parks Commissioner Henry Stern insisted he was "not in the business of running dog hotels and unattended dog toilets."[11] His own dog, a conspicuous golden retriever named "Boomer," was allowed to use the facility in Tompkins Square Park only once each year for his highly publicized birthday bash. The rest of the time, dog owners were left with no support and no other choice. Locations for dog runs have been far less than ideal and space, with few exceptions, is extremely limited. They're squeezed onto tiny traffic islands where they're surrounded by automobile exhaust and dangerous crosswalks. They're crammed onto narrow strips of hot asphalt with chain-link fences in bleak, industrial areas where they won't be seen or smelled. Maintenance of these facilities is always iffy. The precedent that was set and codified by the poop scoop law—the age-old assumption that dog people were responsible for having brought these filthy animals to the city in the first place and should thus be expected to handle all the accommodations—has made for a situation in which average, taxpaying citizens are told to be urban planners, professional zookeepers, animal behaviorists, and cops. Raising funds and then enforcing rules designed for the safety of humans and their pets is difficult enough. The monstrous sanitation problems that arise are beyond description. Picking up the poop is easy—what about all the pee? Containment has led to concentration, and while some communities have acted heroically over the years, others haven't upheld their end of a bargain that was maybe unfair in the first place. Tourists need only step through the twin gates of that famous model dog run in Washington Square Park, the city's most densely populated and overused facility where dozens of gallons of urine are deposited daily, to experience the stench and decide whether "community participation" has been working. Proper maintenance and group efforts have always been sporadic. "George's Run," as it's called, recently went for three years with no maintenance at all. Across the city, other communities are likewise burdened with important responsibilities and given no real authority or means. More often than not, they rely upon the saintliness of one or two of their neighbors in-between jobs who break their backs trying to do the work of thousands, or they fall back on the local nut who has nothing better to do but shout at people. This arrangement has been ad hoc, informal, temporary, and unsatisfactory. If Washington Square is any example, the history of dog runs in New York is one of unending disagreements, fistfights, assaults, gang tactics, and shameful neglect on the part of government. "We had no problems before they put that fence up," recalls one West Villager who actually joined the local Community Board so that the Washington Square dog run would be approved in the mid-1990s. "Everyone got along just fine. Things were simpler back then. As soon as that fence went up, people started trying to tell each other what to do."[12] Impossible situations have served a purpose. By dividing the dog-owning community, once a militant sub-culture and a formidable force, politicians are able to go on dodging their duties, to call for more "community participation," and then to blame the dog owners for not helping out. Currently, threats are being made to shut down the only facility in all of Central Park, a tiny, barren patch of earth that's said to be filthy.

And yet despite all these shortcomings, dog owners have reasons not to trust the City with the important responsibility of caring for their beloved animals. In response to those who want a larger government role, they might point to the rare but faulty fencing the Parks Department has installed and which has led to lost, injured, and dead animals. The few "drainage systems" installed by government (but paid for largely by communities) back up during a good rainfall, making canine play-grounds into open cesspools for several days, off-limits and completely unusable. Understandably, people are concerned about the health risks, for dogs and people alike, and the unwanted exposure to overly vigi-lant poop patrols. Many New Yorkers have given up altogether on dog runs, a nice idea but one that doesn't always work. They've chosen to take their companions and return to the lawns, preferring to take their chances against the ticketing rangers rather than expose themselves or their best friends to these sometimes unwholesome and unpleasant environments. It is a shame that government, after all these years and against the requests of taxpayers, continues to see dog runs as unwanted burdens instead of highly desirable, and desired, additions to communities. When these places are well maintained and the mood is right, they offer unusual opportunities for exchange between people and between dogs. As a result of the few existing dog runs in New York, dogs, if not their owners, are better socialized than they would be in other cities or in suburbs. It is senseless that sincere efforts to open facilities in neighborhoods desperately without them are routinely thwarted by paranoid parent groups, or directors of nearby daycare centers, who persist in believing that dogs, even when kept in enclosed areas, are somehow a threat to children. Parks officials support anti-dog attitudes wholeheartedly and carry on the tradition of playing green politics against a group for which they still harbor deep resentment. It is a sad and ironic fact that dog runs across the country, often inspired by the one first seen in New York City, are ample spaces built and maintained with the proper government cooperation, or at least without official sabotage.

CHAPTER 12

GLOBAL POOP

> "In any problem, if you listen to the extremists . . . DNA databases? The world has bigger problems."
>
> —Sgt. Charles Rudack, Boston Police Department[1]

Tourists stream daily through the arch that announces Fifth Avenue, forging their ways past statues of forgotten heroes in search of that famed and fetid "dog park" they've heard so much about. Despite the overwhelming stench, this tiny patch of pebbles in Washington Square has become a major attraction and some say it's the best show in town. Audiences hold their breaths while dogs of all shapes and sizes play freely off-leash, sending them away with stories of antics and adventures— and hopes of convincing the folks back home to maybe consider this innovation.

Hot on the trail and fresh on the scent, they're sometimes distracted by the local color along the way. One French expedition was recently spotted closing in on an elderly woman whose dog was about to do as nature called. Unaware that video cameras were focusing as she slipped a page from the *New York Times* under the hind quarters of her squatting bichon frise, she crouched with an insouciance that the French found charming to the point of disbelief. They cackled wildly over a tribute that's seldom bestowed upon Parisian pups, this quaint and primitive custom of collecting a dog's mess by hand. Here was one of those eccentric New Yorkers, they thought, self-assured enough to do just about anything in public, an earthy American blessed with all the advantages of blunt informality, and something—finally, something—the French didn't already know.

The team of anthropologists might have yawned without a second thought, bypassed the poop, and forged ahead to all that pee in the dog run, if only they'd looked closer to home. "How can you tell an American in Paris?" asks the old joke. "He's the one picking up after his dog." Any starry-eyed G.I. who's ever slid down the Champs-Elysées with a girl on his arm knows that it's possible to see Paree without ever leaving the farm. It's a well-kept secret but Paris, currently accepted as the reigning poop capital of the world, has a scooping law of its own. Since 2002—a full 25 years after New York's poop scoop law was passed—it has been illegal to deposit any "debris or refuse of animal or vegetal origin on public thoroughfares where they might cause falls." Dog owners used to be allowed to leave the mess in the gutter but now they're required to pick up like New Yorkers. Still, the new law is not taken very seriously and unionized street cleaners would probably declare a general strike if ever it were properly observed. About 150,000 Parisian dogs produce roughly 16 tons of *déjections canines* each day, and on some side streets these seem as unlikely to find a home without public assistance as anywhere else in France.

"Nice, a city paved in dog shit," writes a poop-weary traveler in southern France on one of the many blog sites where those unsavory *baguettes* are among the hottest topics of conversation. "Everywhere in Nice is covered in dog shit and piss. How the residents can have such a lovely city and allow their animals to dump everywhere and anywhere. . . . Yuck." The local *niçois* are no less upset about the situation. Toulousians, too, have an ancient tradition of complaining about the problem that never seems to go away. Slipping into pungent piles has become the stuff of local legend and everyone has a war story to tell. Some 20 years ago, Alan Beck was brought to Toulouse by Pedigree Pet Foods to observe an experimental solution. Dog toilets called *canisettes* had been installed in public areas around the city center. These were sand boxes, not much smaller than the typical New York dog run, constructed in obvious places to draw attention and, in the best of all worlds, to be used. Pedigree was concerned about the rise in anti-dog sentiment due to the Toulousian buildup. Government continues searching for a solution.

Only quite recently has Paris decided to take a precipitous step forward and set an example for other French cities by trying, really trying this time, to make dog owners start scooping. Authorities have a long road ahead of them. Why did they wait so long? The campaign comes with a broader trend seen over the past few years in cities throughout the world where, suddenly and as if from out of nowhere, anti-poop sentiment is taking a more militant turn. For decades after New York took the plunge, many municipalities toyed with the idea by making idle threats and concocting grand schemes, only to try and bury the problem again and again. New evidence, however, indicating that dogs are responsible for an overabundance of *E. coli*, *salmonella*, nitrogen, and phosphorous in more natural settings has stirred up anti-poop fervor and given fodder to pro-scoopers everywhere. And while canine waste's impact on both health and environment in urban centers remains largely theoretical, having feces underfoot in cities, for reasons other than esthetic, is no longer being tolerated.

The worldwide embrace of the poop scoop approach coincides with other recent developments that have nothing whatsoever to do with dogs or their doo. Crackdowns have come with a heightened awareness of the threat of terrorism and more urgent environmental hazards such as global warming and depletion of the ozone layer. From Paris to Budapest to Miami Beach, 2001 appears to be a significant number. Since that time, overall moods have worsened and this has impacted thinking. Just as feelings of impotence before looming threats such as violent crime and pollution incited anti-poop sentiment in New York during the 1970s—and the first wave of AIDS panic probably helped to give a new health law the thrust it needed in the early 1980s—since 9/11 resolve has stiffened internationally and dog owners are being told to act more hygienically. Under all this added stress, changing attitudes on the right to control behavior in dense human populations, to hold individuals accountable for their actions, and to keep track of them if they refuse have played an indirect role in making people keener on addressing dog-related issues more effectively. In the New York tradition of calling people "dog terrorists," greater liberties are being taken to chase down dog owners for any number of infractions and to enforce laws that are basically unenforceable by legal means.[*] Softer, "educational" approaches have been revived with new vigor and some communities want to go a step further. Dresden, Vienna, Edinburgh, and the English town of Bruntingthorpe have moved to create DNA databases that would identify dogs, and their owners, by their droppings. According to these plans, pets would be registered by their DNA at the time of licensing. Specially trained sanitation officers would wander the pavements carrying kits for collecting samples that they would bring to forensic labs for testing. Once the doo was matched to the dog, they'd go knocking on doors. Dresden's proposed fine was the equivalent of $600.

Other cities want to control all kinds of dog "movements" and some are going too far. Geneva is tightening its leash law by trying to make it a crime for any dog, regardless of breed, to walk in parks without a muzzle. In many countries, fines for harming "the environment," meaning both concrete and grass surfaces, have risen astronomically. But the same old questions of enforcement and producing legal evidence in court continue to plague these efforts and some cities are resorting to controversial tactics to overcome these hurdles. Lyon has come under fire by the Big Brother Awards, a group that monitors the abuse of privacy rights, for having secretly planted 48 video surveillance cameras, presumably to control all forms of unlawful behavior. Local authorities in New York have encountered a similar backlash for hiding cameras among tree branches in Washington Square Park. So-

---

[*]Recent revelations that Iraqi insurgents are loading improvised explosive devices (IEDs) with animal waste to better ensure infection in victims also strengthens the dog/terrorism theme first launched by a New York City Parks Commissioner.

cial Democrats stood firm in Vienna and rejected the DNA proposal on the grounds that it would lead to a "police state."[2] Dresden, too, abandoned its database plan, though for a different reason. Predicted to reap hefty profits after passing a break-even point, it was shelved due to extremely high start-up costs and concern over data security. Edinburgh also backed out. Bruntingthorpe, a town of just 200 people and only 30 dogs, has been luckier with peer pressure than with its DNA idea. But in many places, dog owners are simply not responding as well as their neighbors would like. One Montrealer was acquitted of assault charges after a public security officer, who had demanded that the man pick up, claimed he had been attacked with unbagged feces. The alleged flinger then filed his own suit claiming that his character had been defamed by all the publicity generated by a "malicious and illegal prosecution of unfound criminal charges,"[3] *The Gazette* reported. In communities around the world, strong reactions have been countered with equally strong responses. The Spanish town of Tarragona is having some success with its squad of full-time detectives authorized since 2004 to track down, film, and then drag to court polluting pet owners who have no choice but to pay a 15 euro fine. At last count, over twenty offenders had been snagged this way. French reactions to the Catalonian experiment have been enthusiastic. Having such an enforcement campaign in Paris alone, it has been suggested only half in jest, could wipe out the national debt. But Parisian dog owners don't appreciate being followed around by plain-clothed Surveillance Agents who are instructed to take notes on their behavior. And not all of their peers agree that getting those sidewalks clean, at whatever cost, should be a top priority. One blogger recommends letting sleeping dogs lie and leaving the poop right where it is—if only to discourage those ugly Americans from invading.

The French malady will likely spread before it's cured. Dogs are overeating within the hexagon and have grown alarmingly fat in recent years, the obvious result being that they're pooping a lot more. A website called *Rotten.com* says that "obese dogs are rapidly catching up to overweight French kids, with their sagging stomachs and bulging sides capable of depositing larger and more voluminous pockets of dog shit."[4] The Americans, alas, can't be blamed this time and the frustration is mounting. Despite appearances to the contrary, the French hate stepping in dog doo as much as anyone else. Those unappetizing *crottes de chien* are a constant cause for complaint and people would really prefer to avoid them. Turds have tied with cigarette butts as the most-bemoaned blight upon city surfaces. But they aren't going anywhere soon. However strongly the French feel about their fecal dilemma, new attitudes toward poop scoop laws lack that can-do optimism of the Americans and are often sabotaged by the same cynical assumption: The idea will never set well with the French. Instead, the idea remains mostly a thought while an entire subculture grows around the unwholesome matter. Complaining, in fact, seems to be a way of coping with the knowledge that nothing can ultimately be done. Websites are devoted to tracking the sidewalk pestilence and bloggers never tire of making poop jokes. One site includes "The Gallery of Filth," a lurid collection of photographs taken on Parisian pavements displaying those multitudinous mounds in every conceivable circumstance. Poop has become such a fertile topic of study that one wonders what people would do if all that crap were suddenly and miraculously lifted. What is it with the French? The fact that a society with a universal healthcare system has seen fit not to clean up after its dogs suggests a cultural basis for fecal concerns that determines how these problems are viewed and the various approaches, if any, that are taken. Some 600 Frenchmen are wounded each year by slipping on dog doo but, judging from the status quo, these are acceptable casualties. This isn't to say that people have stopped talking about the problem. Paris City Hall reports that 70 percent of citizens interviewed say that dog dirt is the leading cause of uncleanliness. At the same time, 62 percent have come to believe that their neighborhoods are clean. Whatever does this mean? France's poop scoop stance is not so controversial as it is abstract and speculative. It's a theoretical answer to an almost metaphysical question that's discussed ad nauseam in cafés but has limited practical application on the greater sidewalk. Amateur philosopher Gilles Guérin adds a whole new dimension to the topic when he considers this "Parisian Tendency, or Man's Return to an Animal State":

The sidewalks spotted with evacuations or faint traces of fecal matter, the stench that fills the air after a few days of warm and windless weather, the car doors drenched in urine as high as their keyholes, might seem minor concerns when compared to the major problems of this world. However . . . more and more people seem to be accustomed to this state of affairs. Perfectly natural and non-hygienic behavior is becoming more common every day as people grow immune to the most horrendous surroundings. It's not unusual to see someone who's stepped into dog excrement methodically scraping his soles on the edge of the curb and then finishing the job on his doormat. Many people have no problem eating at outdoor restaurants in close proximity to feces.[5]

Shockingly accurate though M. Guérin's descriptions are, the problem is hardly a recent development or a symptom of modern decadence. These laws may not work in France for one simple and timeless reason: the French don't like to follow rules. "That's why the Germans had so much trouble keeping track of us during the Occupation," recalls one Parisian.

Old habits die slowly and French resistance remains strong. But government is finally taking a proactive approach. Traditionally, leaders have paid lip service to the problem but have always ended up dodging the issue of what, exactly, to do about it. Recent steps, however, are offering a glimmer of hope that it's possible to go against the grain of history. "People were afraid of dog owners," recalls Yves Contassot, the Mayor's Deputy for Environmental Affairs, of the pre-scooping days. "In one hand they had a dog, in the other, a vote."[6] Having tried to ignore the situation for centuries, and unwilling to confront anyone with that indelicate request, authorities began by hiring a professional cleanup squad in the early 1990s to do the job that no one seemed willing to do without retirement benefits. A subclass of Parisian sanitation workers—some 60 "pavement saints,"[7] as British journalist Graham Holliday calls them—was paid to scour the sidewalks in large trucks loaded with cleaning fluids and strapped with fire hoses for pavement flushing. Few cities lavish as much as Paris does on poop detail and the French are on the forefront of institutional scooping. Civil servants have also been trained to operate imposing green lawnmower-like machines that inhale dog effluence, among other things. Similar contraptions have since been seen in at least 45 countries throughout the world. They're assigned to the grounds of Buckingham Palace and to Saint Peter's Square, although their suction power has been notoriously ineffective in removing dog dirt. So the French introduced a third type of vehicle known as a *moto-crotte* ("dung-mobile"), or *caninette*, still undergoing a trial stage in many cities. This was the only vehicle designed specifically for canine waste removal. But in Paris these motorcycles with built-on vacuum cleaners were said to be removing only 20 percent of the canine waste left behind, not enough according to Parisian officials who reported that they were costing 4 million euros each year and weren't putting a dent in the dung. "*Moto-crottes* were completely useless," recalls M. Contassot. "They were also causing a great deal of atmospheric and noise pollution."[8] A fire destroyed half of the fleet and City Hall eventually phased out the remaining scooters in 2005.

How long will French street-cleaning machines be an acceptable alternative to scooping? Their obsolescence may be built-in. These high-tech inventions are the objects of ridicule and Luddites abound. One website called *Atypyk.com* brings French sarcasm to a new level with fantastic contraptions that make false promises to solve all of Paris' poop problems. An architect identified as "Rex Bulldogzer" has designed a fleet of imaginary green vehicles that are shown in animation form doing the jobs they might do 24 hours a day, seven days a week, if only someone would believe in them. The first of these, called the "Sucker," moves across the pavement of its own free will collecting dog doo. It looks very much like one of those hovercrafts that dart across the English Channel. The next machine is called the "Broomer." It gets into those hard-to-reach places. The "Hoser" is said to transform bad smells into good ones. The "Waterer," billed as "the final touch to clean sidewalks from any stains," consists of a bowl of goldfish with two leaks. Where does all the poop go once it's been scientifically removed? "Lucky Dog Shit from Paris" is sold in elegant green-and-white canisters. Customers are instructed to remove the lid carefully, place the contents on the ground, and then step into the mess with the left foot. This is guaranteed "to change your life forever instantly." Visitors to the site are encouraged to further improve their lives by printing a down-loadable membership card for "SP," which stands for both "Shit from Paris" and "Souvenir de Paris."[9]

Paris has grown disillusioned with *caninettes* but continues giving *canisettes* a chance. Unfortunately, strategically placed sandboxes with complimentary poop bags aren't the chic spots that were imagined, and they represent yet another expense. Scrapping some of the para-phernalia has been justified for reasons that aren't always economic. Downsizing, it's believed, might also help to prove a point. City Hall suspects that the mere presence of big, costly machines and dedicated workers was actually encouraging dog owners to go on breaking the law and to believe that they themselves were not responsible for the mess. Changing this mentality, and then their behavior, has been the focus of the new campaign. Much like New York's own EPA, whose Depart-ment of Sanitation flatly refused throughout the 1970s to lower itself to picking up after pets, Paris has also decided to turn up the heat on dog walkers by taking that last and desperate resort (peer pressure) by using its right arm (publicity). Any change, it is now believed, will have to come from citizens themselves. The theory, thinly stretched according to some, is that a less permissive society will be a more abrasive incen-tive for keeping those sidewalks clean.

"Zero dung" was the official objective set by Contassot for the spring of 2002, a utopian goal that, despite a marked improvement, still hasn't been met. Like New York's ideal of "zero pollution" in the 1970s, it probably never will be. But public opinion, whether in response to surfaces that are actually cleaner, or to all the attention the program has generated, is changing in government's favor. Many Parisians inter-viewed say that they see an improvement in walking conditions since the new poop scoop imperative has been in effect. "In the beginning," says Contassot, "dog owners were a bit surprised. Fewer than 20 per-cent were picking up. Now two-thirds are."[10] Though these figures are debatable, the program has had some effect. Colorful signs reading "I love my dog/I'm responsible for my dog/I take care of my dog" have been placed in trouble spots across the city. Brochures on "How to lead a good life with your dog in Paris" and a bountiful supply of plastic poop scoop bags are distributed to any willing takers. Dog owner education is provided in public parks by "benevolent monitors," also known as "canine educators." Less friendly tactics have included promoting the city's force of 90 Health Inspectors to the level of "Surveillance Agents" who have the right to issue tickets for littering. Though the number of summonses given is always an unsound measure of a law's success, officials report that over 300 dog owners received fines of 183 euros (the same penalty set for dropping cigarette butts) between January and June of 2006. And while those narrow *trottoirs*, winding cobbled streets, *grands boulevards*, and manicured parks are still bespeckled and far from being declared feces-free, there is, indeed, a difference and the campaign marches on.

After six years of being courted and pursued, many Parisian dog owners still refuse to cooperate, and they have supporters. The local Society for the Protection of Animals, recalling the reaction of New York's ASPCA in the 1970s, has condemned the city's "*anti-crotte*" project for being impractical and unrealistic. How can anyone adequately explain to dog owners, it asks, that they're suddenly being expected to clean even the gutters, which they've grown so accustomed to using, or else pay a large fine? The penalty, which can be as high as the equivalent of $500, is "based on the judge's mood and the state of the National Treasury," says one dog advisory service. Even the "benevolent monitors" have their doubts about the program and are suggesting that more money be invested in equipment. "Just look at how thin this is," says one of the instructors about the government-issued poop scoop bags. "It feels like you're putting your hand right into the stuff!"[11]

French resistance continues but secondary cities haven't lost all faith in their capital. Struggling under the weight of their own massive poop problems, they have welcomed the latest Parisian advances with open arms. Caen has beefed up its efforts with 100 new bag dispensers. Sandboxes are all the rage in Dieppe. Asnières-sur-Seine even gives

A recent advertisement for the anti-poop campaign in Paris reads: "Any left foot will tell you: More and more dog owners are scooping in Paris. That's the new Paris! 30,000 waste baskets are available in Paris. Any dog waste left on public walkways brings a fine of 183 euros."

Source: Image courtesy of Paris City Hall.

perplexed pet owners a choice of curbing, scooping, or using one of 38 *canisites* (a regional variation on *canisettes*). If they soil the side-walk, however, they're hazarding an impressive 450 euro fine. Tours is still giving dung-mobiles a chance. Strasbourg has launched a "sen-sitization" campaign and Bordeaux is dabbling in "conscientious-ness" and creating special dog paths in public parks. Websites like *Cyber-chien.com*, "the site for clean dogs in urban settings," encourage these efforts. Others are skeptical. "Will the war on canine waste take place?" one site asks of Nice's promise to go after a whopping nine daily tons. "Sick and tired of dog-do?" asks a Grenoble blog. "Are you obeying the anti-poop law of Orléans?" asks another in a parental tone that the French don't like. A Parisian dog owner, not a good role model, has consulted *Zonechien.com* on the technicalities of the local law. Is it alright to leave his Baby-Cuddles' mess, he asks, in the gutter, on the grass, or under a tree? "Are these considered the sidewalk?"

Some French cities have lost patience with Parisians and are taking matters into their own hands. Initiatives include Besançon's campaign to handle its modest 3.5 tons of daily *baguettes*. Two special events were held there in 2003, one on the *Esplanade des Droits de l'Homme*, where government tried reaching out to dog owners with "education," and then a less egalitarian phase of "mediation" that con-sisted of having police officers patrol the rest of the city for lawbreakers. "We didn't want to point a finger at dog owners," said the program head to *La Terre de chez nous*. But whom else could they blame? Authorities have considered slipping postcards that read "Better to pick it up than squash it" into the mailboxes of reputed *je-m'en-foutiste* rebels.[12]

That same year, Lyon took a revolutionary approach by resort-ing to "non-verbal communication," *Agence France-Presse* reported. Responding to the 40 tons abandoned per annum by about 140,000 dogs, the City planted 10,000 pieces of fake poop—the kind you used to be able to get in gag gift shops in Times Square but cast in bright red plastic to draw more attention—along Lyon's busiest thoroughfares. The unspoken joke was spoiled by a vast information campaign with a budget of 45,000 euros, and "Pick up or pay" as a verbal reminder.[13]

Toulouse has taken perhaps the most creative and bilious approach of all the French cities. "We're not afraid of being provocative because we want behavior to change," announced Mayor Jean-Luc Moudenc in 2006, when a lavish publicity campaign was launched in a town whose residents have been at each others' throats for generations. The recent rise in militancy recalls New York in its heyday of vigilantism. "The Guide to Cleanliness and Trash Sorting" was the first step in the costly plan to pressure dog owners into compliance. An elaborate animated film was also produced and with a message that isn't cute. Designed to inspire anger, stop-action figures made of multicolored clay are seen walking cobbled streets on a sunny day when, with a crash of thunder, a deluge of dog dirt begins falling from the sky. Umbrellas are useless. Enormous, sloshy piles land on cartoon pedestrians as they scurry for shelter. A mother manages to cover her baby's carriage before three masses land atop with sound effects intended to turn the stomach. "Each day five tons of canine waste fall on Toulouse," says the announcer. "Stop the downpour." The film was distributed to local theaters and shown on French television. An audio version was broadcast on radio stations.[14]

The Toulousian effort draws attention from near and far. Graham Holliday feels strongly enough about the poop problem to have created a flashy website called "Filthy France . . . for a turd-free republik." Here he gives constant updates on the fecal dilemma and proof of its gravity. Included are links to related topics and blog sites, and a photo gallery where he displays his own images from Toulouse that include sidewalk poop before and after someone's slid through and then tracked it for a block or so; a pair of crap-caked Timberlands; scenic squares marred by a single turd; even a mound that's been claimed with a tiny French flag—"Not sure if this is something old or something new," reads the caption, "but it's definitely **something borrowed** [this provides a link to a site detailing the health risks of contact with dog feces]. Alas, it's not something blue. It's brown with a French flag in it near Place Wilson in Toulouse." Holliday encourages amateur photographers to post their own poop pics taken on sidewalks throughout France to *Flickr.com*, the site where they can and do take his advice. "Should my Flickr account and blogs be reserved for the purposes of promotion of the French travel industry with lots of soft focus pictures of lovely chateaus and berets?" asked Holliday about the assumption that it's disrespectful to portray an entire people in such an unflattering light, to make snap judgments of other cultures, or to engage in jokes that only the target group has the right to make. "Or do you mean only French people should be allowed to complain about this problem? And only French people should be allowed to take photos of dog shit on French streets?"[15] Holliday says the condition of streets in Toulouse, despite all the recent efforts, is still shameful. "My feeling is the campaign was an expensive, high-profile, short-term thing more about making the authorities look like they're doing something when they're actually doing nothing. . . . If I took photos of every shit I spotted on the pavements of Toulouse, I'd be uploading 20, 30, or more pics per day."[16]

All the chest-pounding and unflinching displays of empirical evidence don't make France's poop prospects look any more promising. It will be interesting to follow the progress of a recent anti-smoking law, another copycat of an American precedent. Health Law 1310, it should be recalled, was used as a kind of experiment in peer pressure that, many New Yorkers hoped intensely, might help pave the way for similar legislation aimed at smoking. And so it did. But in France, where smokers are used to snuffing out their butts before boarding subway trains, only to light them up again on the next platform, it doesn't seem likely that either target group, smokers or dog owners, will submit very kindly to peer pressure. Most smokers have complied so far, but not without voicing their resentment, and forcing them to smoke in front of cafés rather than in them does mean making a tradeoff between two evils. The first sign of compliance with the smoking ban was the dramatic increase in butts left on sidewalks, which don't seem to be getting any cleaner. The French themselves are among the first to agree with this bleak forecast and the skies don't look sunny. "I think that recent announcements to address the dog problem," says Gilles Guérin, "are nothing more than words designed to satisfy that part of the electorate that's unhappy about

London canine waste can and a few that didn't quite make it.
Source: Irwin Rosenbloom

filth in Paris. There is no visible result. Apart from the major thoroughfares and the tourist spots like the Champs-Elysées, Paris streets are
generally as dirty as they were before. People just learn to get used
to these conditions."[17] Guérin's "Gallery of Filth" includes one recent
photo taken of dog doo and a cigarette butt spread side-by-side near the
wheel of a parked car. A little arrow points to the butt, clearly distin-
guishing it from the feces. Guérin concludes his "Return to an Animal
State" with a few dark words on the moral condition of societies where
public awareness, he says, is in irreversible decline:

> One can easily produce a multitude of similar descriptions detailing
> current behavior and the growing insensitivity toward filth in general.
> One of the unique characteristics of man, the "conscious" species, is
> his disgust for "dirty things." . . . Animals do not reject filth . . . the

lack of disgust and the habit of playing with one's excrement are signs of senility. . . . The current behavioral trend is thus indicative of the degenerating state of mankind in general.[18]

* * *

Cities around the world, refusing to give into French cynicism but seldom matching New York's single-mindedness, continue their marches toward tidier pavements and greener pastures. Because their surfaces tend to be freer of trash of all kinds than New York's could ever hope to be, many can afford to aim for that one form of litter that bothers them more than anything else. But perceptions of the gravity of this single problem, how it is ranked among other issues, and the individual solutions that are proposed would, again, seem to reflect cultural concerns and personal styles. Sometimes the attention paid to canine waste is even inspired by legitimate health and environmental threats that are difficult to deny.

For the Japanese, courtesy is usually enough to make enforcement of local ordinances unnecessary. Despite the recent boom in dog production and a wealth of hideous deformities due to inbreeding, the Japanese can be relied upon to keep their sidewalks clean, though friendly reminders are sometimes posted. The town of Mashiki uses a dose of *kawaii*, or post-war "cuteness," to reach out to dog owners. Brightly colored signs show cartoon dogs with bug-eyes doing their business and suggesting with almost psychotic smiles: "Let's take our dog poop home!" In Denmark, too, dog owners seem to be willing to pick up without much resentment. In fact, they tie their bags with neat little knots. But Mexico City, which has to contend with some of the world's least breathable air, and a host of health problems related to some 3 million stray dogs, hasn't had the time even to begin thinking about how to handle canine waste.

In other countries, where reminders seem necessary and the means exist to get the job done, poop problems are being given at least as much attention as they deserve. London's Dog Act of 1996 was passed for a combination of esthetic and health reasons and it has been taken quite seriously. Once the law was passed by the House of Commons, the House of Lords joined in, vowing "to crack down on dog fouling" by exerting "moral pressure" upon dog owners. A decade later, London sidewalks are infinitely more walkable than those of Paris and without all that heavy machinery. Once a mound is left, however, it tends to stay where it is. Fewer messes also tend to be more noticeable and public outrage has not been altogether calmed. New powers came into force in 2006 with the Clean Neighborhood and Environment Act. Dog bylaws have been replaced with dog control orders that enable local governments and parishes to deal with this dog fouling by banning pets from certain areas, enforcing leash laws, and restricting the number of dogs that a person can walk at one time. Fines for failure to scoop have risen to between 50 and 1000 pounds.

More draconian measures like DNA databases are usually Anglo-German but these seem to be more distinctly Germanic in style. You almost can't blame them. The Federal Republic receives an estimated 1.4 kilos (1400 cubic tons or 3 million pounds) of *Hundekot* each day and is still searching for a solution. Dog owners, along with Turks and assorted Muslims, are among the groups most popularly blamed for litter in general. Some citizens, however, have been able to stay objective and keep their sense of humor in a culture that tends not to shy away from things scatological. Free-spirited Berliners don't like it but they're learning to live with their dog problem. "Rather than the rodent-esque creatures Munich residents like to drag around at the end of a leash—or carry around in bike baskets," says *Spiegel Online*, "a real Berliner wouldn't be caught dead with a mini-mutt. Nor with a pooper-scooper for that matter. When picking a table at a sidewalk café, choose carefully. The wafting scent of dog deposit can ruin a meal no matter how well prepared."[19] Government balances this good-hearted apathy with helpful reminders on kiosks that are stationed throughout the city and a message that's been translated, for some strange reason, for the benefit of English speakers: "Keep clean Berlin!" the signs

Japan uses *kawaii,* or post-war "cuteness," to suggest politely that dog owners pick up. Signs read: "Dog doo prohibited," "If your dog poos while you're out for a walk, perhaps you might clean up after him?" and, finally, a bulldog says "Poop!" over a headline reading: "Let's take our dog poo home!"

Source: Used with permission of Jon Climpson.

implore. Hamburg, too, cares about its poop problem but is trying more seductive measures like "dog stations," the equivalent of the French *canisettes*. Dresden has canned its DNA proposal and is scrambling for a Plan B. Could this be recycling?

While Germans everywhere struggle to convert their irritation into more positive energy, at least one has found a way of devoting poop to a higher purpose. Police in the German town of Bayreuth were baffled in 2005 when an anonymous protester, apparently against the war in Iraq, somehow managed to claim about 3,000 piles of dog offal, over the course of a year, with little yellow flags bearing the image of a smiling George W. Bush. The entire town was covered. Who took the time to count each infraction? "German Police Baffled by Bush Poo-Flags," reported *Indybay.org*. "We have sent out extra patrols to try and catch whoever is doing this act," said a police spokesperson. "But frankly, we don't know what we would do if we caught him red-handed."[20] The idea has taken root and poop-flagging is much more common than one might think. In fact, the act of a lone flagger has become an environmental art installation of global proportions that should make Christo smile. It all started in the good old U.S.A. The instigator is a San Francisco website called *Madeyouthink.org*, which sends free flags, in a choice of colors, to any protesters wishing to claim piles of their own. "You may have to follow your dog around for awhile," the site instructs, "or eat a lot of fiber."[21] So far, photos of these commissioned works have been posted from settings as diverse as Petra and the Pyrenees, the Bavarian Alps and Midtown Manhattan, among many other places where the Bush markers have been used, if not to spearhead a sanitation problem, then to make a political point.

Another colorful approach to the problem comes from Boulder, Colorado, where a combination of esthetic, environmental, and economic concerns have led officials and citizens to take some creative and unapologetic measures to protect wild areas from alleged polluters. Here is an opportunity to consider the impact of canine waste, not in cities but in surrounding areas where it can and sometimes does affect the environment.

The District of North Vancouver, BC, reports a high success rate with this non-confrontational approach to law enforcement.

Source: District of North Vancouver

Feelings about dog leavings tend to be strong for Coloradoans whose admiration for the Great Outdoors is perhaps unmatched. Unspoiled land, essential to the state's economy, is protected by some of the nation's highest tax deductions for property owners who agree never to develop their own. Much of the state's identity has been invested in silent contemplation and recreational activities, among these hiking with dogs. But some people say the extensive trails that make the forests accessible have become obstacle courses in recent years.[†] A greater

---

[†] As is often the case, government's perception of dog problems doesn't necessarily reflect a majority opinion or take into account scientific studies. Marc Bekoff and Carron A. Meaney, for example, took a closer look at the situation in "Interaction Among Dogs, People, and Nature in Boulder, Colorado: A Case Study." Dogs in pub-

awareness of the potentially harmful effects of abundant fecal deposits on ecosystems has drawn more attention to dog owners. Despite a poop scoop law that's been in effect for over a decade, water runoff tainted with canine waste is believed to be having an impact on streams and has been blamed for bacteria levels in Boulder Creek that far exceed state health standards for swimming. No matter what some people are told, they go on assuming that pet feces are fertilizer and thus good for the environment. In response, media attention has been strongly encouraged. Fines have increased from $25 to $100. Catching dog owners in the act, even more unlikely in the deep woods than it is in big cities, has been made a priority for enforcement officers. But more colorfully, Educational Outreach workers have gone on a sweep of trails and hillsides in search of individual piles, then planted two-foot metal rods with bright blue flags into every one of these that they could find. Unlike the German installation, no politician was targeted but faceless dog owners who marred the natural beauty were made to feel uncomfortable. "If they see 100 flags on the landscape," says one official from the Open Space and Mountain Parks Department, "it makes an impression."[23]

As the long and colorful history of approaches to a highly emotional problem has shown, concern over dog doo can push people to some absurd extremes. More colorful still are the efforts of one Boulder resident who's taken it upon himself to confront careless dog fanciers who, he says, have no regard for the indigenous growth. Patrick Murphy, a plant ecologist, has been called "the Pooperatzi" and "the Prince of Poop,"[24] says *The Daily Camera.* Murphy's spent several years plotting piles of dog offal he discovers on Mount Sanitas—apparently no longer living up to its name. The technology is astounding. He uses a Trimble Geoexplorer II global positioning device to create aerial

---

lic parks were reported by trained observers to be much more friendly off leash than on leash. As for their impact on "the environment," polls reported 40 percent more people than dogs disturbing wildlife; 50 percent more people than dogs destroying vegetation; and 50 more people than dogs having harmful effects on bodies of water. Unruly humans, not pets, were seen by eye witnesses to be the greatest threat to parks and 97 percent of those polled said they were comfortable with dogs off leash.[22]

South Jersey Pooper Scoopers, one of many collection services in operation around the world, offers gift certificates.

Source: Image courtesy of South Jersey Pooper Scoopers.

images that he posts online. These pictures bare an uncanny resemblance to the satellite images seen on CNN during the Gulf War. Each pile of poo is painstakingly pinpointed and marked, as is the nearest trash receptacle, which clearly hasn't been used. In November 2001 alone, Murphy documented 1,494 indiscretions laid out in patterned clusters on one Sanitas Valley trail. Every few months, he sets out on a new plotting expedition. The timing of his first formal presentation to the Boulder City Council could not have been more precise. Barely two months after the World Trade Center attacks, he asked the Council to ban dogs from Mount Sanitas for one year in order to stop what the *Camera* called, with a hint of sarcasm, "the evils of canine waste on public lands."[25] Boulder has about 120 miles of trails, many of which are open to off-leash dogs. City Council, which had recently declared dog owners to be "guardians" of their pets, did not welcome Murphy's suggestion to ban dogs from the trails. Instead, the parks department launched a 10-day educational campaign and Murphy set out on another 2-day survey. He's not likely to be discouraged. Just before his presentation to City Council, he had been acquitted on harassment charges after videotaping two dog owners whose pooches were running off-leash in a schoolyard. As for the pollution claims that Murphy has staked, Chris Rudkin, Boulder's Water Quality Coordinator, doubted whether dogs could be held responsible for the damage. "There are lots of sources out there," he told the *Camera*. "To point the finger at only one group like domestic pets might be drawing conclusions beyond the science we have to support it."[26]

Startling revelations, however, were made the following year and confirmed what some people had believed all along. "Water pollution linked to dog do,"[27] read the headline from *USA Today*. Boulder dogs, it turned out, were having an impact on the landscape not with bacteria but with excess nitrogen. As a result, native grasses in a few spots were being overcome by weeds. This alone would not have been national news. Other communities across the country were also presenting new evidence to confirm that dogs were, indeed, causing some environmental problems. Most of these concerned water.

Storm water runoff is the number one source of water pollution in the United States. Human waste, industrial farming, lawn fertilizers from private yards and landscapes overwrought with golf courses, as well as motor oil and a host of other curbside contaminates account for the vast majority of this pollution. But the case against dogs, however miniscule, can no longer be ignored. Unlike big cities where concerns over canine waste tend to be more esthetic, even negligible when diluted by a wealth of more serious pollutants, surrounding areas can now make a harder case that they're being at least partially affected by dog droppings. Algae is overtaking some lakes, and birds and humans aren't the only guilty parties. Excess nitrogen can lower the level of oxygen in water, killing aquatic life. Bacteria, too, seem to be on the rise. More sophisticated DNA testing, and new studies of the antibiotic resistance of microbes of various species, have identified dogs as one of several possible polluters. Interestingly enough, though, new detection methods for identifying pollution sources were available since the mid-1990s but weren't generally talked about until 2002 when the *USA*

Today story appeared—barely nine months after 9/11—and concern over dog doo was skyrocketing.

The "Fido hypothesis,"[28] as researchers call the new thinking, has led to action across the board. Though the seriousness of the damage and the extent that can be blamed on pets remain unclear, communities around the country are operating on the assumption that dogs pose a serious threat to the environment and, even before testing their waters, are putting their money on poop scoop laws. As New York learned a long time ago, this is easier said than done. A survey conducted by the Center for Watershed Protection revealed that 41 percent of Americans admitted they rarely if ever picked up their dogs' mess on the assumption that "it eventually goes away."[29] People also say they feel humiliated when asked to carry scoopers, as did New Yorkers when hit with that same request. Higher fines and awareness campaigns have come in response to beaches that are routinely closed for public safety reasons and contamination found in other waterways. San Diego, Arlington, Boise, and Clearwater, Florida, are among the trouble spots for bacteria and dogs are said to carry as much as 30 percent of the blame in some cases. Burlington, Vermont, is struggling with high levels of phosphorous. Seattle, which discussed handing out "good citizen" tags in the 1990s, has taken a less polite stand by requiring that dog doo be removed from private property within 24 hours. Under the new regime of "zero tolerance,"[30] the fine for leaving canine waste in one's own backyard is twice the amount for failing to scoop in public places. But enforcing this ordinance is as difficult as making sure that dog walkers carry pooper-scoopers with them at all times, another local requirement. The cost of patrolling neighborhoods for accumulation offenses would be exorbitant and Seattleites are expected to inform on each other, which rarely happens.‡

---

‡This is the opposite problem that Tel Aviv encountered in 1999 when it was suggested that getting dog doo off land, public or private, was actually illegal. Canine waste, it was said, had to stay right where it was due to an older agricultural law forbidding the removal of "fertilizer" from another person's land. One lawyer actually demanded the City return all fines collected from the few non-scoopers it had

The delightful absurdity of all these colorful extremes doesn't mean that evidence should be denied across the board. City folk are reminded that pollution isn't just an urban problem. The country isn't as clean as some people would like and industry isn't the only culprit. Confronted with these new findings, however, we should be extremely cautious when assigning blame. Communities around the nation are pointing fingers at dog owners for polluting the environment and it's important to keep things in their proper perspective. An intriguing website called *Poopreport.com*, which covers all matters scatological from every possible angle, has posted an item on its "B.M. Newswire," just in case anyone missed a story that appeared in *USA Today* two months after the dog exposé. This added information places recent developments within a broader context and might help to keep pollution problems on a more human scale, which is probably where they belong.

"It gushes even in dry weather,"[32] said one environmental leader, leaking a story that municipal governments have known for eons but seldom talk about. He was referring to a pipe that expels, as it's been doing for well over 100 years, untold millions of gallons of raw, untreated human sewage directly into a Cincinnati creek. This could have been a scene from Roman Polanski's *Chinatown* but it isn't the water supply that's being drained. Instead, more than 100 pipes like this one are routinely dumping human effluence into waterways around the metropolitan area. Cincinnati is not alone. Since the 1800s, dozens of other American cities have also been engaging in this practice, illegal since the Clean Water Act of 1972, of flushing toilet "overflow"[33] directly into waterways. Population growth has been used as a reason for doing what's become customary in many places. Rainwater, too, which seeps into old, cracking pipes and causes them to overload, is often blamed. For whatever reasons, these flushes occur an estimated 40,000 times each year across the country and will no doubt continue because cities simply don't have the financial means, they say, to handle

---

been able to catch over the years. The courts disagreed with this interpretation and no monies were refunded.[31]

the excess sewage in any other way. Cincinnati's sewer rates, it's been estimated, would increase by as much as 1500 percent if the problem were ever taken seriously. "It would bankrupt us," said the director of the Metropolitan Sewer District of Greater Cincinnati. "It would be, last one out, turn out the lights. Cincinnati would just be another wide spot on I-75."[34] As the problem is left unremedied, populations continue to expand in cities across the nation. Old pipes grow older, rusting, cracking, and leaking harmful bacteria, viruses, and assorted parasites before they can even reach their destination—which is the local water supply. So raw human sewage continues to pollute both soil and water, and to sicken about 1 million people each year, according to the Centers for Disease Control and Prevention. This poisons shellfish, forces beaches to close, and contaminates drinking water sources. Perhaps for these reasons, many environmentalists agree that, in the vast majority of cases and among all forms of animal waste, the human kind poses by far the greatest threat to the environment. "Sewage overflows occur in every city," Nancy Stoner of the National Resources Defense Council told *USA Today*. "These pipes are out of sight, out of mind."[35] Federal authorities have, nonetheless, taken some of the heat off themselves by fining some cities a few hundred thousand and requiring them to spend hundreds of millions to fix their overflow problems. But cities are challenging these moves and the dumping will continue into the foreseeable future.

If the country isn't safe from humans, then how can we protect it from dogs? Once again, it's possible to conclude that the canine damage is being overestimated. "Most dog waste in any real concentrations comes through city run-off," says Alan Beck, "which in cities with combined systems gets processed. In cities with direct run-off, this gets diluted. All studies related to nitrate-type contamination find agricultural run-off the main issue. Cows and pigs do a hell of a lot more damage but city people are better targets. The 'Fido hypothesis' should be the intensive farming hypothesis. But we all know that city people, especially those in New York, are heathen, minority criminals who love their dogs while mugging other people. Why not blame them for contamination in the water as well?"[36]

Since *USA Today* reported the new evidence of dog pollution, papers around the country have covered the problem. But seen in a broader context, is canine waste really a threat in natural settings? Consistent with this history of approaches to the many problems dogs are said to cause, it appears that an undue portion of blame is once again being foisted on them and their caretakers. In the interest of political expediency, governments are tiptoeing around those gargantuan threats that seem to defy all human intervention, and are aiming instead for the one that they can, in some small way and with vast press coverage, get a handle on. "Zero pollution" has always been a noble but unrealistic goal, though helping the environment in some small way seems better than doing nothing at all. If governments could afford to do more, then maybe they would. But for the moment, lone acts of "community participation"— which is to say, poop scoop laws—are once again being called upon to do the job that governments cannot or will not do. These laws, among many possible approaches to the problem, are becoming more popular. But even if they worked at 100 percent capacity, they would have a very limited impact on the environment.

Whomever or whatever is to blame for pollution, one thing is for certain: Dog owners should be on their guards. Historically, dogs have been feared for two closely related reasons that are two sides of the same coin, if not both ends of the beast. Over the years, teeth and hindquarters have been regulated, respectively, with leash laws and poop scoop laws. Many anti-dog people consider these to be equally important. And now they have a way of enforcing both in a single blow. If dogs are said to be polluting the environment because they're running off-leash and the owners couldn't find their leavings in the deep woods even if they wanted to, then crazier enforcement of leash laws is sure to follow shortly. Dogs will be denied the exercise and freedom of movement they need in order to lead happy, healthy lives, not only in cities that tend to shy away from the dog run idea (or to accept it with appalling complacency as New York does) but in wide open country where pets, and indigenous wildlife, will be blamed for pollution. Just as dogs were held accountable for the urban crisis in the 1970s, which came at a time of greater awareness of ecological disaster, once again they're said to be ruining the world's natural environment.

Assuming that dog deposits should and could be collected from surfaces in town or country, then what's to be done with them? Poop scoop laws without biodegradable bags ensure that individual parcels will be buried in landfills, like the one that makes up a large part of Staten Island, where they're mummified for generations. Is this the best solution? Not since the sixties or seventies have New Yorkers had much interest in "goin' to California," but they might look to their polar opposite for some guidance now. That state is on the cutting edge of environmental reform and has been for many years. We forget that California set auto emissions standards in the 1960s before New York's EPA even existed. In recent years, residents see no reason not to devote vast stretches of beach to off-leash dogs, and yet they choose not to back down when government and industry try to sabotage their clean air efforts. San Francisco, the first city in the world to declare a ban on smoking in indoor public areas, is now the first to make a serious, city-wide attempt at recycling dog doo into energy. Following the example of less extensive European efforts, and practices already in place at a few dairy farms in the United States, San Francisco is turning animal waste into methane to reduce its dependency on natural gas. After years of discussion, this is finally happening. Human waste products could be next. "There's no question poop is profitable," said the President of Intelligent Products in Kentucky to the *Boston Herald*, prophetically in 1998 when marketing his patented pooper-scooper called the Mutt Mitt. "Gasoline was once dinosaur poop. There's no reason we can't turn human poop into gasoline. Human waste has a commercial value of $19 billion a year."[37]/§ The environment, too, profits from this alterna-

---

§Victor Hugo would have agreed. "A big city," he wrote in *Les Misérables*, "is the most powerful of dunging animals. To use the town to manure the country is to ensure prosperity. If our gold is so much waste, then, on the other hand, our waste is so much gold. . . . A sewer is a mistake."[38] The idea that human feces might be better appreciated somewhere else is not a new one. For centuries in London, waste was

tive fuel source because so little energy is used in the conversion process. Canine waste, for example, is collected in biodegradable bags and placed in "digesters" that capture methane as the matter decomposes. Will Brinton, a biowaste expert with Wood Ends Laboratory, recently told *NPR* that canine waste is an extremely efficient producer of energy. Many cities, he said, already have digesters in place for breaking down organic waste, so no new technology is needed. America produces roughly 10 million tons of pet feces each year and this most recent advance makes the stuff more exciting than ever before. San Francisco has taken another giant leap forward by outlawing the use of plastic bags in retail stores. Biodegradable bags made of potato starch will be used instead, thus decreasing the demand for the oil used in manufacturing plastic and making scooping more environmentally friendly all around. Whether shopping or walking their dogs, people will be making the smart choice. Once again, dogs are solving at least as many problems as they cause. Reckoning with canine waste has played a role in making the city confront more extensive environmental threats. Dogs are earning their keep.

But whether poop is fermented, flagged, photographed, filmed, DNA-encoded, or just plain talked about, we return to that eternal question of how to get it off the ground. If dog owners won't cooperate, and the social cost of trying to change their minds is simply too high, then it's always possible to hire people who don't mind all that much. The world is chock-full of professional poop-scooping services that will arrive on time to remove the mess before it can enter the streams or offend too many passersby. If governments are really as concerned about these problems as they say they are, then they'll stop pussyfooting around and get a grip on the situation. An entire industry has grown around the failure of poop scoop laws and it's about time to start tapping into this resource. Dog owners, too, stand to benefit from having their own yards cleaned. "Love your dog but hate cleaning up after it?" asks

---

collected in buckets by night and spread to the countryside. China continues to use human excrement extensively as a fertilizer.

one company. "You've labored all week and took a lot of crap at work," says *PoopButler.com*, a site that lists removal companies around the world. "Do you really need to be taking it at home, too?" The following list of poop-scooping companies is by no means exhaustive. Hundreds of other services are waiting for the business.

A1 Pooper Scoopin'	Calgary
Bowser's Bomb Vanishers	Connecticut
Delta Doggy Doo	Vancouver
Dig-A-Dung	British Columbia
The Do Do Crew	Ontario
Dog Dooty	Ontario
Dog-Gone Waste	Los Angeles
The Doggy Doo Wagon	British Columbia
Doody Duty	British Columbia
The Dung Beetle	El Dorado City, CA
Following Fido	Ontario
Got Poop?	Alaska
The Grand Poobah	Colorado
K-9 Pollution Solutions	Auckland, New Zealand
Mutt-Minders	Modesto, CA
Muttley's Maid	Colorado
Ooh Pooh!	Colorado
Pet Maid	Ontario
Pooh Doody	Yuba City, CA
Poop Patrol	Toronto
The Poop Squad	Ottawa
Pooper Troopers	Seattle
Scooperhero! Defender of the Clean Yard	Baltimore, MD
Scoopy Doo	Winnipeg
Tidy Tails	San Bernardino, CA
We Do Doo Doo	Los Angeles
Yucko's	Illinois and Missouri

WHO COULD HAVE KNOWN?

> "Then I looked down at the water immediately beneath me, and knew that New York was a real city. All kinds of refuse went floating by: bits of wood, straw from barges, bottles, boxes, paper, occasionally a dead cat or dog, hideously bladder-like, its four paws stiff and indignant towards heaven."
>
> —Rupert Brooke, *Letters from America*[1]

Back in old New York, the question of whose duty it is to clean up after dogs has been settled for some time. A necessary law has encouraged a useful custom, one so blended into daily life that its practice has become matter-of-fact and the results, for those unfamiliar with the unruly pre-scooping days, invisible but for the clearings on pavements and lawns where there once was something to shout about. Dogs are now the responsibility of their owners. People have the right of way. New York can move on.

What with all the free walking space, newspaper coverage of dogs has changed dramatically since Health Law 1310 went into effect. Poop and pet problems of all kinds, for years the subjects of lengthy articles and angry letters, have lost much of their appeal. People today tend to like their animal news to be happy and carefree. The post-9/11 flurry of activity, and the renewed effort to blame dogs for destroying "the environment" across the globe, are recent developments. With a little luck, these will also be short-lived. But the curious silence of the intervening years shows how pivotal the poop scoop law really was. In New York, as soon as the new decree appeared to be working in the early 1980s and the city seemed well on its way toward recovery, serious attention to dogs came to a screeching halt with the scope of coverage and the sheer number of articles devoted to them dropping, like the city's human birth rate in the previous decade, to almost zero. This four-legged dilemma that once divided New York and soured community relations has pretty much fallen off our radar. With all due respect to the law and its many helpful effects, could anything else explain this utter loss of interest?

The appeal of a juicy topic didn't dry up completely. On the contrary, a central part of Rudolph Giuliani's "quality of life" campaign in the 1990s—after arresting those homeless windshield cleaners who held idling motorists hostage at traffic lights until the light changed and their cars could go polluting the rest of the city—was engaging in hot pursuit of the handful of dirty dog people who continued to break a social contract. Crime and dirt, or what little was left of them from the seventies, were the targets of a two-pronged attack that turned against dogs near the end of Giuliani's second term. The mayor's decision to play the dog card, and the renewed campaign against canine waste that followed, came at a time when his career had suffered tremendous damage. Like John Lindsay and his own last-minute endorsement of a poop scoop law in 1972 when his popularity was at a low point, Giuliani's sudden interest in dog doo was the act of a desperate man.

But before the law-and-order mayor began reviving the specter of a civil war, his Parks Commissioner, Henry Stern, tried a less confrontational approach by celebrating the 20th anniversary of the poop scoop law in Washington Square Park. Promptly on August 1, 1998, Stern stood in the shadow of the great arch, at a tolerable distance from a raunchy dog run, with a conspicuous golden retriever named "Boomer" panting and drooling by his side and Sanitation Commissioner John Doherty, who had come to lend moral support. Old Ed Koch, Stern's former boss and a veteran from the dog wars, looked down approvingly from his apartment at no. 2 Fifth Avenue. Seen from above, crowning the center of activity were television crews, newspaper reporters, and a small group of dog owners who wanted nothing more in the world than to see themselves and their pets on the evening news. Nearby a table was laid out with free dog toys and treats, as well as a cake baked for human consumption in the hope that people wouldn't bite the hand that fed them. But there were no skirmishes in Washington Square Park, the grass museum that had once been a setting for civil resistance. On the contrary, a few participants were almost overeager to outline, in sycophantic detail, their own personal scooping styles to the reporters who took notes dutifully. One woman with a pug named "Winnie" said she used Ziploc bags, which she sealed quickly. Another law-abiding citizen used paper towels. Someone else used Dixie cups. Proud scoopers were rudely pushed aside by Bash Dibra, the celebrity dog trainer whom Stern, clearly unfamiliar with how to handle a dog, kept around to help with "Boomer" the golden retriever at public appearances—and who had every intention of being seen, as agreed, smiling next to the Commissioner. Stern himself was not known to smile much but he praised responsible, scooping citizens who took pride in their city. Thanks to Health Law 1310, he said, New Yorkers had learned to "coexist" despite their many differences.

Attitudes toward dogs had undergone a radical change since the 1970s in both the news and politics. These once-controversial animals had become so desirable that some officeholders wanted to be seen holding leashes at all times. The Parks Commissioner had gone perhaps too far with this strategy and was being taken to court by Manhattan Borough President Ruth Messinger for spending public money on a campaign to insert his conspicuous golden into the *Guinness Book of World Records* as "the world's most-petted dog." Mayor Giuliani, who was also expected to attend that day but never showed, was coming under fire himself for all the undue attention being drawn to his personal but very public yellow

Lab named "Goalie." It was bad enough that the dog he had promised to his unruly son when they moved into Gracie Mansion was shamelessly spread across the pages of *Pethouse*. "But Goalie has now appeared on the cover of a national magazine as many times as Mr. Giuliani has since he took office,"[2] remarked the *Times* with a dose of doggy skepticism that seemed almost out of place in the current setting.

If anyone had been able to back him into a corner, the mayor would have been forced to admit, like his Parks Commissioner, that the sidewalk situation was enormously improved. Koch's bold move to bring a militant subculture into the mainstream had been, with rare exceptions, a stellar success. Despite the occasional hot flashes on city surfaces, community relations had calmed down, and official endorsements of dog ownership reflected a broader acceptance by society. Though some people still thought that helpful hygienic reminders were needed from time to time, overall feelings toward pets had turned overwhelmingly positive, and the single most important factor was the simple fact that dog owners were cheerfully picking up. On the sidewalks, innocuous animals were inspiring more smiles than arguments. Practically every New Yorker, leashed or leashless, was going out of the way not to dodge something offensive but to testify—loudly, publicly, and whether or not anyone had even asked—that he or she was a confirmed "dog person" who could be counted on to defend these animals and their owners no matter what. Perceptions had changed. Dog-as-protector/predator and dog-as-harbinger-of-disease had given way to dog-as-saint, dog-as-conversation-piece, and dog-as-family-crest. An abrasive obstacle had become a social lubricant, a way of feeling good about oneself, a sign of status, and a reason for getting to know the neighbors that New Yorkers never knew they had (many of whom they would soon wish they hadn't). In advertising, the more fashionable breeds were being linked to other sought-after items like expensive cigars, fine wines, leather sofas, and tight abs. On the same streets that set these trends for the rest of the world, scenes of domestic bliss kept coexisters from ever imagining that these delightful, lovable creatures who brought so much richness to daily life could be mistreated in any way, especially when the owners were behaving so responsibly. New York settled into softer, more complacent times and forgot about all the *other* animal issues placed on the bargaining table back in those bellicose seventies. The press enabled this innocence by confining its attention to diligent coverage of poop scoop anniversaries, to vicious attacks by pit bulls—the latest incarnation of urban violence and the final threat to the perfect peace of reclaimed American cities—and to stupid stories about Labrador and golden retrievers.

Against a convincing backdrop of urban wellness, in a new age of mindless conformity, a numbing revelation was made. Two months after the celebration organized to remind dog owners of their responsibilities toward society, news of a meatier kind was finally laid on New York's table. A story called "Gimme Shelter"[3] appeared on the cover of *New York* magazine, blowing the lid off a well-kept secret. It seemed that while Mayor Giuliani was gearing up to chase down the last remaining "dog-doo deadbeats"[4]—and while he and his Parks Commissioner were busy publicizing their own Labrador and golden retrievers—the ASPCA had been forced to shut down all but one of its facilities. How could anyone have missed this? The oldest and single most important humane organization in the country hadn't, in fact, closed its doors 20 years earlier, as promised while the poop scoop law was being debated in Albany. But its demise was only a matter of time.[*] In 1994, after 100 years of half-measures and neglect, and with virtually no media coverage whatsoever, the ASPCA, under the direction of Roger Caras—one of the leading opponents of Health Law 1310—had finally resigned from its job as official dog catcher and did not renew its contract with the City. Having been a traditional scapegoat for animal abuse, the ASPCA announced that it would be operating on a smaller scale as a "no-kill" facility. The tired and battered humane organization could no longer be blamed for New York's inhumane acts because its dirty job had been handed over to something called the

---

[*]The City gave the ASPCA $4.5 million in 1993. But the ASPCA was still losing about $1 million each year and had lost $6 million in the previous four.

Center for Animal Care and Control (CACC). Billed as a separate entity, this newly formed agency was in reality a division of the Department of Health. Taxpayers joined license-paying dog owners to share in the responsibility of handling New York's enormous stray population—still present and growing 20 years after Health Law 1310 had gone into effect—through the CACC.

Was the City of New York up for the unpopular task it had been spared for a century? One of the unintended side effects of the poop scoop law was that, in making dogs more socially acceptable, it had also made for more dogs. New York would have an estimated 1.5 million dogs by 2006, though the actual figure was much higher because countless animals were either unlicensed or homeless. However many animals New York did or didn't have, someone responsible was needed to look after them when their owners didn't. Who would that be? The CACC wasn't as disinterested as Giuliani wanted to project to anyone who cared enough to know. Its seven board members included three City Commissioners and four other members also appointed, and able to be fired, by the mayor himself. The "independent" body was designed for more control than care, its top priorities being to discourage innovation and to minimize controversy. CACC employees, even high-level directors, were routinely fired for speaking out against shelter conditions and the utter lack of adoption efforts. "What does the CACC have to hide?"[5] asked Elizabeth Hess, the animal rescuer and author who wrote the article that did further damage to Giuliani's fading career prospects.

Government had plenty to hide. In fact, the mayor's reputation wouldn't be fully redeemed, or his career dragged from the political graveyard, until the aftermath of the World Trade Center attacks. Unlike San Francisco, whose municipal shelter program was a model of success for other cities, New York under Rudolph Giuliani had created what was probably the most horrific government-run pet extermination camp in the nation. Dogs, cats, and animals of all kinds, readers learned in the hideous but accurate exposé, were being kept in crowded cages where they went unfed, unwatered, unwalked, and covered in their own feces and urine until pried loose for almost certain death. Since 1994, the year in which Giuliani took office, about 40,000 animals had been dying annually in terror and without dignity—and nobody seemed to know a thing about this disgrace. "The goal is just to euthanize as quickly as possible," said the CACC's former director of publicity, who had been fired and then denied severance for failing to sign a confidentiality agreement. "And to make sure the mayor's reputation isn't tarnished."[6] City Hall, having thwarted several efforts to recruit managers who might have improved the situation, sent Giuliani's own personal choice from the inside to run the mysterious, semiprivate agency that might be compared to those outside security firms contracted to fight the nation's semi-legal wars around the world. To care for stray animals, Giuliani appointed a woman from his Office of Operations whose affection for dogs leaned toward bearded collies and whose expertise was—you can't make this stuff up—Solid Waste Management.

A subtler and more insidious irony hovered over the celebration, organized a few months before, to remind dog owners of their responsibilities toward society. Following the initial success of the poop scoop law in the 1980s, successive administrations had not made good use of the opportunity presented by their predecessors who had worked so hard to bring pets into the future in some decent and humane way. Caring for animals was not supposed to stop at cleaning up after them. By choosing to focus entirely on the precedent this law established, to view dogs only in terms of sanitation and as the responsibilities of individuals alone, and then by their own examples to encourage citizens to treat them as consumer items with brand names and built-in (inbred) obsolescence—in other words, to treat dogs like automobiles—some politicians were about as guilty as they possibly could have been for the appalling truth that had finally come to light. Despite strenuous warnings from animal rights advocates in the 1970s that a canine waste law would, in the long run, work *against* animals, the prophesy had come to pass in a way that even the doomsdayers had failed to predict. The dogs themselves, and pets of all kinds, were being treated no better than disposable waste products.[†]

A year after the *New York* story appeared, public outrage over the shelter situation had calmed down and many New Yorkers had forgotten there ever was a CACC. Government marked yet another anniversary of Health Law 1310 and Giuliani got started on his anti-poop campaign. His career, however, was still in a state of apoplexy when the fading mayor started stirring up anti-poop vigilantism by encouraging wounded pedestrians, in press and radio interviews, to go after the "slobs" who violated sacred public spaces. After 21 years, the faintest trace amounts of errant feces proved to be enough to rally a small but devoted mob. Public sentiment shifted back into high gear for a time, distracting from any number of other problems, human or humane, the city continued to face. In the future, New Yorkers could always expect someone in Albany to try, every few years, to double the lowest fines for poop-related offenses.

New York made no mention of the underlying canine waste theme that's been the subject of this book. But seen in the perspective of the city's age-old battle over this single issue, a more inclusive story would have given dog owners more cause for outrage, if such a thing is possible to imagine. They had been cheated. The sidewalks and parks were only cleaner since the 1970s because they had swallowed their pride and complied with a controversial law on the assumption that if they went along with this idea and acted hygienically, then the City would do its own part by accommodating animals in some responsible and thoughtful way. But dog owners were left holding the bag, and strays were left out in the cold.

[†]It might be said that the mass extermination of animals was an *alternate* solution to trying stricter enforcement of the poop scoop law. In 1993, the number of Sanitation officers assigned specifically to the "pooper scooper brigade" had been cut. The following year, while Giuliani was setting up the CACC, he continued this strategy by shifting the remaining manpower only to those areas where poop was the most highly concentrated.

While the scope of *New York*'s story didn't include the broader picture of a tragic tale, it did sum up the post-Lindsay years and managed to ask the only relevant question about pets in New York when it said: "We've cut crime. We've fixed up the parks. So why does a city rich with animal lovers have one of the poorest shelter systems in the country?"[7]

It's been a goal of this book to answer that question. Dogs may have come to New York for the wrong reasons. They were imported in scores to serve us by making up for our shortcomings. The arrival of unprecedented numbers of pet animals coincided with the urban crisis, a time when cities themselves began to look like mistakes. Dogs helped out for a while by offering people protection against each other and providing a tonic for some of the indignity of urban life. They filled a desperate emotional void in an ever-harsher environment. But as soon as New York started toward recovery, all that changed. With living conditions improving, it was possible to ask, once again, why New York needed so many dogs. Rather than reward them for services rendered, we treated them with a curious mixture of overblown affection, outright contempt, and shameful neglect.

Much of New York's failure to accommodate dogs has been due to unending disagreements over the proper uses of shared spaces. Sidewalks were only part of the problem. Whether in times of friendly hellos or civil strife, dogs and lawns can be incompatible wherever land is extremely scarce. *New York* was right: One of the more obvious advances of the post-Lindsay years has been the growing safety and greenness of public parks. And if the outward appearance of grass museums has been the traditional gauge of a population's state of mind, then dogs have appeared as either heroes or villains, depending on the circumstances. When parks were dangerous and safety was the first concern, dogs were seen in a positive way by their owners and much of law enforcement. But by destroying the public's green areas while making them accessible to unarmed pedestrians, dogs were also adding to society's stress by reducing that other measure of human happiness, the state of the lawns. The retreat of the public green had, in fact, accompanied the advance of crime and fiscal austerity and these animals were often seen as accomplices, if not as the downright causes of New York's predicament. As living conditions improved, so did the city's green areas, and it should come as no surprise that the runoff of a newfound prosperity didn't trickle down very far. Dogs, unofficially tolerated in more chaotic times, could no longer be justified if they impinged on purely esthetic concerns in a society that had come to place outward appearances before all else. A new era of public works, and changing definitions of "quality of life," had tipped the balance decidedly out of their favor and left the caretakers to their own devices.

From the struggle to keep New York relatively green during an urban crisis, when a leash law was enacted and a mayor, already sensing that government was losing ground in a turf war, tried to disguise the pavements to look like parks—to later years when most pretensions to "environmentalism" were swept under the rug—government's first concern has been to keep the city as green as humanly possible.[‡] Rather than accommodate dogs in a meaningful way, leaders have sought to exclude them at any cost. Providing them and their guardians with adequate living space has never been a priority. The turf war continues to rage as government, instead of investing a few thousand dollars each year in dog run maintenance, spends millions on stage-set parklets with historically accurate fencing that are seldom, if ever, open to the public.[§] While developers and City planners are continually chipping away at exercise space for dogs, government is resorting to the most absurd of extremes: Astroturf. Across New York, spaces once used informally for off-leash purposes have been permanently reclaimed in the name of a

---

[‡]Adele Bender wrote a prophetic 1976 letter to the *New York Times* in which she remarked, "Animals are a very good diversion from the real issues—what will be next, plants?"[8]

[§]The traditional use of greenery as a salve for urban disorder is best exemplified by a series of imposing, neo-Gothic gardens recently installed along Sixth Avenue below West Fourth Street. For decades the location of an unsightly recycling center and several mini riots, this area has been remodeled and added to the City's collection of dead space.

natural appearance. No dogs allowed—in fact, they're less welcome on fake grass than they were on the real kind. This latest improvement is found not only in parks but on the redeveloped piers, first promised in the Lindsay years and only recently completed. New York dogs, allowed for decades to run happily on surfaces that no one else wanted, have been banished to tiny, paved enclosures where they and their owners sit in urine and feces to bake in the summer sun and freeze in the winter wind while lush, artificial lawns cut unseasonably across the Hudson toward the Garden State, New Jersey. Swathed in thousands of yards of green plastic, and accented with clumps of surgically implanted "native" grasses, the riverfront announces to the world that passes on cruise ships: "New York is clean and green. Life is orderly. Please come back, and don't forget to bring the kids"—enough to make some of us yearn for those lawless, lawnless seventies.[¶]

*   *   *

And yet despite the overwhelming weight of hard evidence, more than enough to create a stir should New Yorkers be inclined to make one, assigning responsibility is a tricky business. Blame, indeed, is the lifeblood of both politics and a good conscience, but a sober approach demands some consideration of historical factors, changing attitudes, shifting priorities, and so many other aspects of the problem. Blame, moreover, is a precious commodity and should be used sparingly or it loses its value. But considering how central dogs have become to our city lives, we might at least try and understand what went wrong.

Long before our best friends were accepted, or barely tolerated in New York—before the law that made this possible—they were already the unwitting vehicles for virtually every human emotion and agenda. This could go either way. Being in favor of keeping them could mean being in favor of all that was pure and noble. At the same time,

---

[¶]New York's Department of Parks and Recreation announced in 2006 that an additional $150 million would be spent on fake grass across the city. Real grass, the Department said, was becoming too expensive to maintain. It went without saying that dogs would be banned from all green-colored plastic surfaces.

these animals could be used to describe all that was impure and lowly. One person's sense of well-being was another's primal fear. Before cities even existed, dogs were faithful protectors and hunting companions. But they've also been seen as a source of disease and danger. In modern urban areas, their candid squatting in public places, in full view of everyone and without the slightest embarrassment, has surely added to anti-dog prejudice. Filth is a reminder of civilization's fragility, and of our own mortality. The dogs have had very little to say for themselves, and a subject open to multiple meanings is easily appropriated and used for whatever purpose. Being for banning dogs, or just their waste products, has sometimes been construed as taking a pro-people stand, though we forget that in the heyday of environmentalism, humanity was often considered a lost cause. Thus the complexity of the problem.

It's understandable that governments, which are supposed to be concerned mainly with people, try to avoid too much involvement in animal care and control, an area that is simply too volatile. Public criticism can be extremely damaging and might prevent leaders from accomplishing human goals, which, many humans agree, should be the absolute priorities of government. Whenever leaders cross the line by taking firmer stands for or against other animals, they're exposing themselves, and society, to potential risk. Extreme reactions from both pro- and anti-dog people assure that little or nothing gets done. The surplus of emotion surrounding the mere mention of dogs, as either friends or foes, hasn't been in the dogs' own best interests.

But people are people and they'll always need someone to blame. In fact, it might be said that the only reason we have leaders at all is so that we'll have someone to hold accountable for all of our problems. We want to believe that government is a machine and not a group of individuals with weaknesses and faults like us. We think, against reason, that justice is always served and things get done automatically. Animal lovers forget that it was the Friends of Animals, not some heartless fiend or faceless monolith, that suggested in 1982 to have all assets stripped from the ASPCA and transferred to a City-run shelter system.

They also like to forget who's to blame for buying pets in the first place and then dumping them into incapable hands. The front lobbies of shelters are relay points for feelings of guilt and self-loathing. Here, blame is transferred, as if by osmosis, from individuals to institutions. Most self-proclaimed animal lovers don't even have the courage to visit these awful places unless they're dropping something off. They say the thought of seeing or hearing all those homeless little furry creatures just makes them feel too sad—but how do they think the poor animals feel? More lives could surely be saved if only more people could bear a few moments of personal discomfort. Those who bite the bullet and abandon their former friends try to make it easier on themselves. They say that good homes will be found in no time and that it's all for the best. But there's no kind farmer at the end of the road. If they dare to ask, they're told that their pets will be given lethal injections within a few days, which doesn't stop most people from leaving them just the same. They console themselves on the way out by blaming someone else for being cruel, forgetting that they're the ones who couldn't resist buying that doggy in the window.

The shame that we're made to feel each time we inadvertently step into a mess of dog doo pales by comparison to what we might feel about a dynamic that's changed very little in all these years. Rule no. 1 in New York City: Don't do anything that you can get someone else to do. Looking back at the single issue that made so many New Yorkers take note of dogs in the first place—the presence of feces in quantities that could no longer be ignored—we see that blame has been cast like seeds in the wind. Some irate pedestrians blamed dog owners for the mess. Others blamed the Department of Sanitation for not doing its job. Government agencies blamed citizens, or the fiscal crisis for which pets were often considered the cause. Parents blamed pet owners for the inherent risks of daily life in concentrated urban areas, instead of keeping their kids in the suburbs. They and like-minded allies pressured government to exploit unfounded fears for public health.

A growing anti-poop, often anti-dog lobby blamed City Council for failing to address a mounting problem. State leaders, too, blamed local legislators, even though Council had more pressing problems to solve. Once a law was barely passed, Albany blamed the slow start on City Hall. But much of local government had never wanted a poop scoop law in the first place. Citizens, in turn, blamed law enforcement officers for being unable to perform superhuman tasks. Law enforcement blamed dog owners for their lack of cooperation. While the city's canine waste problem was gradually solved through social pressure and re-education, the issue that had kept so many people from accepting this difficult law all along—the unsolved problem of stray animals—was blamed on the ailing ASPCA, which blamed a government in recovery, which blamed the ASPCA. All the while, New Yorkers went on buying dogs instead of recycling.

In an atmosphere of wild accusations and widespread innocence, it's no wonder that the simplest problems take forever to solve. Nobody wants to assume responsibility for animals because failing in any way makes someone a bad person. At the risk of offending millions, it should be said, contrary to popular opinion, that having a dog or claiming to love animals is no proof of virtue, no more so than being seen pushing a stroller. On the other hand, laboring in quiet anonymity to help an animal, human or non-human, to lead a happy, healthy life is commendable, indeed. The City of New York has recently taken steps to improve its image and maybe to help other animals in the process. But much of the real work is being done by individuals, either alone or in foster care networks, who give pets temporary homes until they can find permanent ones with responsible owners. New Yorkers aren't all bad. They sometimes even turn down publicity, if not out of modesty, then for brute survival. "If more people knew about what I'm doing," says the founder of one of the animal rescue networks that don't like to advertise, "they'd be dumping dogs on me round-the-clock. I'd rather shoot myself in the head."

"Community participation" takes many forms but government shouldn't be let off the hook entirely. Like the poop scoop law, this quaint notion is deeply rooted in another era. Still used anachronistically by politicians, the expression is a variant of "citizen participation," which originally referred to welfare distribution and school decentralization in the early 1960s. During the fiscal crisis, as New York plunged into debt and government could no longer provide the most basic services, the idea was extended and applied to everything under the sun from park maintenance and sanitation to police protection and animal care and control. Individual citizens were asked to help out in a time of crisis, and they did.

It's important to remember that the poop scoop law was first conceived as a *temporary* measure. In later years of fiscal health, government could, in theory, reclaim its duties. Citizens could rightly expect more from their hired hands. But for some strange reason, leaders seldom addressed the needs of pet animals. They continued to view canine waste and stray animals as aspects of the same problem—called "pollution"—but the kind for which individuals, not institutions, were to be held accountable. Rather than break with tradition and take on a problem that had not been cleaned up, they turned their energies toward enforcing still more "community participation," and long after they could legitimately fall back on the excuse that there wasn't enough money for local government to handle dog runs, shelters, or even street cleaning. Instead, an old idea was repeatedly taken off the shelf, dusted off, and held up as an example. When not bullying dog owners in public parks, threatening them with fines and imprisonment, officials have created diversions by turning them against each other, or their dogless peers against them. Private efforts are celebrated with awards and pats-on-the-back to the few lone individuals who've struggled, against all odds and with nearly negligible results, to make a difference. But official congratulations should always be treated with suspicion. These honors are dubious because they help government to get away with murder.

Practical suggestions? These sound simpler than they are. Set better examples for the rest of the world. Keep urban problems in their proper perspectives. Don't let politicians or special interest groups blow any single issue out of proportion to its true importance. Risks should not be overstated. Neuroses should not be indulged. Progress has for centuries been measured by advances made in human health, particularly in the management of waste and the prevention of disease in cities. We'd be very sorry if this weren't the case. There's always room for improvement, but maybe we can afford to obsess a little less about human health and focus a little more on protecting pets from people—that is, if we care about them as much as we say we do.

Priorities need to change. Health and happiness are solid goals. But to measure society's well-being and government's performance in square feet of public green or the number of scraggly trees and bushes is an extremely wasteful hobby. Though the color itself seems to be essential to feelings of calm in humans, and thus to their mental health, taking potted plants too seriously, as we've seen, can cause more frustration than happiness. Confusing cities with natural ecosystems allows governments to overlook the more vital tasks at hand such as garbage collection, enforcement of clean air standards, or accommodation of dogs. Tree-worship also encourages an almost animistic approach to decoration, with people meditating upon lawns, real or plastic, to simulate a state attainable only by the few New Yorkers who have summer homes. While we're indulging our green urban fantasies, leaders are free to enlist noble causes like environmentalism to protect concrete surfaces, thus distracting residents from what little unspoiled nature is left in the world and is still in need of our help. New Yorkers could really improve their lives, and the rest of the world, by trying to see dogs—living, breathing dogs, not stuffed or cartoon—as the more direct and wholesome link to the nature for which they so chronically yearn. The fauna group consists of higher life forms than anything in flora. Protecting and nurturing other animals—not gardening or scenic design—should be the priorities of government. These won't be until individual citizens learn to use "peer pressure" for something more substantive than making a city block look more like a suburban front yard.

Finally, cities should be accepted for what they are. Residents who, whether for their families or themselves, will not tolerate the inherent risks and annoyances of urban life probably shouldn't be living in places like New York. They're why we made the suburbs. To kick and scream about overcrowding, noise, unsightliness, and the shortage of rolling estate lawns and assorted ornamental greenery; to be in a constant state of fear over crime and disease; to claim more than one's fair share of buffer space; and then to blame the nearest party for anything less than gated or pristine—this sort of anti-social behavior makes cities more unpleasant than they need be. Cities are not the suburbs. They're loud and brassy. They're dirty but interesting. Large, concentrated urban centers have always been where crime and disease happen, and they always will be. But New York is also a breeding ground for new ideas, and neither rising rents nor an Internet will change that for at least a few more years.

Considering how much dogs have enriched our private and social lives, we need to reward our companion species for all they've given us. It's the very least we can do.

APPENDIX

Since New York's poop scoop law was enacted in 1977, most people have come to assume that picking up is a kind of moral duty that all dog owners have had, since some ancient time immemorial, toward the rest of society. It is not. Picking up is a custom like any other, the product of a specific set of circumstances. Today, most dog owners do it automatically. But this wasn't always the case. Making this act into a daily habit took years of hard work. How could this have been?

"It shall be the duty of each dog owner," the law proclaimed, "to remove any feces left by his dog on any sidewalk, gutter, street, or other public area." We might try to imagine how utterly alien these words must have sounded at the time. The mere thought of handling feces was enough to make dog owners retch. The fear of disease prevented many from complying. But it was also "the fear of social embarrassment," said EPA Administrator Jerome Kretchmer, that kept them from accepting their fate. Kretchmer assured dog owners that, in time, they could overcome their many fears and reservations. Still, there seemed to be something almost unnatural about picking up feces. Even today, when scooping is considered a normal part of human behavior, first-time dog owners must go through a brief period of desensitization. They should be praised for the lengths to which they're willing to go out of love for a pet and consideration for other humans.

INSTRUCTIONS FOR SCOOPING POOP IN NEW YORK CITY

1. The dog's walker prepares by sliding a hand, usually the writing hand, into a plastic bag. Any plastic bag will do, so long as it's large enough to cover all five digits as well as the palm. Some people prefer newspapers, paper towels, or even Dixie cups. But a plastic bag is the universal scooper of choice with a species unique for its two opposable thumbs to use for gripping. The bag will serve as a kind of prophylactic glove.

    Now, the condition of the bag is crucial. Many dog owners agree that it's better not to pick up at all than to have a bag with even the tiniest tear and end up with what's known as "poop finger." Having first examined the glove for safety, making certain it is in no way flawed, the dog owner is ready to do his or her civic duty—and fast, before somebody steps into it!

2. Novices should at this point brace themselves. If absolutely necessary, the dog owner may address the subject from the corner of an eye and, voluntarily suspending all breathing, bend over or squat to feel for the target (by the way, blind persons with Seeing Eye dogs are exempted from scooping in New York City). Constant practice enables some of the more seasoned pros to perform the task without ever addressing the nasty business directly or catching the unpleasant aroma. Regardless of one's personal poop-scooping style, the business must be grabbed securely through the plastic gauntlet and held for a second or two in the palm of the hand.

    This doesn't have to be as traumatic as it sounds. The warmth that a dog owner feels through the plastic is the warmth of life. Most agree that handling cold feces is much more revolting than handling the fresh kind. Under optimal conditions, the dog has no tummy problems—but if he does, the experienced and skillful dog owner wipes up as much as possible, often leaving behind a long mark on the pavement that would rival the best brushstroke from New York's Abstract Expressionist School.

3. The next part requires even more dexterity. Standing upright again, the human takes the other hand, the one holding the dog's leash, and with whatever fingers are free (it is vital to maintain a firm grip on the dog's leash at all times on a busy city street), quickly flips the bag inside out, thereby removing the unspeakable from its handheld position and, before it can return to earth, containing it safely in the reversed plastic bag. Ideally, this act of scooping, with each of its necessary components, is performed in one swift, elegant, and unbroken movement that lasts approximately three to four seconds. ("This is pet hysteria," said a leading dog advocate of the 1970s, insisting there was no practical way for a dog owner to hold the leash in one hand and, at the same time, clean up. Upon this platform he would unite some 310,000 outraged New Yorkers who, likewise, believed it was impossible to do two things at once. History has proven them wrong.)

4. Don't start breathing easily. It's not over yet. The part that people find most difficult comes next. This is where the possibility for "social embarrassment" is made painfully apparent. The dog owner must at this point hold the bag out awkwardly (it's not the sort of thing one likes to put into a pocket or a handbag) and pass any number of strangers on the street before finding a public waste basket in which to deposit the parcel. Typically, the person tries to avoid direct eye contact with passersby while rushing to the nearest receptacle, which might mean covering a long distance across an entire city block. The goal is to drop the refuse before attracting too much attention to oneself. Passersby (and there's an endless supply of these in New York) pretend not to notice the sight or smell. But they do. They even seem a bit embarrassed. For all parties involved, these painfully slow trajectories from squat-to-toss can seem like small eternities. Suburbanites with big backyards must try very hard to imagine how uncomfortable a New York dog owner must feel carrying a load of feces along a crowded city sidewalk. Occasionally, an obnoxious kid from New Jersey will

laugh aloud and express disgust to a New Yorker who is, after all, only following the law. To make matters even more difficult, New York's Department of Sanitation has never been able to keep up with the city's waste disposal needs. The search for a public waste basket, one that is not already full and brimming over onto the street, typically ends with the dog owner carefully placing the bag on top of an enormous pile of trash, which threatens to topple at any moment. After all that effort and embarrassment, the poop will very likely end up on the pavement once again, this time in a plastic bag. But that's of no concern to the dog owner, who has followed the law as best as possible, placing the poop, if not exactly *in* a trash basket, then at least *over* one, in a ritual gesture of consideration toward fellow humans.

Sources Consulted

City Council Collection, La Guardia and Wagner Archives, La Guardia Community College, CUNY.

City Hall Library, New York.

Governor's Bill Jacket: Chapter 464 of Laws of 1977. New York State Library, Albany, New York.

Transcript of New York State Assembly Floor Debate, 23 May 1977. Bill no. 464 sponsored by Edward H. Lehner. New York State Assembly Public Information Office. Albany, New York.

Transcript of New York State Senate Floor Debate, 23 June 1977. Bill no. 464 sponsored by Franz S. Leichter. New York State Department of Microfilm and Records, Albany, New York.

Anthrozoös.

Boston Herald.

Chicago Daily Tribune.

The Daily Camera.

Daily News.

Dog Run, A Publication of the Washington Square Dog Run Association.

The Jerusalem Post.

The Montreal Gazette.

New York.

New York Post.

New York Times (NYT).

New York Times Magazine.

Newsday.

Our Town.

Le Point.

PoopReport.com

Soho Weekly News.

Spiegel Online.

La Terre de chez nous.

USA Today.

The Washington Post.

Westsider.

Village Voice.

Auletta, K. (1979). *The Streets Were Paved with Gold.* Random House.

Bailey, Robert W. (1984). *The Crisis Regime.* State University of New York Press.

Beck, A. M. "The Impact of the Canine Clean-up Law." *Environment,* Vol. 21, No. 8, October 1979.

Blackmar, E., Rozenweig, R. (reprint 1998). *The Park and the People: A History of Central Park.* Cornell University Press.

Brooke, R. (1916). *Letters from America.* Charles Scribner's Sons.

Browne, A. (1985). *I Koch: A Decidedly Unauthorized Biography of the Mayor of New York City, Edward I. Koch.* Dodd, Meade.

Buckley, W. F. (1966). *The Unmaking of a Mayor.* Viking Press.

Burnstein, D. E. (1993). *Clean Streets and the Pursuit of Progress: Urban Reform in New York City in the Progressive Era.* (Dissertation). Rutgers.

Cannato, V. J. (2001). *The Ungovernable City: John Lindsay and His Struggle to Save New York.* Basic Books.

Caro, R. (1974). *The Power Broker: Robert Moses and the Fall of New York.* Knopf.

Cartwright, D. S., Schwartz, H., Tomson, H. S. (1975). *Gang Delinquency.* Brookes/Cole Publishing Company.

Eisenbud, M. (1978). *The Environment, Technology and Health*. New York University Press.

Eisenbud, M. (1990). *An Environmental Odyssey*. University of Washington Press.

Ferretti, F. (1976). *The Year the Big Apple Went Bust*. Putnam.

Flippen, J. B. (2000). *Nixon and the Environment*. University of New Mexico Press.

Glickman, L. T., Shofer, F. S. "Zoonotic Visceral and Ocular Larva Migrans," *Veterinary Clinics of North America: Small Animal Practice*, Vol. 17, No. 1, January 1987.

Goldstein, R. C. (1970). *New York: Civic Exploitation*. Macmillan.

Hacker, A. (1975). *The New Yorkers: A Profile of an American Metropolis*. Mason/Charter.

Heckscher, A. (1974). *Alive in the City: Memoir of an Ex-Commissioner*. Scribner.

Herrman, N., Glickman, L. T., Schantz, P. M., Weston, M., Domanski, L. M. "Seroprevalence of Zoonotic Toxocariasis in the United States: 1971–1973." *American Journal of Epidemiology*, Vol. 122, No. 5, 1985.

Hugo, V. (1976). *Les Misérables*. Folio Press.

Kelly, K. (1973). *Garbage: The History and Future of Garbage in America*. Saturday Review Press.

Kenney, D. J. (1987). *Crime, Fear, and the New York City Subways: The Role of Citizen Action*. Praeger.

Klein, W. (1970). *Lindsay's Promise: The Dream That Failed*. Macmillan.

Koch, E. I. (1984). *Mayor*. Simon and Schuster.

Lebowitz, F. (1981). *Social Studies*. Random House.

Lewin, R. A. (1999). *Merde: Excursions in Scientific, Cultural, and Socio-Historical Coprology*. Random House.

Lindsay, J. V. (1970). *The City*. W. W. Norton.

Lindsay, J. V. (1976). *The Edge*. W. W. Norton.

Merlen, R. H. A. (1971). *De Canibus—Dog and Hound in Antiquity*. J. A. Allen & Co. LTD.

Morris, C. R. (1980). *The Cost of Good Intentions: New York City and the Liberal Experiment 1960–1975*. McGraw-Hill.

Nowell, I. (1978). *The Dog Crisis*. St. Martin's Press.

Ponting, C. (1991). *A Green History of the World*. Penguin Group.

Rich, J. (1964). *How to Be a New Yorker*. DoubleDay.

Sayre, N. (1974). *Sixties Going on Seventies*. Arbor House.

Schneider, E. C. (2001). *Vampires, Dragons and Egyptian Kings: Youth Gangs in Postwar New York*. Princeton University Press.

Shefter, M. (1987). *Political Crisis/Fiscal Crisis: The Collapse and Revival of New York City*. Columbia University Press.

Siegel, F. (1997). *The Future Once Happened Here: New York, D.C., L.A. and the Fate of America's Big Cities*. Free Press.

Tannenbaum, A. (2003). *New York in the 70s*. Feierabend.

Taylor, G. R. (1970). *The Doomsday Book*. Thames and Hudson, Ltd.

Whalen, R. J. (1965). *A City Destroying Itself: An Angry View of New York*. William Morrow and Company.

INTERVIEWS:

Steven Armstead, Open Space and Mountain Parks Department, Boulder, CO.

Alan M. Beck, Director of the Center for the Human-Animal Bond, Purdue University School of Veterinary Medicine; former Director of NYC Bureau of Animal Affairs.

Yves Contassot, Mayor's Deputy for Environmental Affairs, Paris.

Adrienne Eldred, former Member of Community Board Two, NYC.

Frank R. Fioramonti, former Legislative Counsel to Councilman Carter Burden, New York City Council.

Carol Greitzer, former Member of New York City Council.

Pascal James Imperato, MD, Professor and Chair, Department of Preventative Medicine and Community Health, SUNY Downstate Medical Center; former Commissioner of NYC Department of Health and Mental Hygiene.

Don Jordan, Director, Seattle Animal Shelter.

Jerome Kretchmer, former Administrator of NYC Environmental Protection Agency.

Patricia Livingston, PhD, CRC, Professor Emerita, New York University; Founder, New York Coalition for Dog Control.

Frank McLaughlin, New York City Council Staff Member 1970–1972.

Carmen Orechio, former Senator, New Jersey; Commissioner of Department of Public Safety, Nutley, NJ.

Sergeant Charles Rudack, Acting Director of Animal Control and Hearing Officer, Boston Police Department.

Stephen Zawistowski, Executive Vice President, National Programs, and Science Advisor, ASPCA.

. . . and countless chats with people in dog runs across New York City.

FILMS, DOCUMENTARIES, ETC.:

Crimes and Misdemeanors. Woody Allen, Metro-Goldwyn-Mayer, 1989.

Lewis Mumford on the City (documentary film). "The City: Cars or People?" Directed by Christopher Chapman. National Film Board of Canada. Original film release: 1963.

The Out of Towners. Arthur Hiller; written by Neil Simon, Paramount Pictures, 1969.

The Prisoner of Second Avenue. Melvin Frank; written by Neil Simon, Warner Brothers Pictures, 1975.

Saturday Night Live. "Mr. Bill Goes to N.Y." © 1975–1980 National Broadcasting Company, Inc.

Taxi Driver. Martin Scorsese; written by Paul Schrader, Columbia Pictures, 1976.

NOTES

INTRODUCTION

1   Victor Hugo, *Les Misérables* (Folio Press, 1976), p. 1068.

2   *Carmen Orechio interview.*

CHAPTER 1: INVASION OF THE DOG PEOPLE

1   *NYT*, 23 July 1978. Dena Kleiman, "Owners of Dogs Face Orders to Clean Up."

2   Ibid.

3   *NYT Magazine*, 20 August 1972. Gini Kopecky, "To scoop or not to scoop."

4   *NYT*, 21 December 1974. "Curb Those Dogs!"

5   *Chicago Daily Tribune*, 4 December 1938. Bob Becker, "Curb Your Dog."

6   *NYT Magazine*, "To scoop or not to scoop."

7   *NYT*, "Curb Those Dogs!"

8   *NYT*, 27 May 1975. Russell Baker, "Beastly Manhattan."

9   *NYT*, 1 February 1978. Anna Quindlen, "City Dog: A Mixed Breed."

10   *Newsday*, 22 May 1974. Coleman McCarthy, "For City Dwellers, It's a Dog's Life."

11   Ibid.

12   *NYT Magazine*, 7 September 1970. Claire Berman, "New York: A city going to the dogs?"

13 "Sweet Virginia," Jagger-Richard, Abkco Music, BMI, 1972.

14 *NYT*, 1 February 1976. Carl Glassman, "For Dogs, City Is the Big Biscuit."

15 *NYT*, "City Dog: A Mixed Breed."

16 Iris Nowell, *The Dog Crisis* (St. Martin's Press, 1978), p. xiv.

17 Ibid., p. xiii.

18 *NYT*, 11 March 1973. Michael Knight, "'Newspaper' Gives Advice on Paper-Training Dogs."

19 Glenn Howell, Letter to the Editor, *NYT*, 29 February 1976.

20 Leonard H. Goldberg, Letter to the Editor, *NYT*, 7 May 1974.

21 Anonymous dog run interview, 2007.

22 Douglas Brin, Co-Founder of New York Coalition for Dog Control, Letter to the Editor, *NYT*, 15 February 1978.

23 *NYT Magazine*, "To scoop or not to scoop."

24 *Daily News*, 3 June 1974. Owen Moritz, "There'll Be No Dogs in City of the Future on Roosevelt Island."

25 *NYT*, 28 February 1976. William Farrell, "Urban Dog Population Is a Rising Problem."

26 *NYT*, 28 July 1977. Pat Gleason, "Environmentalist Shows Widespread Concern for Owners and Dogs."

27 *NYT*, 10 November 1972. David Bird, "City Asks a Law on Dog Littering."

28 *NYT*, 26 May 1972. James M. Markham, "Dogs Upsetting Brooklyn Heights."

CHAPTER 2: ENVIRONMENTALISM AND GRASS ROOTS

1 *NYT*, 1 March 1971. "Dog Owners May Have to Clean Up After Pets."

2 Paul Schrader, *Taxi Driver*.

3 Allan Tannenbaum, *New York in the 70s* (Feierabend, 2003), p. 5. Text used: © 2003 P. J. O'Rourke.

4 *NYT*, 1 August 1970. Frank Lynn, "Con Ed's Plans Opposed by Kretchmer."

5 Richard M. Nixon, 1 January 1970. State of the Union Address.

6 Merril Eisenbud, *The Environment, Technology and Health* (New York University Press, 1978), p. 62.

7 *NYT*, 12 March 1970. David Bird, "Pollution Officials Say Cleanup Delayed by Emotional Outcry."

8 *NYT Magazine*, 25 April 1971. Grace Lichtenstein, "Running for Mayor on a Garbage Truck."

9 Merril Eisenbud, *An Environmental Odyssey* (University of Washington Press, 1990), p. 201.

10 *NYT*, 26 January 1970. "Democrat in Line for Eisenbud Job."

11 *NYT Magazine*, "Running for Mayor on a Garbage Truck."

12 Ibid.

13 Ibid.

14 Ibid.

15 Ibid.

16 Ibid.

17 Ibid.

18 *NYT*, 14 October 1970. David Bird, "Kretchmer Is Seeking $1.2 Billion."

19 Robert Caro, *The Power Broker: Robert Moses and the Fall of New York* (Knopf, 1974), p. 1118.

20 *NYT*, 19 April 1971. Paul L. Montgomery, "Earth Week Stresses 'Grass-Roots Action': Lindsay Joins Marchers in Central Park and Bikers on the Grand Concourse."

21 Ibid.

22 Ibid.

23 *Lewis Mumford on the City* (documentary film), "The City: Cars or People?" Directed by Christopher Chapman. National Film Board of Canada. Original film release 1963.

24 Ibid.

25 John Lindsay, *The City* (W. W. Norton, 1970), p. 62.

26 *NYT*, "Earth Week Stresses . . ."

27 *NYT*, 24 March 1976. "New York's Loss . . ."

Chapter 3: Cautionary Tales: Doggy Politics 101

1 *NYT*, 22 August 1996. Elizabeth Bumiller, "Most Political of Animals."

2 *New York*, 24 July 1978. R. V. Denenberg, Eric Seidman, "Dogs Are Going to the Law."

3   R. Fagan, Letter to the Editor, *NYT*, 30 March 1974.

4   Margaret Doretta Meixner, Letter to the Editor, *NYT*, 28 March 1974.

5   Charles Steir, Letter to the Editor, *NYT*, 1976.

6   Albert Husted, Letter to the Editor, *NYT*, 29 February 1976.

7   William P. Armstrong, Letter to the Editor, *NYT*, 1976.

8   Fran Lebowitz, *Social Studies* (Random House, 1981), pp. 239–240.

9   *NYT*, "Most Political of Animals."

10   Ibid.

11   *Associated Press/NYT*, 29 January 1972. "President Consoles Boy Whose Pet Dog Has Leg Amputated."

12   *NYT*, 2 July 1972. Frances X. Clines, "Mayor Proposes a Stricter Law on Dog Littering."

13   *NYT*, "Dog Owners May Have to Clean Up After Pets."

14   René H. A. Merlen, *De Canibus—Dog and Hound in Antiquity* (J.A. Allen & Co., LTD., 1971), pp. 100–101.

15   *NYT*, 10 November 1972. David Bird, "Dog Owners Protest Bill to Force Street Cleanup."

16   *NYT*, "Dog Owners May Have to Clean Up After Pets."

17   *NYT*, "City Asks a Law on Dog Littering."

18   *NYT*, "Dog Owners May Have to Clean Up After Pets."

19   *Village Voice*, Clark Whelton series on the canine waste problem.

20   Ibid.

21   *NYT*, "Dog Owners Protest Bill to Force Street Cleanup."

22   Ibid.

23   *NYT Magazine*, "To scoop or not to scoop."

24   Ibid.

25   *NYT*, "Dogs Upsetting Brooklyn Heights."

26   Ibid.

27   Ibid.

28   *NYT*, "City Asks a Law on Dog Littering."

CHAPTER 4: KEEP OFF THE GRASS

1   *NYT*, 23 May 1972. Ralph Blumenthal, "City Will Restrict Dogs' Use of Parks."

2   *NYT Magazine*, "To scoop or not to scoop."

3   Vincent J. Cannato, *The Ungovernable City: John Lindsay and His Struggle to Save New York* (Basic Books, 2001), p. 523.

4   August Heckscher, *Alive in the City: Memoir of an Ex-Commissioner* (Scribner, 1974), p. 5.

5   Ibid., p. 4.

6   Cannato, p. 147.

7   Carol Hillman, Letter to the Editor, *NYT*, 8 May 1975.

8   *NYT Magazine*, 7 September 1970. Claire Berman, "New York: A city going to the dogs?"

9   *NYT*, 22 April 1971. Marya Mannes, "Up in Central Park—Ugh!"

10 *NYT*, "City Will Restrict Dogs' Use of Parks."

11 Heckscher, p. 1.

12 Ibid., p. 83.

13 Ibid., p. 5.

14 Ibid., p. 83.

15 Charles Zaug, Letter to the Editor, *NYT*, 23 May 1975.

16 Anonymous Letter to the Editor, *NYT*, 1975.

17 Heckscher, p. 6.

18 *NYT*, 12 December 1993. "Bruised Dog Frays Nerves on 33rd Street."

CHAPTER 5: . . . AND DON'T EAT THE DAISIES

1   Woody Allen, *Crimes and Misdemeanors*.

2   *NYT*, "City Will Restrict Dogs' Use of Parks."

3   Ibid.

4   Ibid.

5   Ibid.

6   Ibid.

7   *NYT*, "Mayor Proposes a Stricter Law on Dog Littering."

8   Ibid.

9   Ibid.

10 Ibid.

11 *NYT*, 12 July 1972. "Dog Owners Say City Errs."

12 *NYT*, "City Will Restrict Dogs' Use of Parks."

13 *NYT Magazine*, "To scoop or not to scoop."

14   *NYT*, "Dog Owners Protest Bill to Force Street Cleanup."

15   *NYT*, 13 September 1970. "Beame Seeking 'Envirmaids' to Fight Litter and Pollution."

16   *NYT*, 6 August 1972. "Women Urged as 'Envirmaids.'"

17   *Yves Contassot interview.*

18   *NYT*, "Dog Owners Protest Bill to Force Street Cleanup."

19   *NYT*, "For Dogs, City Is the Big Biscuit."

20   Albert Husted, Letter to the Editor, *NYT*, 29 February 1976.

21   George Schoncite, Letter to the Editor, *NYT*, 27 August 1975.

22   Joan Rubin, Letter to the Editor, *NYT*, 29 February 1976.

23   Albert Husted, Letter to the Editor, *NYT*, 29 February 1976.

24   Marliese Daglian, Letter to the Editor, *NYT*, 7 July 1972.

25   Max Kline, Letter to the Editor, *NYT*, 17 July 1972.

26   Glenn E. Fant, Letter to the Editor, *NYT*, 7 July 1972.

27   *Daily News*, 23 July 1972. Fred Loetterle, "Great Debate: Doggy Do or Doggy Don't."

28   *NYT Magazine*, "To scoop or not to scoop."

29   Ibid.

30   *Our Town*, 29 August 1975. Patricia E. Polak, "Public Debates Anti-Dog-Fouling Measure."

31   *NYT Magazine*, "To scoop or not to scoop."

32   *NYT*, 3 February 1972. "Dog-Littering Foe Puts the Onus on the Owners."

33   Lawrence T. Glickman and Frances S. Shofer, "Zoonotic Visceral and Ocular Larva Migrans," *Veterinary Clinics of North America: Small Animal Practice*, Vol. 17, No. 1, January 1987.

34   *NYT*, "Dog-Littering Foe . . ."

35   Nira Herrman, Lawrence T. Glickman, Peter M. Schantz, Marian G. Weston, Linda M. Domanski, "Seroprevalence of Zoonotic Toxocariasis in the United States: 1971–1973." *American Journal of Epidemiology*, Vol. 122, No. 5, 1985.

36   *Pascal James Imperato interview.*

37   *NYT Magazine*, "To scoop or not to scoop."

38   *NYT*, "Dog Owners Protest Bill to Force Street Cleanup."

39   *NYT*, "City Asks a Law on Dog Littering."

40   *NYT Magazine*, "To scoop or not to scoop."

41   Ibid.

CHAPTER 6: A SHOWDOWN

1   All letters, telegrams, etc., from City Council Collection, Laguardia and Wagner Archives.

2   Marliese Daglian, Letter to the Editor, *NYT*, 7 July 1972.

3   *NYT*, 6 July 1972. "Action of Dog Litter and Graffiti Put Off for Months by Council."

4   Ibid.

5   Alvin Frankenberg, Letter to the Editor, *NYT*, September 1972.

6   *Carol Greitzer interview.*

7   All speeches from *City Council Collection*, Laguardia and Wagner Archives.

8   *Village Voice*, Clark Whelton series.

9   *Daily News*, "Great Debate: Doggy Do or Doggy Don't."

10   All letters, telegrams, etc., from *City Council Collection*, Laguardia and Wagner Archives.

11   *NYT*, "City Asks a Law on Dog Littering."

12   *NYT*, "Dog Owners Protest Bill to Force Street Cleanup."

13   Ibid.

14   *NYT*, "Mayor Proposes a Stricter Law on Dog Littering."

15   *NYT*, "Dogs Upsetting Brooklyn Heights."

16   Ibid.

17   *NYT*, 6 February 1973. "Kretchmer Quits His Post to 'Explore' Mayoral Bid."

18   *NYT*, 7 June 1981. Ralph Blumenthal, "Condemnation Issue on the West Side Arouses Distrust."

19   *Jerome Kretchmer interview.*

20   *NYT*, "City Asks a Law on Dog Littering."

21   Heckscher.

22   William F. Buckley, *The Unmaking of a Mayor* (Viking Press, 1966), p. 33.

23   John V. Lindsay, *The Edge* (W. W. Norton, 1976), p. 125.

24 *NYT*, 16 June 1980. Robert D. McFadden, "Lindsay Hurt as Bike Hits Running Dog."

CHAPTER 7: NEW STRATEGIES, ODD IDEAS

1 *NYT*, 24 December 1977. Alan S. Oser, "Environment Reviews Hinder Federal Aid."

2 Margot Barkham, Letter to the Editor, *NYT*, 14 July 1974.

3 *NYT*, 26 March 1972. "Towns Try to Reduce Dog Litter."

4 Ibid.

5 *NYT*, 28 December 1973. "$1 Million Urged to Fight Dog Excreta."

6 Ibid.

7 Cannato, p. 565.

8 Robert A. Makla, Letter to the Editor, *NYT*, 22 December 1976.

9 *NYT*, "Environment Reviews Hinder Federal Aid."

10 *NYT*, "Curb Those Dogs!"

11 *NYT*, 20 August 1975. Edward Ranzal, "Sewer Drains to Be Tried as Street Toilets for Dogs."

12 Ibid.

13 Ibid.

14 Ibid.

15 *NYT*, 7 July 1975. Tom Buckley, "Dogs, Dirt, Psychology."

16 Ibid.

17 Ibid.

18 Ibid.

19 Ibid.

20 Ibid.

21 Ibid.

22 Ibid.

23 Ibid.

24 Ibid.

25 Ibid.

26 *NYT*, 15 March 1976. Peter Khiss, "Mrs. Beame Joins Protest Against Dog Litter."

27 William J. O'Malley, Letter to the Editor, *NYT*, 15 April 1975.

28 *NYT*, "Curb Those Dogs!"

29 *Our Town*, "Public Debates Anti-Dog-Fouling Measure."

30 *NYT*, "Dog-Littering Foe Puts the Onus on the Owners."

31 Anonymous dog run interview, 2006.

CHAPTER 8: POOP PANIC: PINNING NEW YORK'S DOWNFALL ON DOGS

1 *NYT*, 26 April 1974. Jane Brody, "Bites Reported on the Increase in City as More People Acquire Watchdogs."

2 Joseph Caldwell, 2007. Letter to the author.

3 *New York Post*, 17 July 1976. Tom Topor, "City Dogs Big and Small."

4 Anonymous dog run interview, 2006.

5 *Soho Weekly News*, 22 January 1976. Maxwell Firbank, "Cathouse for Dogs in Village?"

6 Neil Simon, *The Prisoner of Second Avenue*.

7 Ibid.

8 Ibid.

9 Ibid.

10 Ibid.

11 Ibid.

12 Ibid.

13 Dennis Jay Kenney, *Crime, Fear, and the NYC Subways: The Role of Citizen Action* (Praeger, 1987), p. 59.

14 *NYT*, 14 November 1976. "Dog Walkers Consider Park Safe at Night."

15 Ibid.

16 Ibid.

17 Ibid.

18 *NYT*, 16 March 1974. "Dog Companions Found to Help Schizophrenics."

19 Ibid.

20 *NYT*, 5 January 1973. John C. Devlin, "Cynophobists Find Way to Get Over Their Fear of Dogs."

21 Bernard Weiss, Letter to the Editor, *NYT*, 10 October 1974.

22 Thomas Russell Jones, Letter to the Editor, *NYT*, 27 August 1974.

23 *Daily News*, 15 November 1973. Ken McKenna, "The stray dog dilemma: It's getting worse."

24 *Stephen Zawistowski interview.*

25 *Soho Weekly News*, "Cathouse for Dogs in Village?"

26 *NYT*, 12 November 1972. Alan M. Beck, "Packs of Strays Part of the Brooklyn Scene."

27 R. Fagan, Letter to the Editor, *NYT*, 30 March 1974.

28 *NYT*, 24 February 1973. Deirdre Carmody, "A.S.P.C.A. Shift Heartens Critics."

29 Carter Burden, Letter to the Editor, *NYT*, 10 April 1974.

30 Ibid.

31 *NYT*, 8 March 1974. "Fit for a Dog."

32 Carter Burden, Letter to the Editor, *NYT*, 10 April 1974.

33 Encil E. Rains, Letter to the Editor, *NYT*, 9 March 1974.

34 R. Fagan, Letter to the Editor, *NYT*, 30 March 1974.

35 *NYT*, "Bites Reported on the Increase in City as More People Acquire Watchdogs."

36 *NYT*, 28 February 1976. William E. Farrell, "Urban Dog Population Is a Rising Problem."

37 *Daily News*, 25 August 1975. Beth Fallon, "The Worst Doggy Do Is Biting."

38 *NYT*, 27 July 1978. John Duka, "The City Dog: For Better or Worse?"

39 Jack Gasnick, Letter to the Editor, *NYT*, 1976.

40 *NYT*, "Environmentalist Shows Widespread Concern for Owners and Dogs."

41 *NYT*, "Sewer Drains to Be Tried as Street Toilets for Dogs."

42 *NYT*, "For Dogs, City Is the Big Biscuit."

43 Ibid.

44 Ibid.

45 *Alan Beck interview.*

46 *NYT*, 4 March 1976. Murray Schumach, "2 German Shepherds Terrorize Queens Community."

47 Ibid.

48 Ibid.

49 Ibid.

50 Ibid.

51 Ibid.

52 Ibid.

53 Ibid.

54 Ibid.

55 Ibid.

56 Marc D. Kantrowitz, Letter to the Editor, *NYT*, 8 March 1976.

57 *NYT*, 21 May 1976. Leslie Maitland, "Superintendent and Dog: Friends Take Their Side."

58 Ibid.

59 *NYT Magazine*, 7 March 1976. Russell Baker, "Dog Day Evening."

60 *Daily News*, "The Worst Doggy Do Is Biting."

CHAPTER 9: A NEW PRAGMATISM

1 *NYT*, 18 May 1981. "A Serious Health Problem: When People Bite People."

2 *NYT*, "Mrs. Beame Joins Protest Against Dog Litter."

3 Ibid.

4 Ibid.

5 Ibid.

6 Ibid.

7 *Our Town*, 17 October 1975. Dewing Brabac, "Muttering Majority Becomes More Vocal."

8 *NYT*, "Mrs. Beame Joins Protest Against Dog Litter."

9 Ibid.

10 Ibid.

11 Ibid.

12 Ibid.

13 Ibid.

14 *Daily News*, 31 March 1977. Arthur Browne, "He'd Tax Doggie Intake to Curb Output."

15 Ibid.

16 Ibid.

17 Edward I. Koch, *Mayor* (Simon and Schuster, 1984).

18 Ibid., p. 111.

19   Ibid., p. 111.

20   *Daily News*, 20 May 1977. Alton Slagle, "How come they do-do us like they do?"

21   *New York*, 24 July 1978. "Dogs Are Going to the Law."

22   Ibid.

23   *NYT*, 19 May 1978. E. J. Dionne, Jr., "Albany Gets Around to Handling of Dogs."

24   Transcript of NYS Assembly Floor Debate, Bill no. 464, 23 May 1977.

25   Transcript of NYS Senate Floor Debate, Bill no. 464, 23 June 1977.

26   Governor's Bill Jacket, Chapter 464 of Laws of 1977.

27   *NYT*, 28 June 1977. "Carey Won't Sidestep Bill on Curbing Dogs."

28   *NYT*, 6 July 1977. "Walking Tall."

29   *NYT*, "Carey Won't Sidestep Bill on Curbing Dogs."

30   Ibid.

31   *New York*, "Dogs Are Going to the Law."

32   *NYT*, "Carey Won't Sidestep Bill on Curbing Dogs."

33   *NYT*, "The City Dog: For Better or Worse?"

34   Governor's Bill Jacket: Chapter 464 of Laws of 1977.

35   Ibid.

36   Ibid.

37   *Westsider*, 27 July 1978. Allan Jalon, "Scoop That Poop!"

38   Ibid.

39   Governor's Bill Jacket.

40   *Westsider*, "Scoop That Poop!"

41   *NYT*, "Walking Tall."

42   Governor's Bill Jacket.

43   *Westsider*, "Scoop That Poop!"

44   Ibid.

45   Ibid.

46   Ibid.

47   *New York*, "Dogs Are Going to the Law."

48   Ibid.

49   *Westsider*, "Scoop That Poop!"

50   Ibid.

51   Ibid.

52   Ibid.

53   Ibid.

54   *NYT*, 8 April 1977. David Bird, "A.S.P.C.A. Eliminates Pickup of Stray Dogs in New York City."

CHAPTER 10: NO MORE MR. NICEGUY: THE FINAL CONFRONTATION

1   *NYT*, "The City Dog: For Better or Worse?"

2   Ibid.

3   *Saturday Night Live*, "Mr. Bill Goes to N.Y." © 1975–1980 National Broadcasting Company, Inc.

4   *NYT*, "Owners of Dogs Face Orders to Clean Up."

5   *NYT*, 2 August 1978. Fred Ferretti, "Dog Owners Cope with Cleanup Law."

6   *NYT*, 11 November 1978. Laurie Johnston, "Success of Dog-Filth Ban Is Called 'Spotty.'"

7   *NYT*, "Dog Owners Cope with Cleanup Law."

8   Ibid.

9   Ibid.

10   Ibid.

11   *NYT*, 19 March 1980. "Elegant Dirt."

12   Ibid.

13   Ibid.

14   Ibid.

15   *NYT*, "Dog Owners Cope with Cleanup Law."

16   Ibid.

17   Ibid.

18   *NYT*, "Success of Dog-Filth Ban Is Called 'Spotty.'"

19   *NYT*, 15 February 1979. Clyde Haberman/Albin Krebs, "Sandy Goes to the Suburbs."

20   *NYT*, 29 June 1984. "Meaner Streets, Cleaner Streets."

21   *UPI/The Washington Post*, 22 August 1978. "New Yorkers Leave Dogs Rather Than 'Scoop Poop.'"

22   Ibid.

23   *Stephen Zawistowski interview.*

24   *NYT*, "Dog Owners Cope with Cleanup Law."

25   Ibid.

26   Ibid.

27   Ibid.

28   Ibid.

29   *NYT*, 9 August 1979. "Dog-Cleanup Law Is Upheld by Judge."

30   Ibid.

31   *NYT*, "Success of Dog-Filth Ban Is Called 'Spotty.'"

32   *NYT*, 2 February 1979. Laurie Johnston, "City Opens a Full Drive on Dog Litter."

33   Paul Sawler, Letter to the Editor, *NYT*, 2 February 1979.

34   Office of the Mayor, The City of New York. Press Release, 1 August 1979.

35   *NYT*, "City Opens a Full Drive on Dog Litter."

36   Ibid.

37   Ibid.

38   *NYT*, "Success of Dog-Filth Ban Is Called 'Spotty.'"

39   Ibid.

40   *NYT*, 2 August 1979. Lee A. Daniels, "Dog-Cleanup Praised After a Year."

41   *NYT*, "Success of Dog-Filth Ban Is Called 'Spotty.'"

42   *NYT*, 8 June 1986. Eleanor Blau, "Canine Waste."

43   *Alan Beck interview.*

44   *NYT*, 30 May 1988. "Curbing Dogs with Kindness."

45   Ibid.

46   *NYT*, "Success of Dog-Filth Ban Is Called 'Spotty.'"

47   *NYT*, 5 January 1980. "Mayor Renews Efforts on Dog Cleanup Law, Doubling Lowest Fine."

48   Office of the Mayor, The City of New York. Press Release, 1 August 1979.

49   Ibid.

50   Department of Sanitation, The City of New York. Press Release, 1 August 1985.

51   Ibid.

52   *NYT*, 1 August 1986. "A Matter of Communication—or a Lack of It."

53   Ibid.

54   Ibid.

55   Ibid.

56   Ibid.

57   *NYT*, "Success of Dog-Filth Ban Is Called 'Spotty.'"

58   Ibid.

59   Ibid.

60   Ibid.

61   *NYT*, 16 June 1984. James Brooke, "6 Years of Canine Waste Law: All in All, a Cleaner New York."

Chapter 11: Summary: Why It Happened Here First

1   "25th Floor," Smith-Kral, Arista Records, Inc., 1978.

2   *NYT*, "6 Years of Canine Waste Law: All in All, a Cleaner New York."

3   Alan M. Beck, "The Impact of the Canine Clean-up Law." *Environment*, October 1979, Vol. 21, No. 8.

4   *NYT*, "6 Years of Canine Waste Law: All in All, a Cleaner New York."

5   *Alan Beck interview.*

6   Lawrence T. Glickman and Frances S. Shofer, "Zoonotic Visceral and Ocular Larva Migrans."

7   *NYT*, "Dog Owners May Have to Clean Up After Pets."

8   Alan M. Beck, "The Impact of the Canine Clean-up Law."

9   *NYT*, "6 Years of Canine Waste Law: All in All, a Cleaner New York."

10   *Daily News*, 21 August 1999. Michael R. Blood, "Dog Poop Rebuke: Don't suffer stool gladly, Rudy tells caller."

11   *Dog Run, A Publication of the Washington Square Dog Run Association*, Fall/Winter 1998. Philip Nobel, "Public Space Goes to the Dogs: An Outsider's View."

12   *Adrienne Eldred interview.*

Chapter 12: Global Poop

1   *Charles Rudack interview.*

2   *Associated Press*, 16 June 2005. "Des tests ADN contre les crottes de chien."

3　*The Montreal Gazette*, 17 March 1992. "Dog Owner Who Didn't Scoop Sues for Defamation."

4　*Rotten.com*, 21 February 2008. "Dog Shit."

5　*Gillesguerin.com*, 21 February 2008. Gilles Guérin, "Tendance Parisienne, ou Le retour de l'homme à l'animal."

6　*Yves Contassot interview.*

7　*FilthyFrance.com*, 2007. Graham Holliday, "Filthy France . . . for a turd-free republik."

8　*Yves Contassot interview.*

9　*Atypyk.com*, 21 February 2008.

10　*Yves Contassot interview.*

11　*Le Point*, April 2002. "Paris butte sur les crottes de chien."

12　*La Terre de chez nous*, 8 November 2003. "Halte aux crottes de chiens!"

13　*Agence France-Presse*, 17 November 2003. via *FunnyNews.fr*, "Dix milles fausses crottes de chiens dans les rues de Lyon."

14　*Toulouse.fr*, 24 October 2006. "Déjections canines: arrêtons le deluge!"

15　*FilthyFrance.com*, 2007. Graham Holliday.

16　Graham Holliday, e-mail, 13 April 2007.

17　Gilles Guérin, email, 13 April 2007.

18　*Gillesguerin.com*, 21 February 2008. "Tendance Parisienne . . ."

19　*Spiegel Online*, 17 March 2006.

20　*Indybay.org*, 21 March 2005. "German Police Baffled by Bush Poo-Flags."

21　*Madeyouthink.org*, 21 February 2008.

22　Marc Bekoff and Carron A. Meaney, "Interactions Among Dogs, People, and Nature in Boulder, Colorado: A Case Study," *Anthrozoös*, 10, pp. 23–31, 1997.

23　*Steven Armstead interview.*

24　*The Daily Camera*, 5 December 2001. Chris Burge, "City, County Leaders Hear Dog Poop Pleas."

25　Ibid.

26　Ibid.

27　*USA Today*, 7 June 2002. Traci Watson, "Water pollution linked to dog do."

28   Ibid.

29   Ibid.

30   *Don Jordan interview.*

31   *The Jerusalem Post*, 19 March 1999. Liat Collins, "A Poop Scoop."

32   *USA Today*, 19 August 2002. Tom Vanden Brook, "Sewage pouring into lakes, streams."

33   Ibid.

34   Ibid.

35   Ibid.

36   *Alan Beck interview.*

37   *Boston Herald*, 9 August 1998. "Mutt Mitt Inventor: Poop Is Profitable."

38   Hugo, p. 1061.

AFTERWORD: WHO COULD HAVE KNOWN?

1   Rupert Brooke, *Letters from America* (Charles Scribner's Sons, 1916), pp. 8–9.

2   *NYT*, 7 August 1994. Steven Lee Meyers, "First Dog Is Latest Family Member to Outshine Mayor."

3   *New York*, 19 October 1998. Elizabeth Hess, "Gimme Shelter."

4   *Daily News*, "Dog Poop Rebuke: Don't suffer stool gladly, Rudy tells caller."

5   *New York*, "Gimme Shelter."

6   Ibid.

7   Ibid.

8   Adele Bender, Letter to the Editor, *NYT*, 1976.

INDEX

Betros, Emeel, 187, 188, 189, 190, 191,
  197, 198
Biaggi, Mario, 41
Bide-A-Wee, 52, 222
Big Brother Awards, 268
Bite problem
  canine, 144, 153, 154, 161, 164–176, 235
  human, 176, 235
  See also New York City/Bureau of Animal
  Affairs
Blind persons, exemption for, 116, 212, 314
Blindness, exposure to canine waste as a po-
  tential cause of, 92, 110, 207
Bloomingdale's, 75, 76, 77, 79
Boise, canine waste problem in, 288
"Boomer" (Parks Commissioner Henry
  Stern's dog), 262, 296, 297, 299
Bordeaux, canine waste problem in, 276
Bosch-Fischer, E., 109
Boston, canine waste problem in, 246, 265
Boston Herald, 292
Boston, leash law in, 72
Boulder, canine waste problem in, 283–287
Boy Scouts of America, 107
Breeding, 15–16, 157–158, 161, 165–166,
  206, 246, 298, 301, 308
Brinton, Will, 293
Bronx County Kennel Club, 220
Brooke, Rupert, 295
Brooklyn Cat Club, 109
Bruntingthorpe, canine waste problem in,
  268, 269
Brussels, canine waste problem in, 246
Buckley, William F., 122–123
Budapest, canine waste problem in, 267
Buffalo
  canine waste problem in, 195, 198, 199,
  204, 205, 206, 216, 218, 230
  SPCA, 216
Burden, Carter, 59, 86, 105–106, 112, 115,
  161, 162, 163, 164, 167, 178
Burlington, canine waste problem in, 288
Bush, George W., 283

Caemmerer, John, 202
Caen, canine waste problem in, 274
Cahill, Kevin, 207
Caldwell, Joseph, 145–146
Campbell, John, 186
Caninettes, 272, 273
Canisettes, 267, 273, 274, 276, 283

Canisites. See Canisettes
Cannato, Vincent, 63, 65, 123, 130
Cap, Marjorie, 113
Caras, Roger, 25, 26, 167, 168, 299
Carey, Hugh, 130, 160, 204, 205, 206,
  219, 227
Carl Schurz Park, 134, 136, 137, 139, 140,
  176, 178, 240–241, 244
Carl Schurz Park Association, 137, 139, 140,
  177, 236
Caro, Robert, 39
Center for Animal Care and Control
  (CACC). *See* New York City/CACC
Center for Watershed Protection, 288
Centers for Disease Control and
  Prevention, 290
Central Park, 12, 32, 40, 42, 45, 65–71, 73,
  75, 76, 77, 78, 79, 86, 98, 112, 147, 148,
  149, 153, 155, 166, 181, 204, 209, 221,
  233, 263
Central Westchester Humane Society, 226
Checkers Speech, 50–52
Chelsea Committee for Canine Calm, 109
Chesapeake Bay, canine waste problem in, 86
Chicago
  canine waste problem in, 8, 11, 100, 127,
  245, 246
  effects of the urban crisis upon, 29
Children Before Dogs, 60, 90, 91, 94–95,
  110, 250
  See also Fran Lee
China
  ban on large dogs, 25
  human waste as fertilizer, 293
  rabies epidemic, 25
Chinatown, 289
"Chopper" (wounded dog belonging to the
  boy consoled by Richard Nixon), 50
Cicero, Carla, 114
Cincinnati, water pollution in, 289–290
Citizens for Animals, 162, 164
City, The, 41
City Club of New York, 234
Clean Air Act, 34
Clean Water Act, 34, 289
Clearwater, canine waste problem in, 288
Cleopatra's Needle, 78
Coalition for Dog Control, 21, 139, 236
  See also Livingston, Patricia
Cohen, Monroe, 100
Columbia University, 99, 111